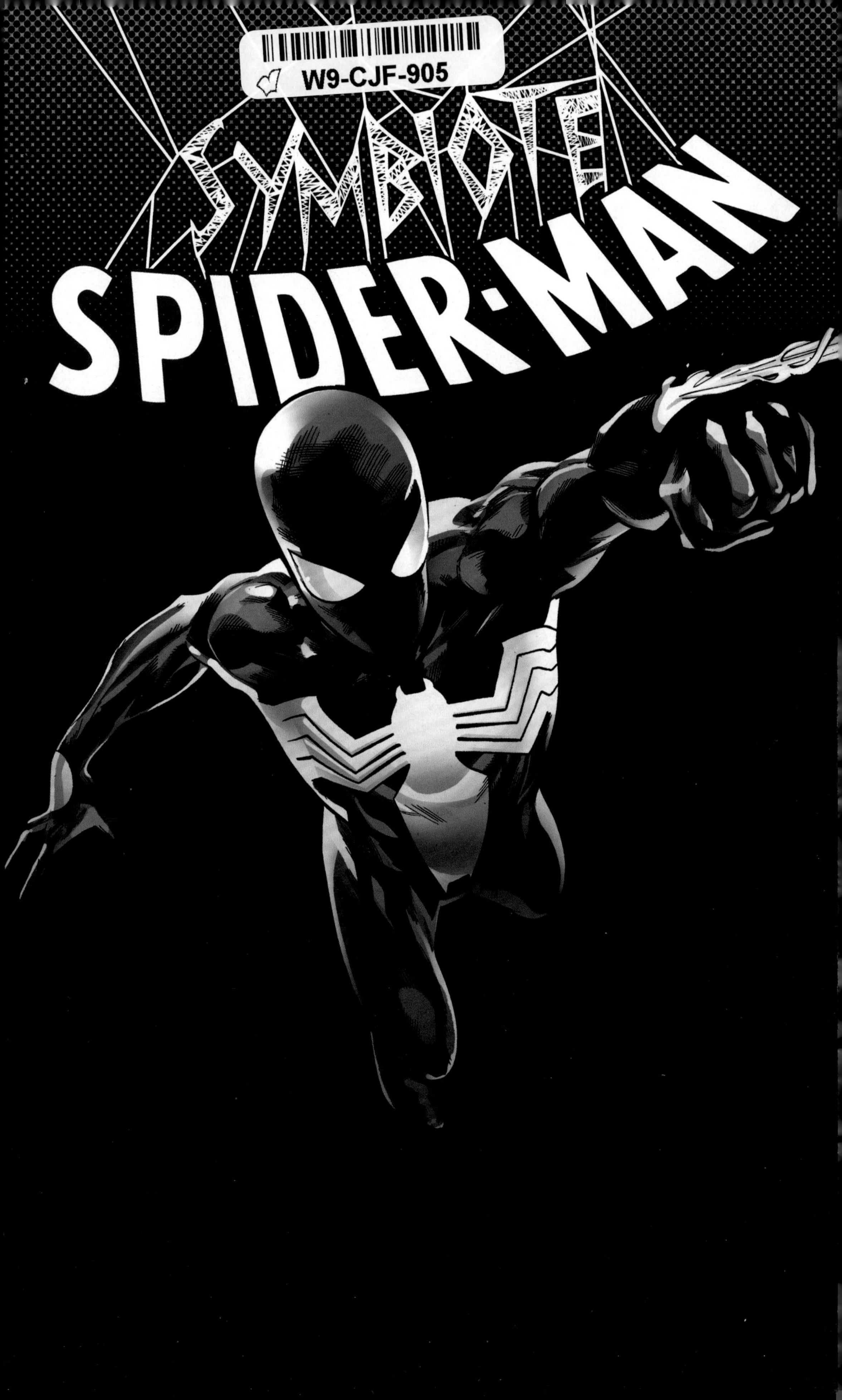
SYMBIOTE
SPIDER-MAN

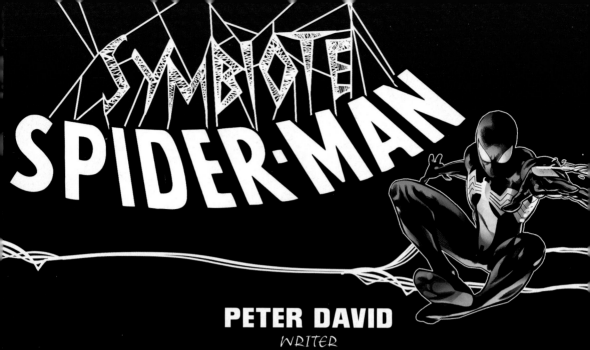

SYMBIOTE SPIDER-MAN

PETER DAVID
WRITER

GREG LAND
PENCILER

JAY LEISTEN
INKER

IBAN COELLO
FLASHBACK SEQUENCE

FRANK D'ARMATA
COLORIST

VC'S JOE SABINO
LETTERER

GREG LAND & **FRANK D'ARMATA**
COVER ARTISTS

DANNY KHAZEM & **LAUREN AMARO**
ASSISTANT EDITORS

DEVIN LEWIS
EDITOR

NICK LOWE
EXECUTIVE EDITOR

SPIDER-MAN *CREATED BY* **STAN LEE** & **STEVE DITKO**

Collection Editor: MARK D. BEAZLEY
Assistant Editor: CAITLIN O'CONNELL
Associate Managing Editor: KATERI WOODY
Senior Editor, Special Projects: JENNIFER GRÜNWALD
VP Production & Special Projects: JEFF YOUNGQUIST
Book Designer: SALENA MAHINA

SVP Print, Sales & Marketing: DAVID GABRIEL
Director, Licensed Publishing: SVEN LARSEN
Editor in Chief: C.B. CEBULSKI
Chief Creative Officer: JOE QUESADA
President: DAN BUCKLEY
Executive Producer: ALAN FINE

SYMBIOTE SPIDER-MAN. Contains material originally published in magazine form as SYMBIOTE SPIDER-MAN #1-5. First printing 2019. ISBN 978-1-302-91904-7. Published by MARVEL WORLDWIDE, INC., a subsidiary of MARVEL ENTERTAINMENT, LLC. OFFICE OF PUBLICATION: 135 West 50th Street, New York, NY 10020. © 2019 MARVEL No similarity between any of the names, characters, persons, and/or institutions in this magazine with those of any living or dead person or institution is intended, and any such similarity which may exist is purely coincidental. **Printed in Canada.** DAN BUCKLEY, President, Marvel Entertainment; JOHN NEE, Publisher; JOE QUESADA, Chief Creative Officer; TOM BREVOORT, SVP of Publishing; DAVID BOGART, Associate Publisher & SVP of Talent Affairs; DAVID GABRIEL, SVP of Sales & Marketing, Publishing; JEFF YOUNGQUIST, VP of Production & Special Projects; DAN CARR, Executive Director of Publishing Technology; ALEX MORALES, Director of Publishing Operations; DAN EDINGTON, Managing Editor; SUSAN CRESPI, Production Manager; STAN LEE, Chairman Emeritus. For information regarding advertising in Marvel Comics or on Marvel.com, please contact Vit DeBellis, Custom Solutions & Integrated Advertising Manager, at vdebellis@marvel.com. For Marvel subscription inquiries, please call 888-511-5480. **Manufactured between 9/6/2019 and 10/8/2019 by SOLISCO PRINTERS, SCOTT, QC, CANADA.**

10 9 8 7 6 5 4 3 2 1

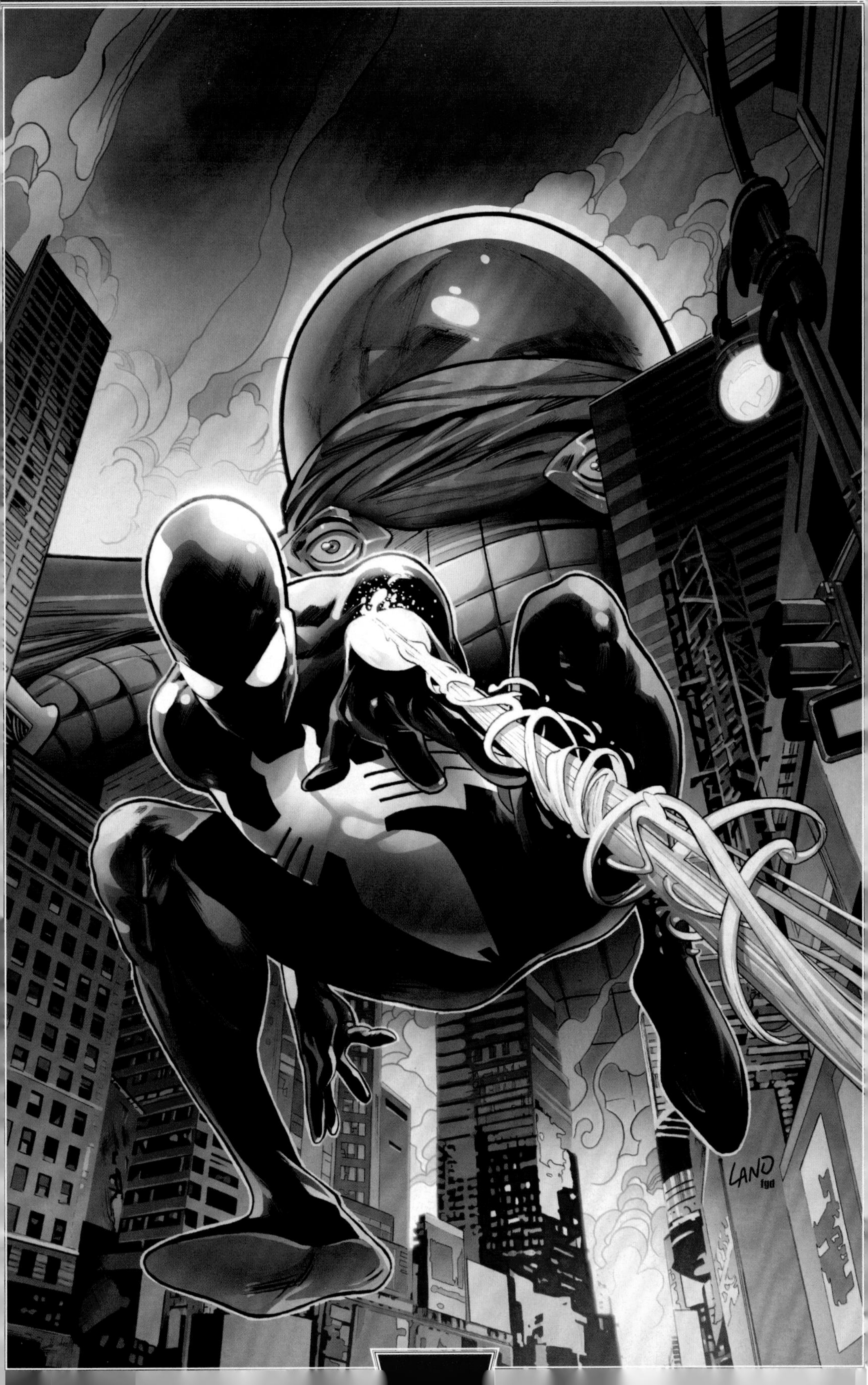
LAND
fgd

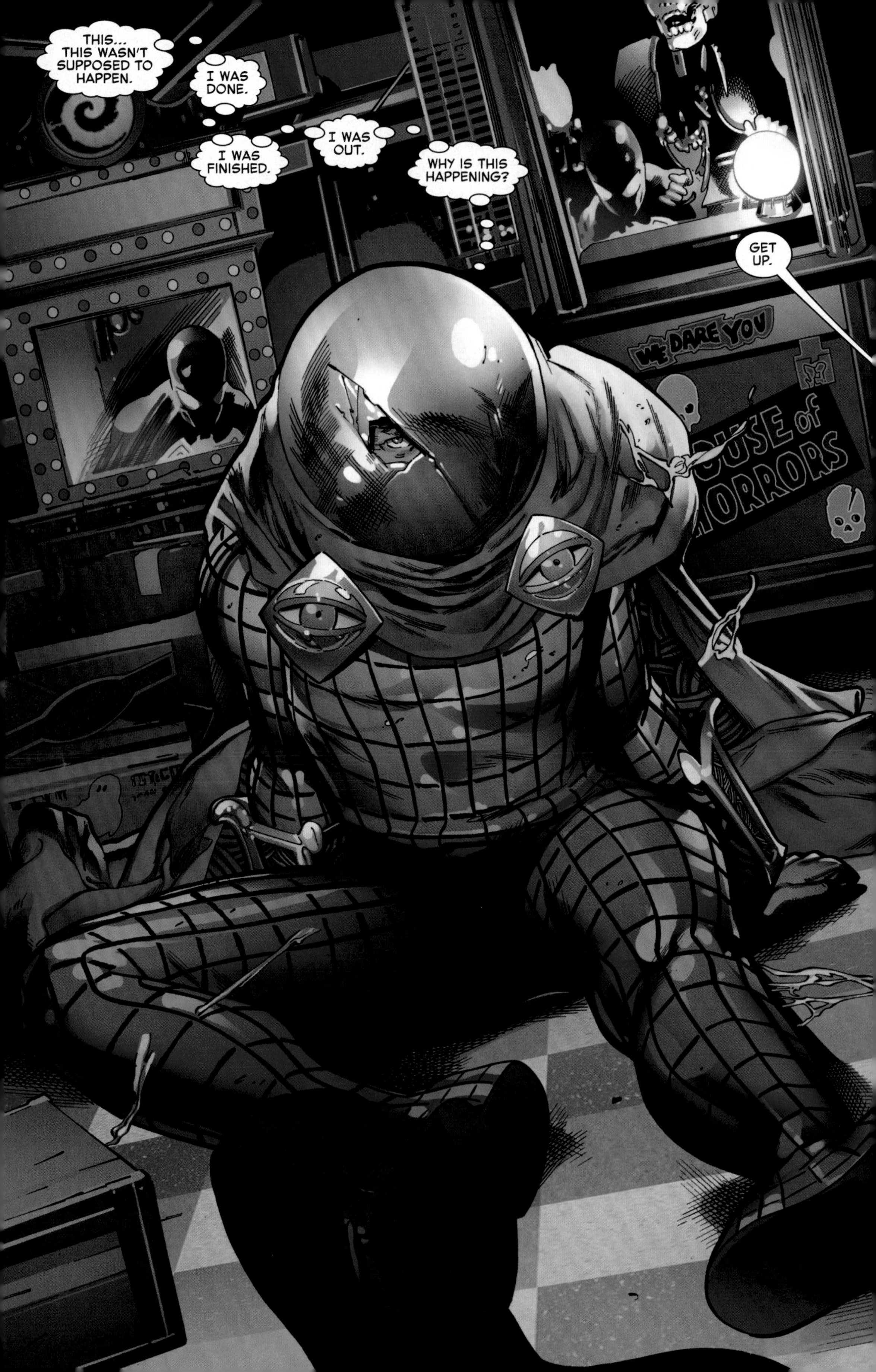
THIS... THIS WASN'T SUPPOSED TO HAPPEN.
I WAS DONE.
I WAS FINISHED.
I WAS OUT.
WHY IS THIS HAPPENING?
GET UP.
WE DARE YOU
HOUSE of HORRORS

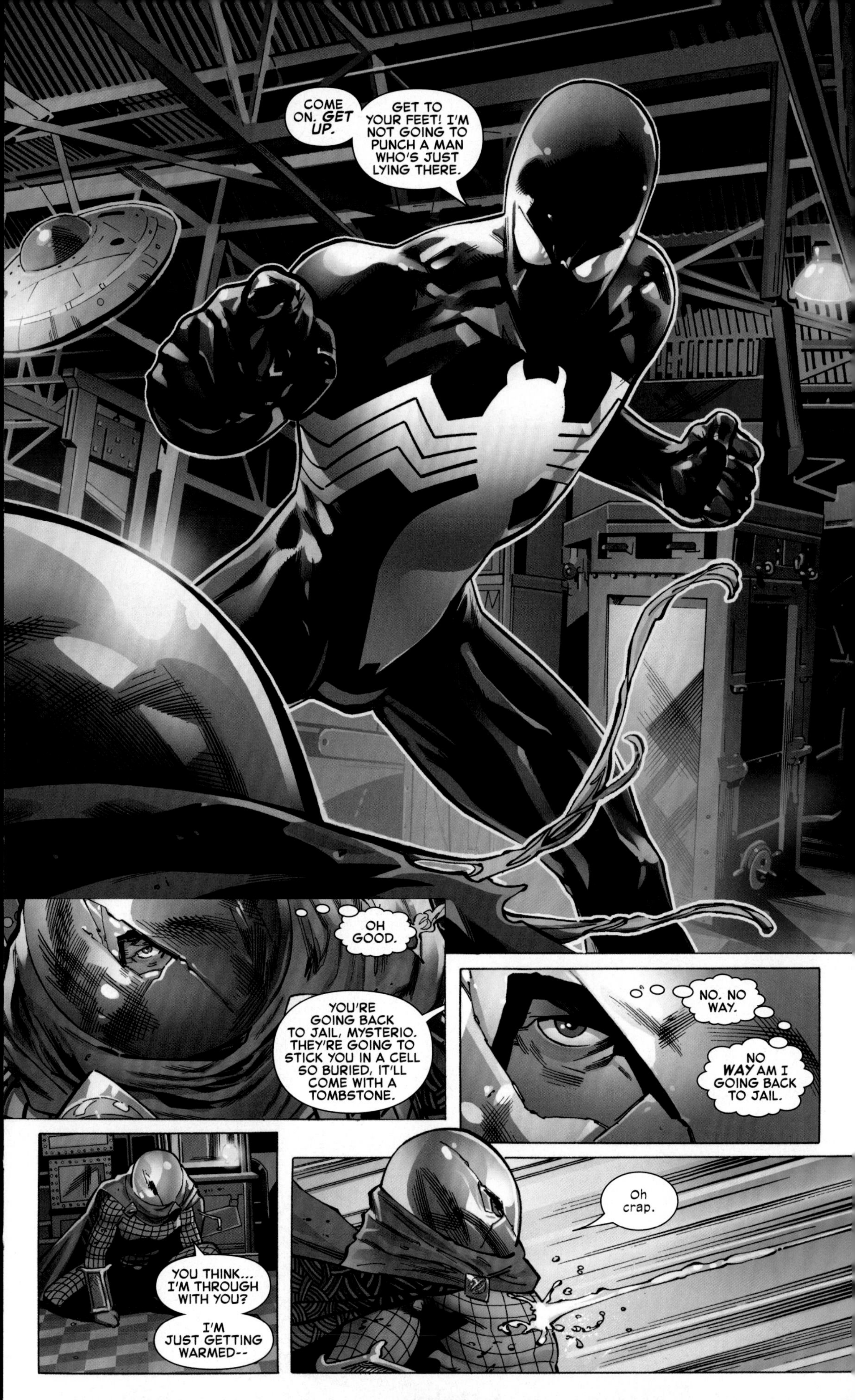
COME ON. GET UP.
GET TO YOUR FEET! I'M NOT GOING TO PUNCH A MAN WHO'S JUST LYING THERE.
OH GOOD.
YOU'RE GOING BACK TO JAIL, MYSTERIO. THEY'RE GOING TO STICK YOU IN A CELL SO BURIED, IT'LL COME WITH A TOMBSTONE.
NO. NO WAY.
NO WAY AM I GOING BACK TO JAIL.
YOU THINK... I'M THROUGH WITH YOU?
I'M JUST GETTING WARMED--
Oh crap.

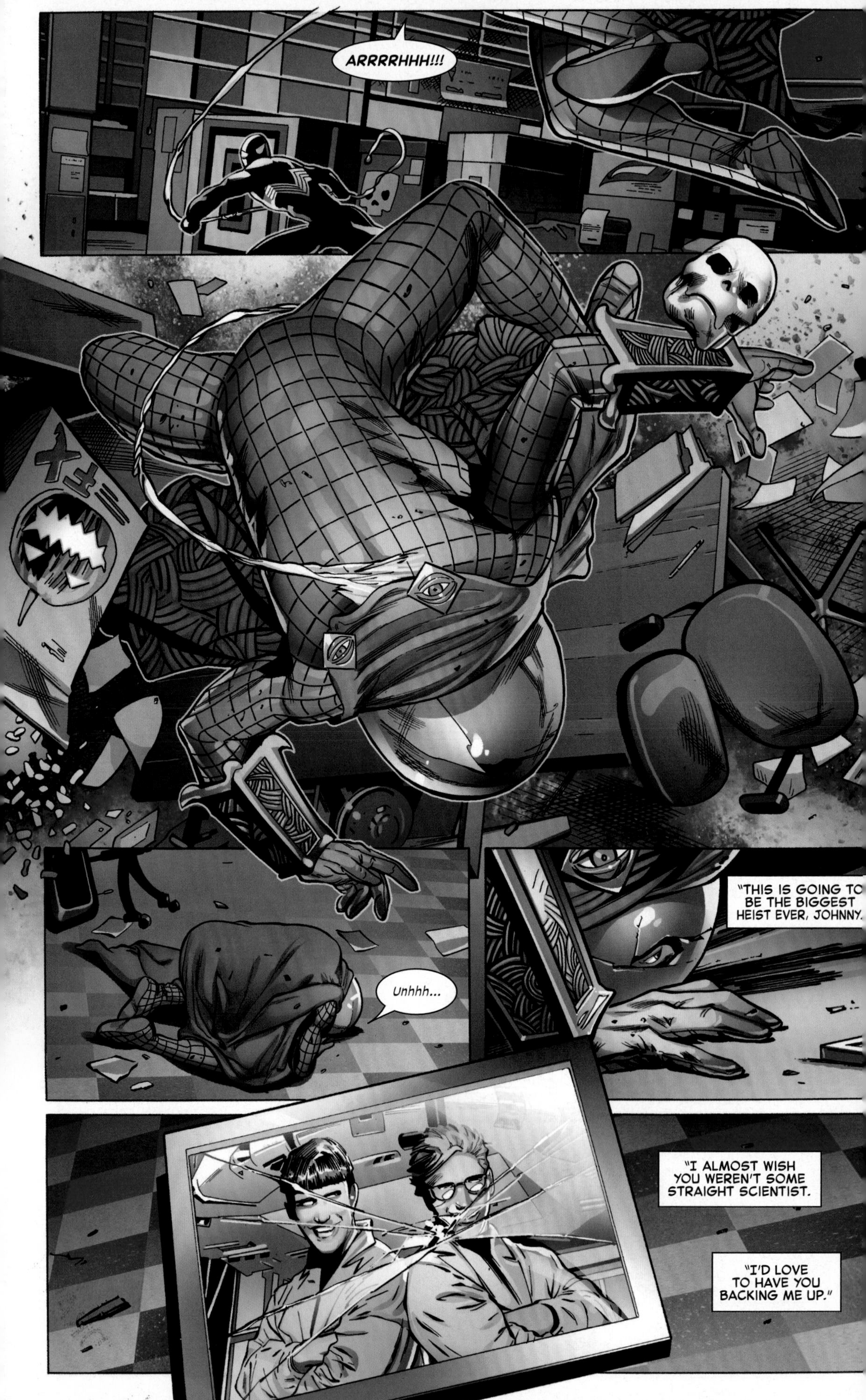
ARRRRHHH!!!
Unhhh...
"THIS IS GOING TO BE THE BIGGEST HEIST EVER, JOHNNY.
"I ALMOST WISH YOU WEREN'T SOME STRAIGHT SCIENTIST.
"I'D LOVE TO HAVE YOU BACKING ME UP."

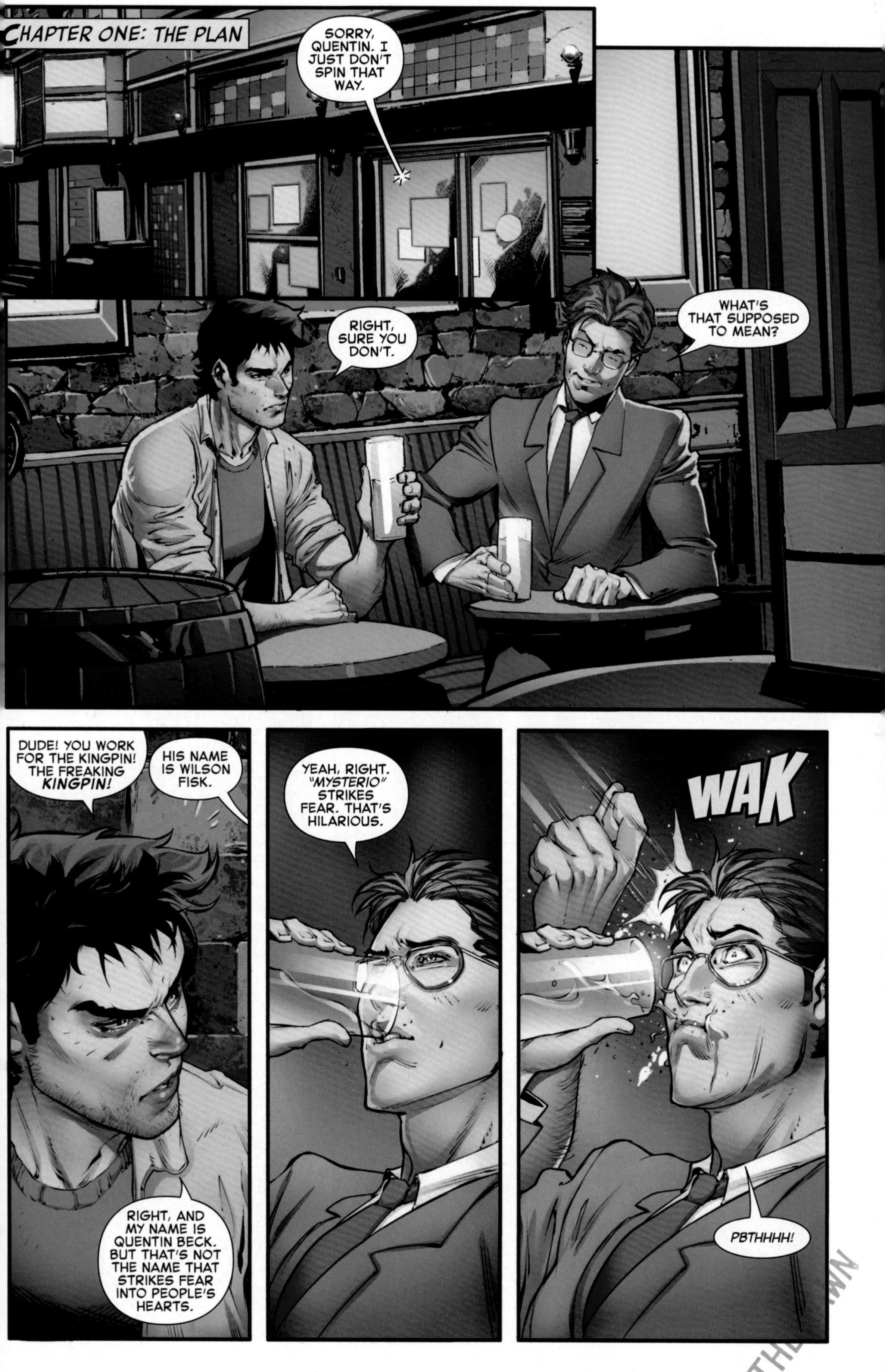
CHAPTER ONE: THE PLAN
SORRY, QUENTIN. I JUST DON'T SPIN THAT WAY.
RIGHT, SURE YOU DON'T.
WHAT'S THAT SUPPOSED TO MEAN?
DUDE! YOU WORK FOR THE KINGPIN! THE FREAKING KINGPIN!
HIS NAME IS WILSON FISK.
RIGHT, AND MY NAME IS QUENTIN BECK. BUT THAT'S NOT THE NAME THAT STRIKES FEAR INTO PEOPLE'S HEARTS.
YEAH, RIGHT. "MYSTERIO" STRIKES FEAR. THAT'S HILARIOUS.
WAK
PBTHHHH!

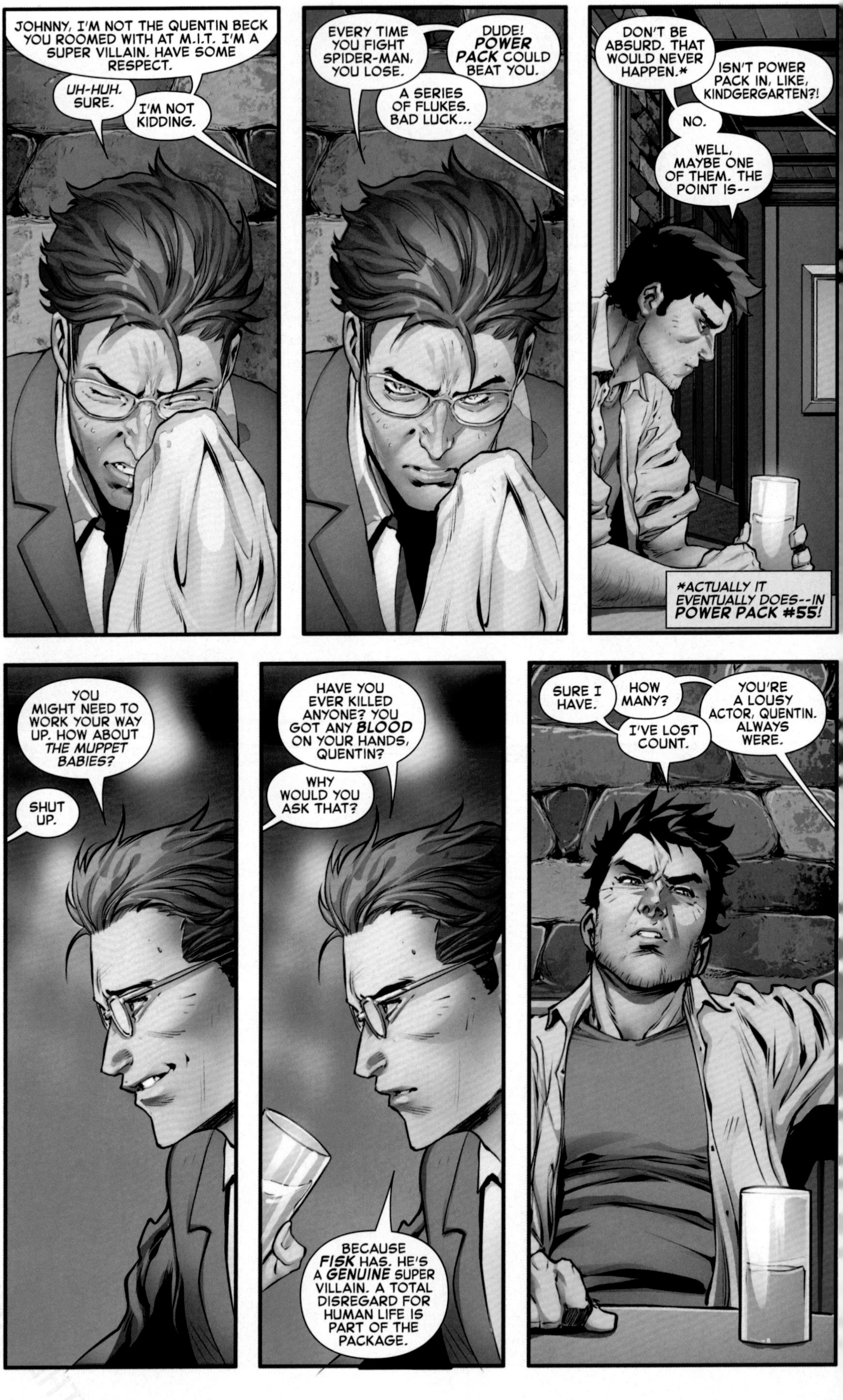
JOHNNY, I'M NOT THE QUENTIN BECK YOU ROOMED WITH AT M.I.T. I'M A SUPER VILLAIN. HAVE SOME RESPECT.
UH-HUH. SURE.
I'M NOT KIDDING.
EVERY TIME YOU FIGHT SPIDER-MAN, YOU LOSE.
DUDE! POWER PACK COULD BEAT YOU.
A SERIES OF FLUKES. BAD LUCK...
DON'T BE ABSURD. THAT WOULD NEVER HAPPEN.*
ISN'T POWER PACK IN, LIKE, KINDERGARTEN?!
NO.
WELL, MAYBE ONE OF THEM. THE POINT IS--
*ACTUALLY IT EVENTUALLY DOES--IN POWER PACK #55!
YOU MIGHT NEED TO WORK YOUR WAY UP. HOW ABOUT THE MUPPET BABIES?
SHUT UP.
HAVE YOU EVER KILLED ANYONE? YOU GOT ANY BLOOD ON YOUR HANDS, QUENTIN?
WHY WOULD YOU ASK THAT?
BECAUSE FISK HAS. HE'S A GENUINE SUPER VILLAIN. A TOTAL DISREGARD FOR HUMAN LIFE IS PART OF THE PACKAGE.
SURE I HAVE.
HOW MANY?
I'VE LOST COUNT.
YOU'RE A LOUSY ACTOR, QUENTIN. ALWAYS WERE.

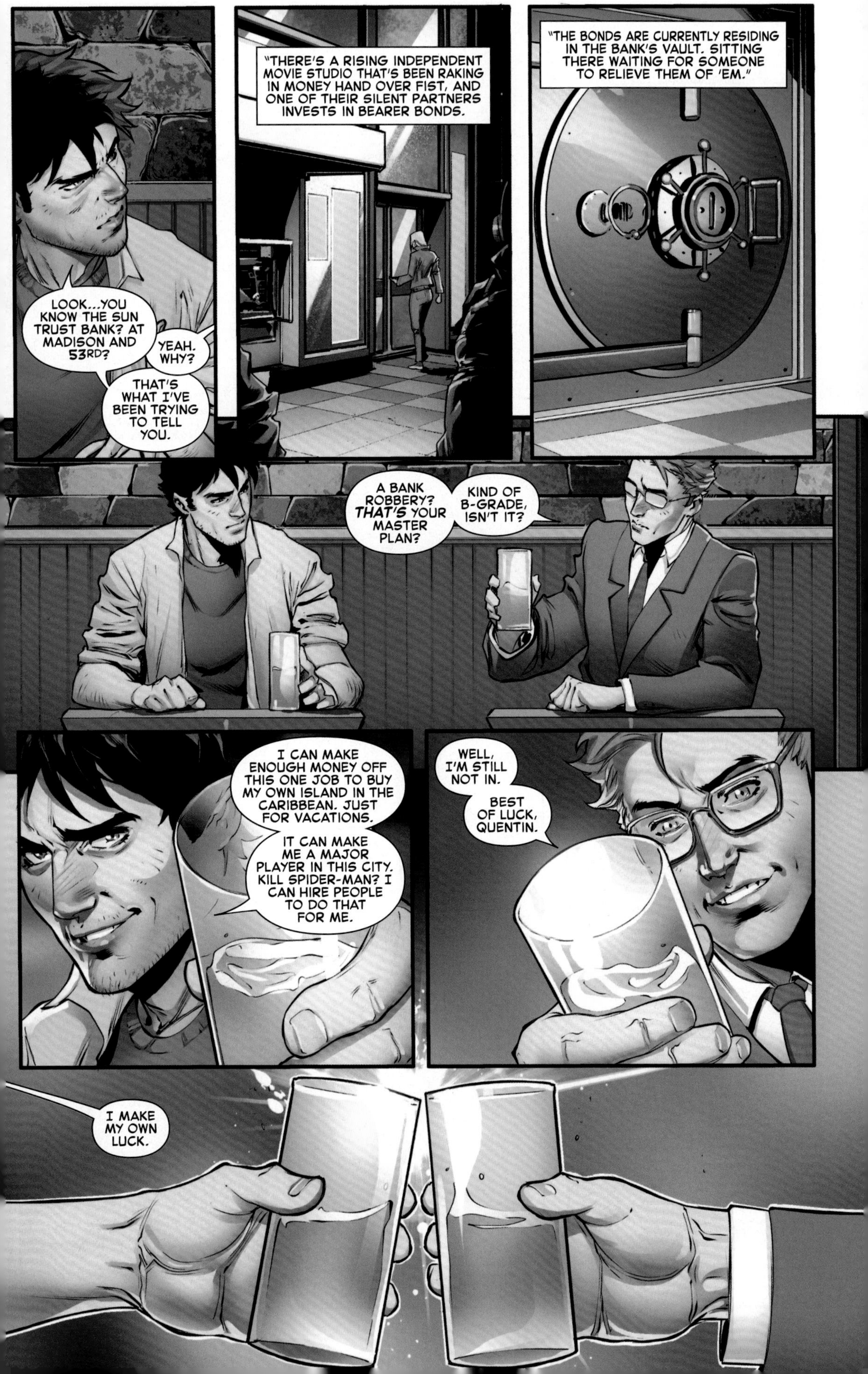
LOOK...YOU KNOW THE SUN TRUST BANK? AT MADISON AND 53RD?
YEAH. WHY?
THAT'S WHAT I'VE BEEN TRYING TO TELL YOU.
"THERE'S A RISING INDEPENDENT MOVIE STUDIO THAT'S BEEN RAKING IN MONEY HAND OVER FIST, AND ONE OF THEIR SILENT PARTNERS INVESTS IN BEARER BONDS.
"THE BONDS ARE CURRENTLY RESIDING IN THE BANK'S VAULT. SITTING THERE WAITING FOR SOMEONE TO RELIEVE THEM OF 'EM."
A BANK ROBBERY? *THAT'S* YOUR MASTER PLAN?
KIND OF B-GRADE, ISN'T IT?
I CAN MAKE ENOUGH MONEY OFF THIS ONE JOB TO BUY MY OWN ISLAND IN THE CARIBBEAN. JUST FOR VACATIONS.
IT CAN MAKE ME A MAJOR PLAYER IN THIS CITY. KILL SPIDER-MAN? I CAN HIRE PEOPLE TO DO THAT FOR ME.
WELL, I'M STILL NOT IN.
BEST OF LUCK, QUENTIN.
I MAKE MY OWN LUCK.

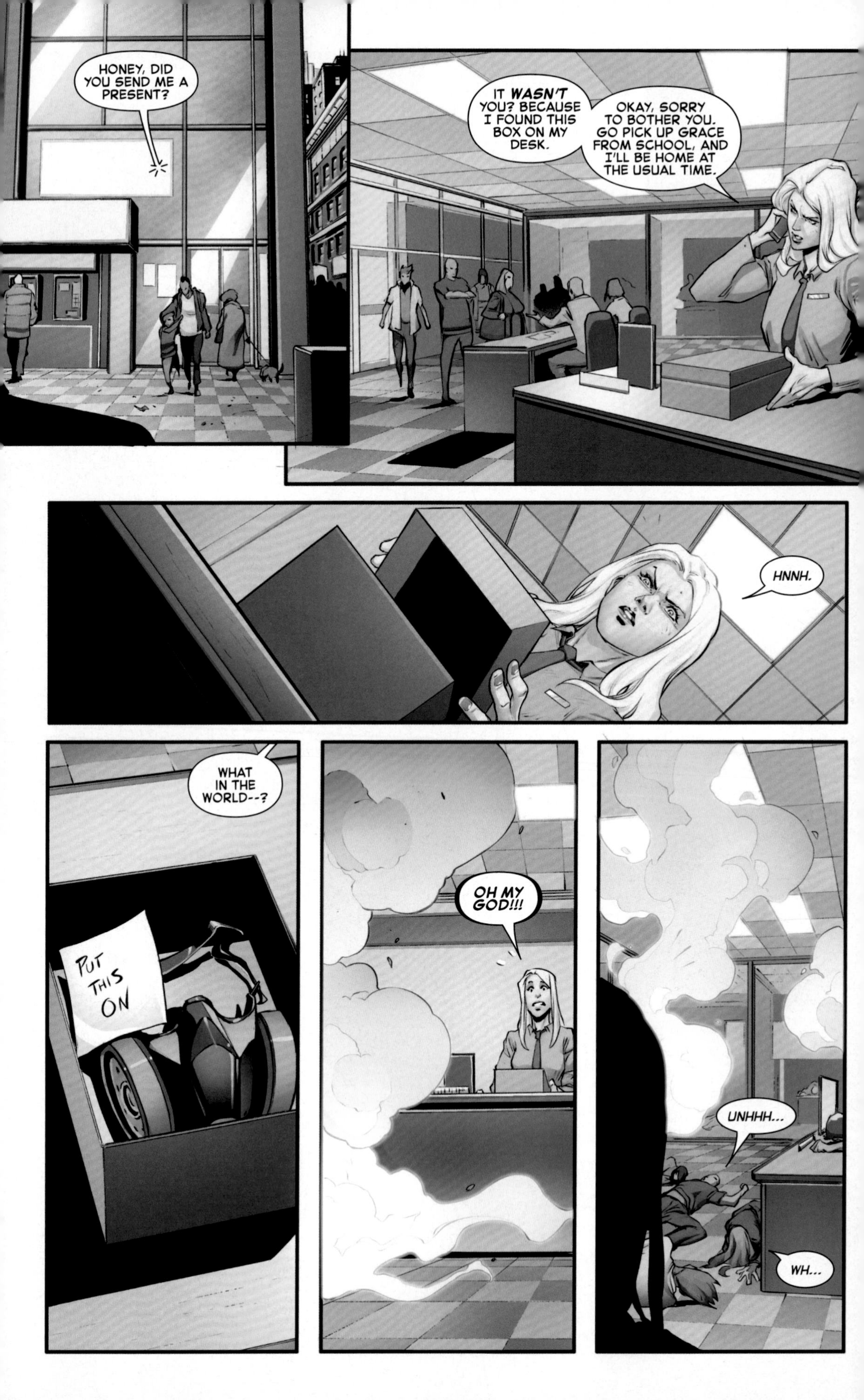
HONEY, DID YOU SEND ME A PRESENT?
IT WASN'T YOU? BECAUSE I FOUND THIS BOX ON MY DESK.
OKAY, SORRY TO BOTHER YOU. GO PICK UP GRACE FROM SCHOOL, AND I'LL BE HOME AT THE USUAL TIME.
HNNH.
WHAT IN THE WORLD--?
PUT THIS ON
OH MY GOD!!!
UNHHH...
WH...

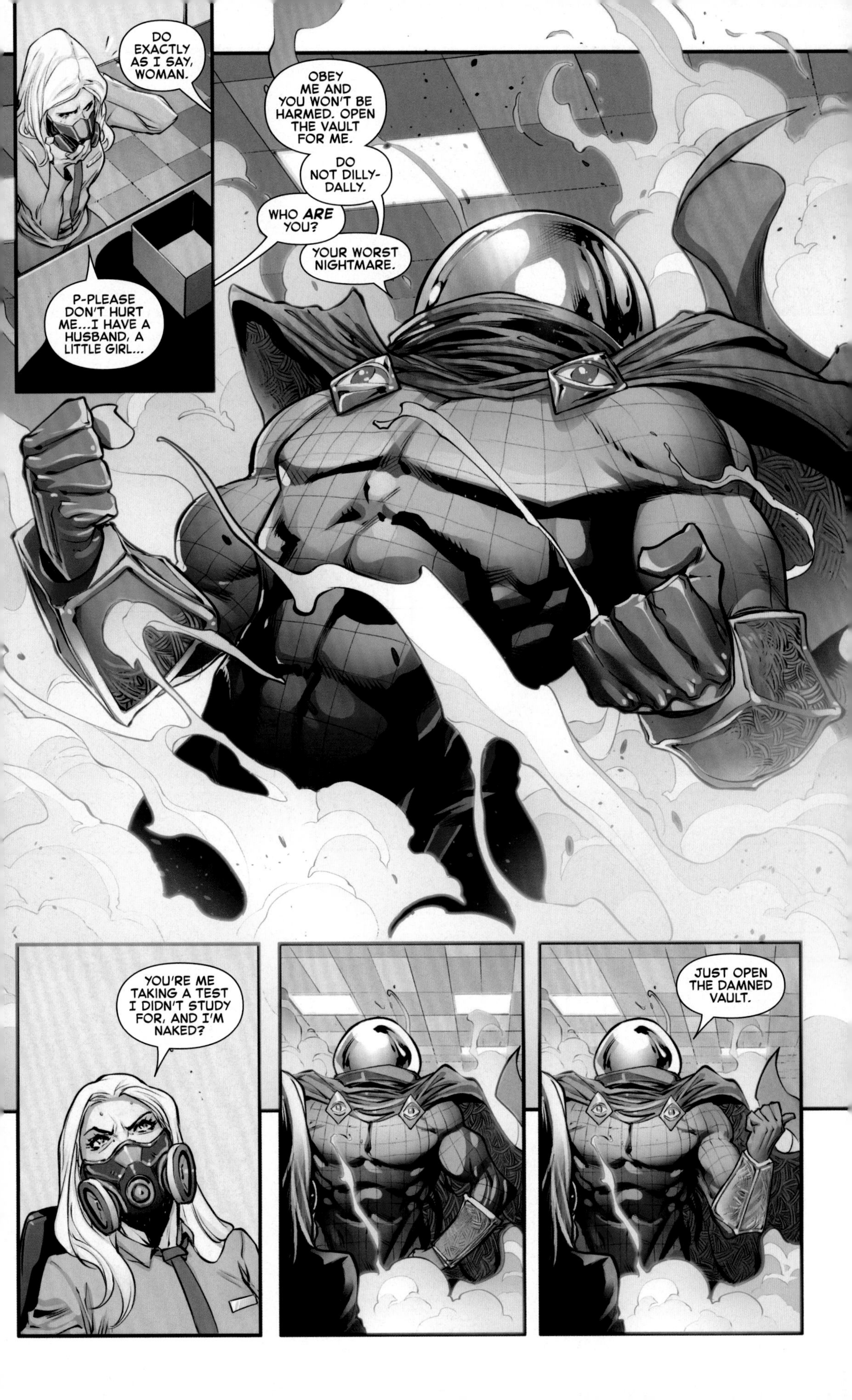
DO EXACTLY AS I SAY, WOMAN.
OBEY ME AND YOU WON'T BE HARMED. OPEN THE VAULT FOR ME.
DO NOT DILLY-DALLY.
P-PLEASE DON'T HURT ME...I HAVE A HUSBAND, A LITTLE GIRL...
WHO ARE YOU?
YOUR WORST NIGHTMARE.
YOU'RE ME TAKING A TEST I DIDN'T STUDY FOR, AND I'M NAKED?
JUST OPEN THE DAMNED VAULT.

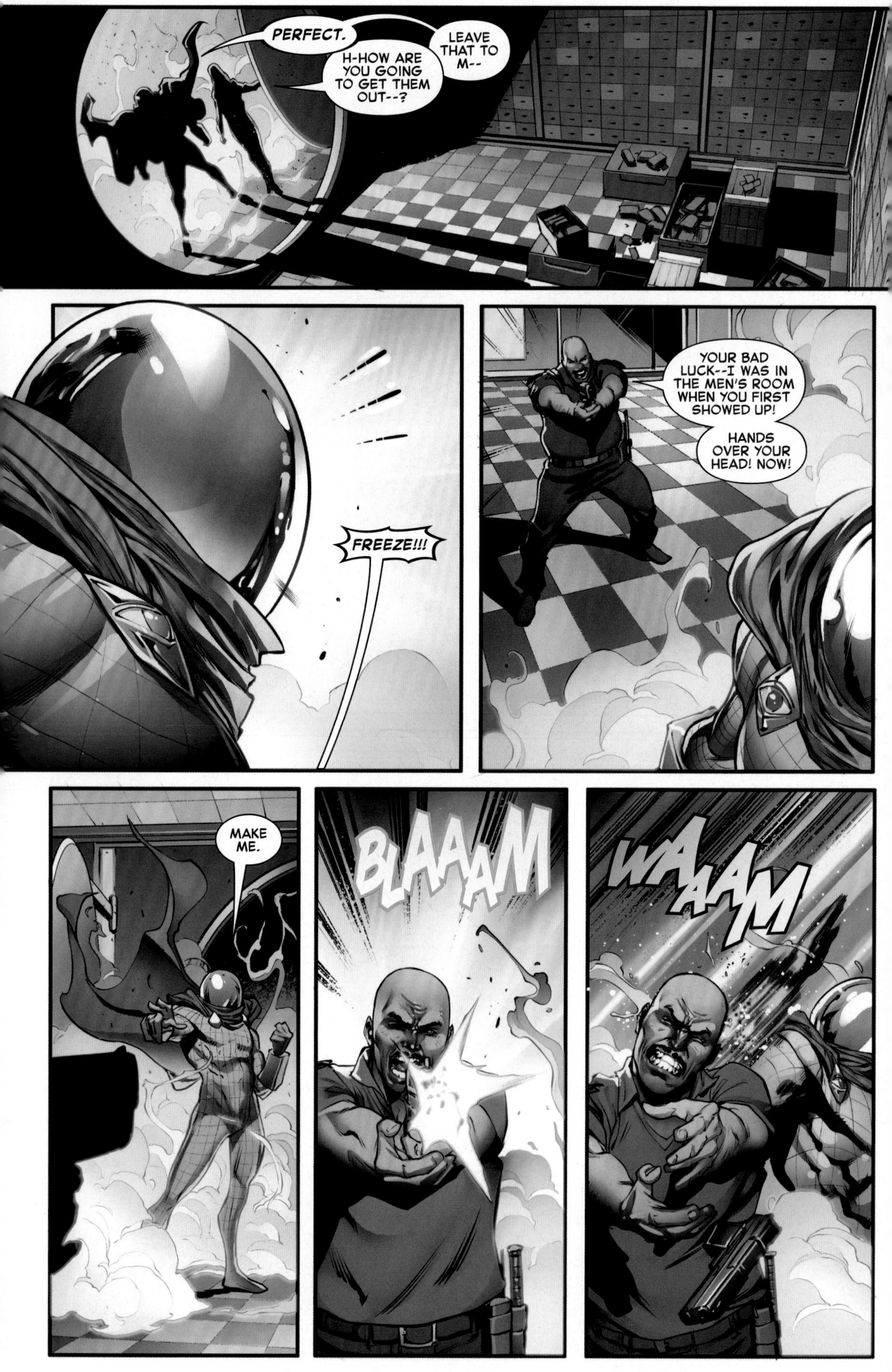

PERFECT.
H-HOW ARE YOU GOING TO GET THEM OUT--?
LEAVE THAT TO M--
FREEZE!!!
YOUR BAD LUCK--I WAS IN THE MEN'S ROOM WHEN YOU FIRST SHOWED UP!
HANDS OVER YOUR HEAD! NOW!
MAKE ME.
BLAAAM
WAAAM

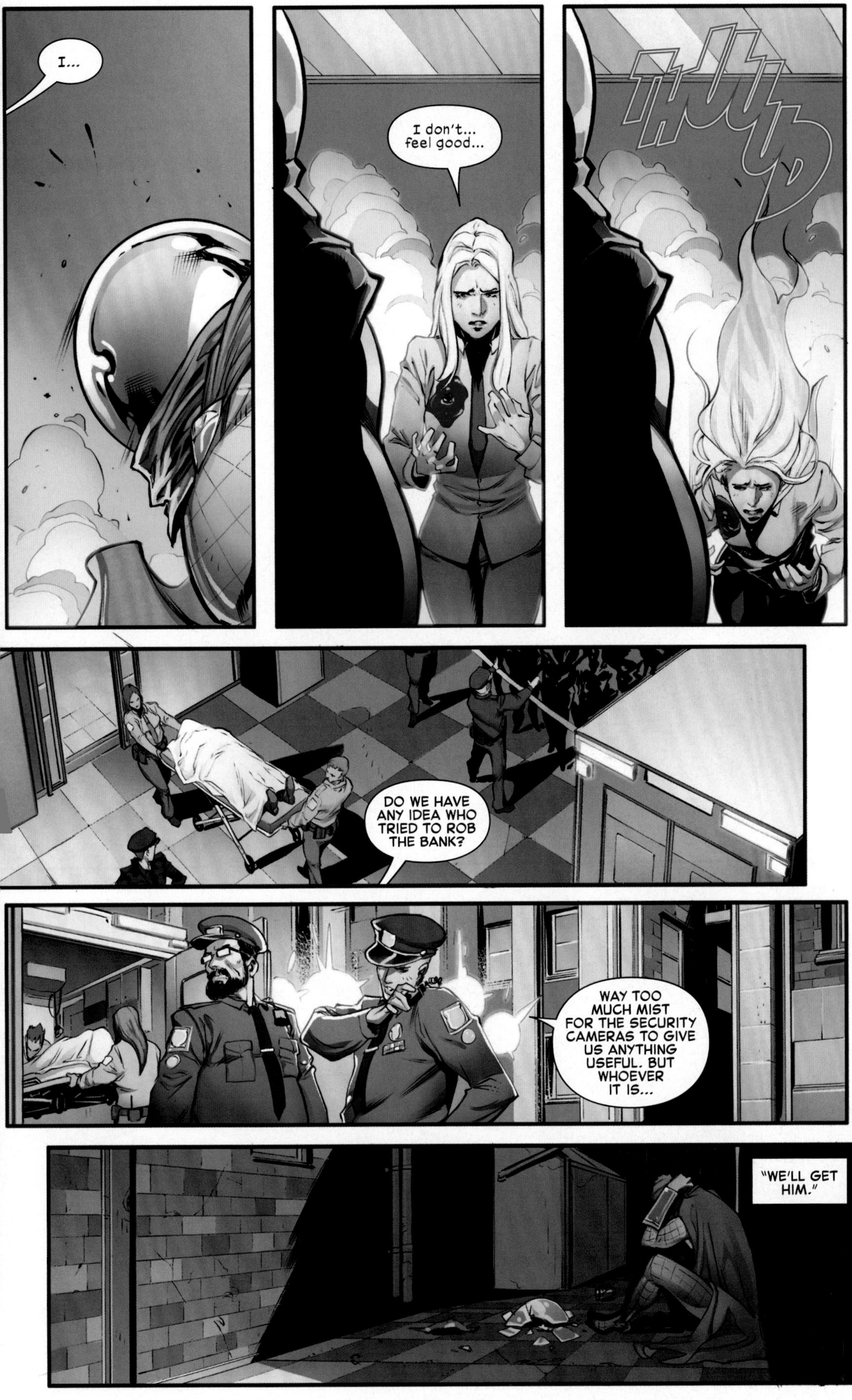
I...
I don't... feel good...
THUUD
DO WE HAVE ANY IDEA WHO TRIED TO ROB THE BANK?
WAY TOO MUCH MIST FOR THE SECURITY CAMERAS TO GIVE US ANYTHING USEFUL. BUT WHOEVER IT IS...
"WE'LL GET HIM."

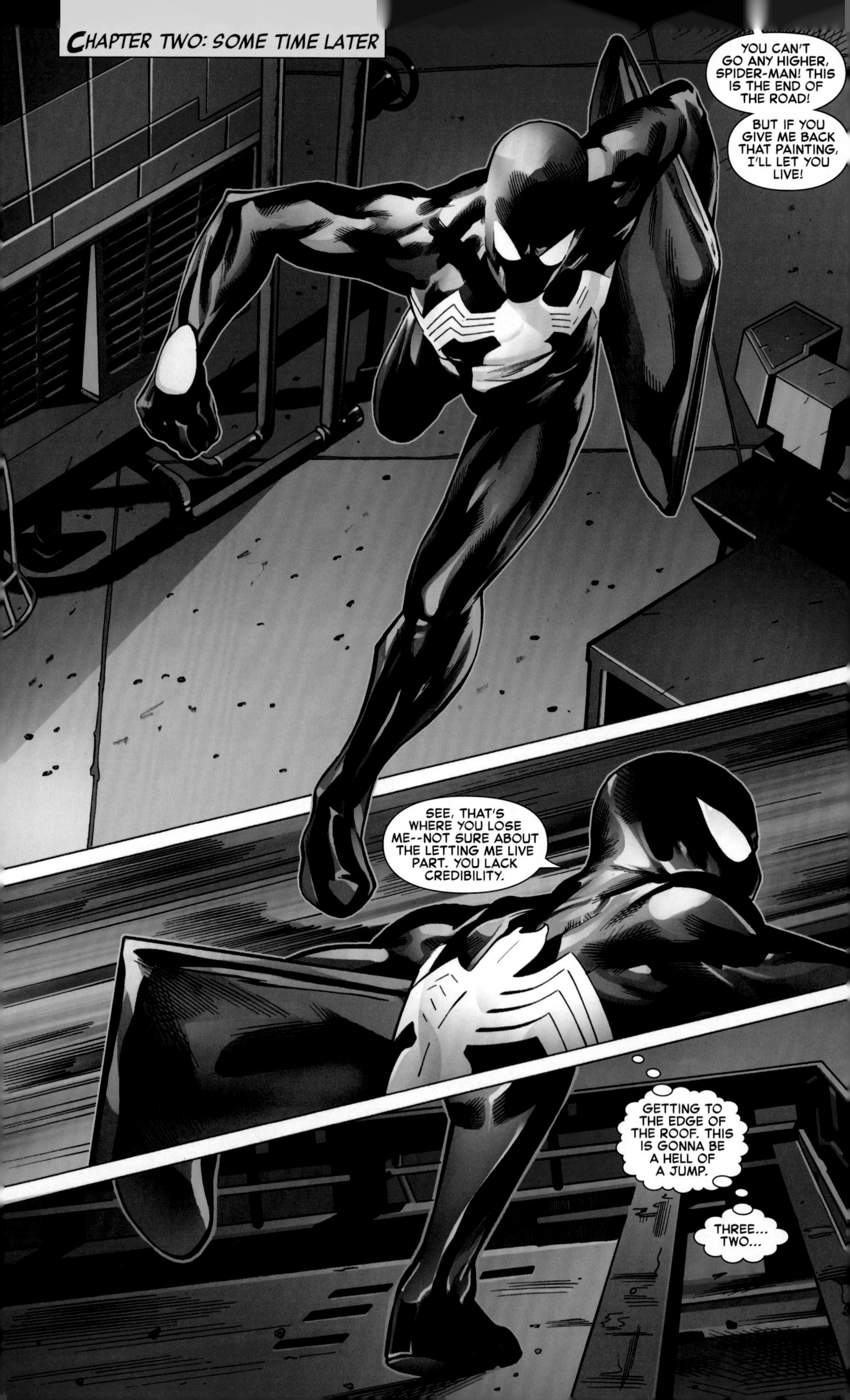
CHAPTER TWO: SOME TIME LATER
YOU CAN'T GO ANY HIGHER, SPIDER-MAN! THIS IS THE END OF THE ROAD!
BUT IF YOU GIVE ME BACK THAT PAINTING, I'LL LET YOU LIVE!
SEE, THAT'S WHERE YOU LOSE ME--NOT SURE ABOUT THE LETTING ME LIVE PART. YOU LACK CREDIBILITY.
GETTING TO THE EDGE OF THE ROOF. THIS IS GONNA BE A HELL OF A JUMP.
THREE... TWO...

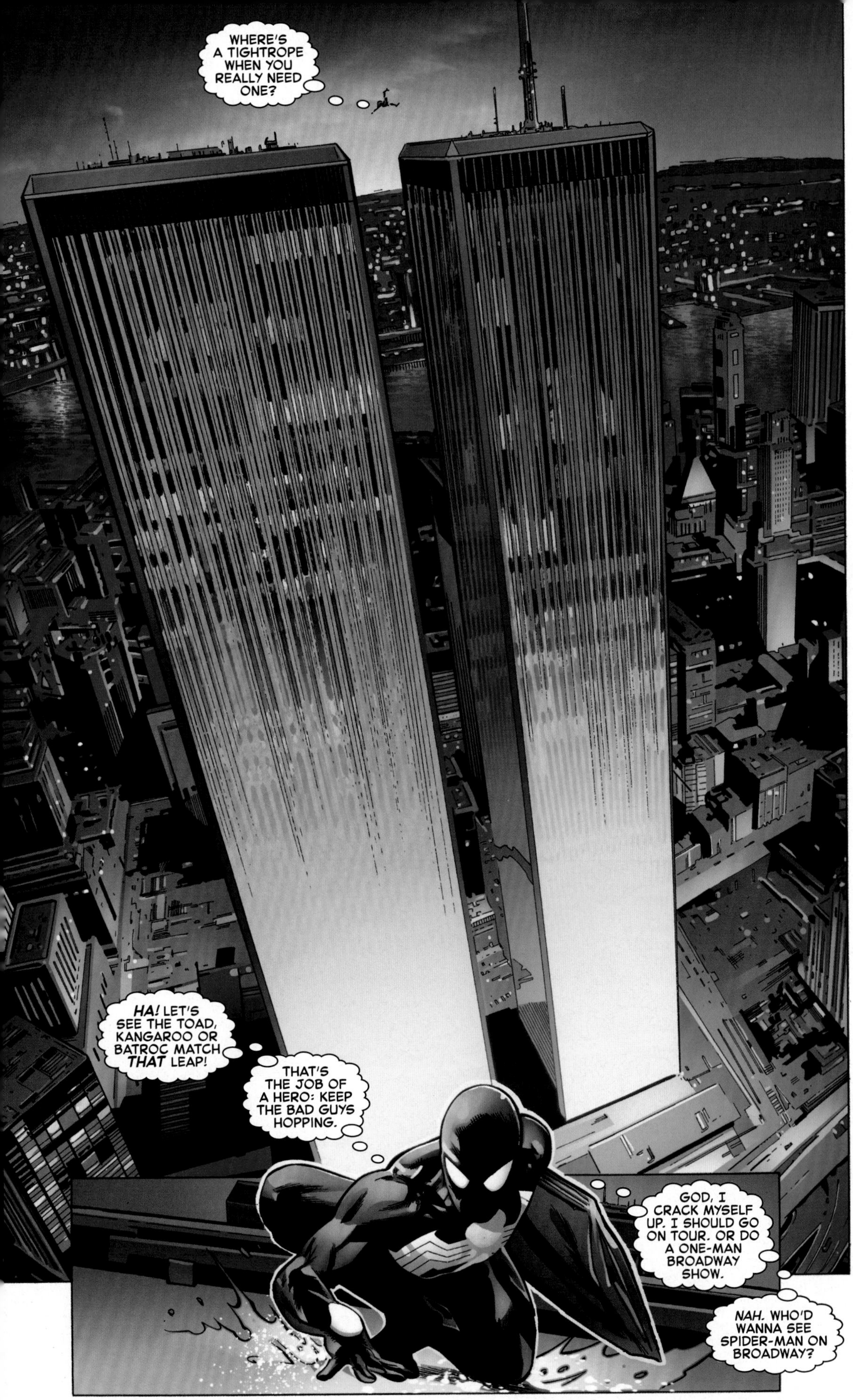
WHERE'S A TIGHTROPE WHEN YOU REALLY NEED ONE?
HA! LET'S SEE THE TOAD, KANGAROO OR BATROC MATCH THAT LEAP!
THAT'S THE JOB OF A HERO: KEEP THE BAD GUYS HOPPING.
GOD, I CRACK MYSELF UP. I SHOULD GO ON TOUR. OR DO A ONE-MAN BROADWAY SHOW.
NAH. WHO'D WANNA SEE SPIDER-MAN ON BROADWAY?

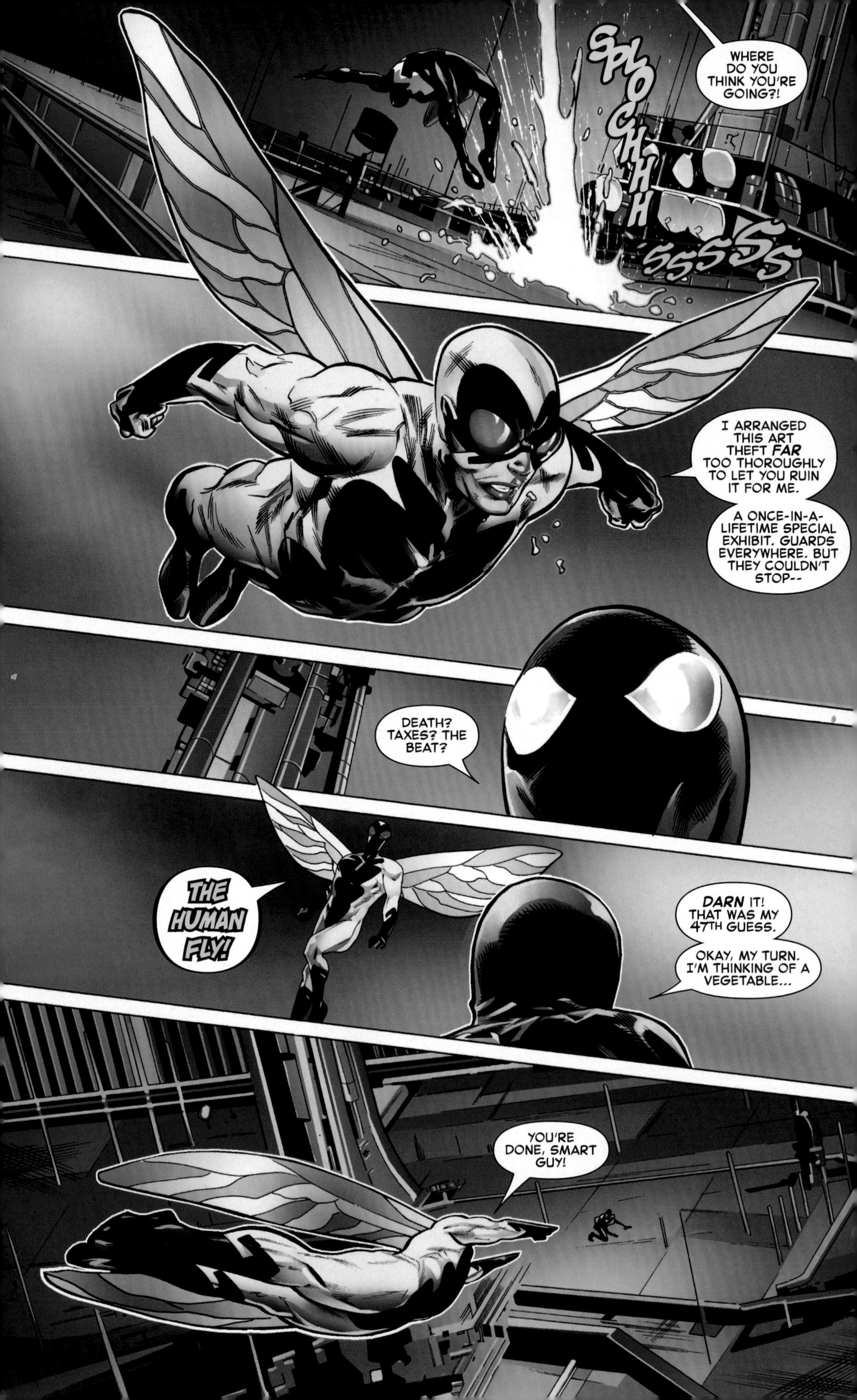

WHERE DO YOU THINK YOU'RE GOING?!
SPLOCHHH
SSSSSS
I ARRANGED THIS ART THEFT FAR TOO THOROUGHLY TO LET YOU RUIN IT FOR ME.
A ONCE-IN-A-LIFETIME SPECIAL EXHIBIT. GUARDS EVERYWHERE. BUT THEY COULDN'T STOP--
DEATH? TAXES? THE BEAT?
THE HUMAN FLY!
DARN IT! THAT WAS MY 47TH GUESS.
OKAY, MY TURN. I'M THINKING OF A VEGETABLE...
YOU'RE DONE, SMART GUY!

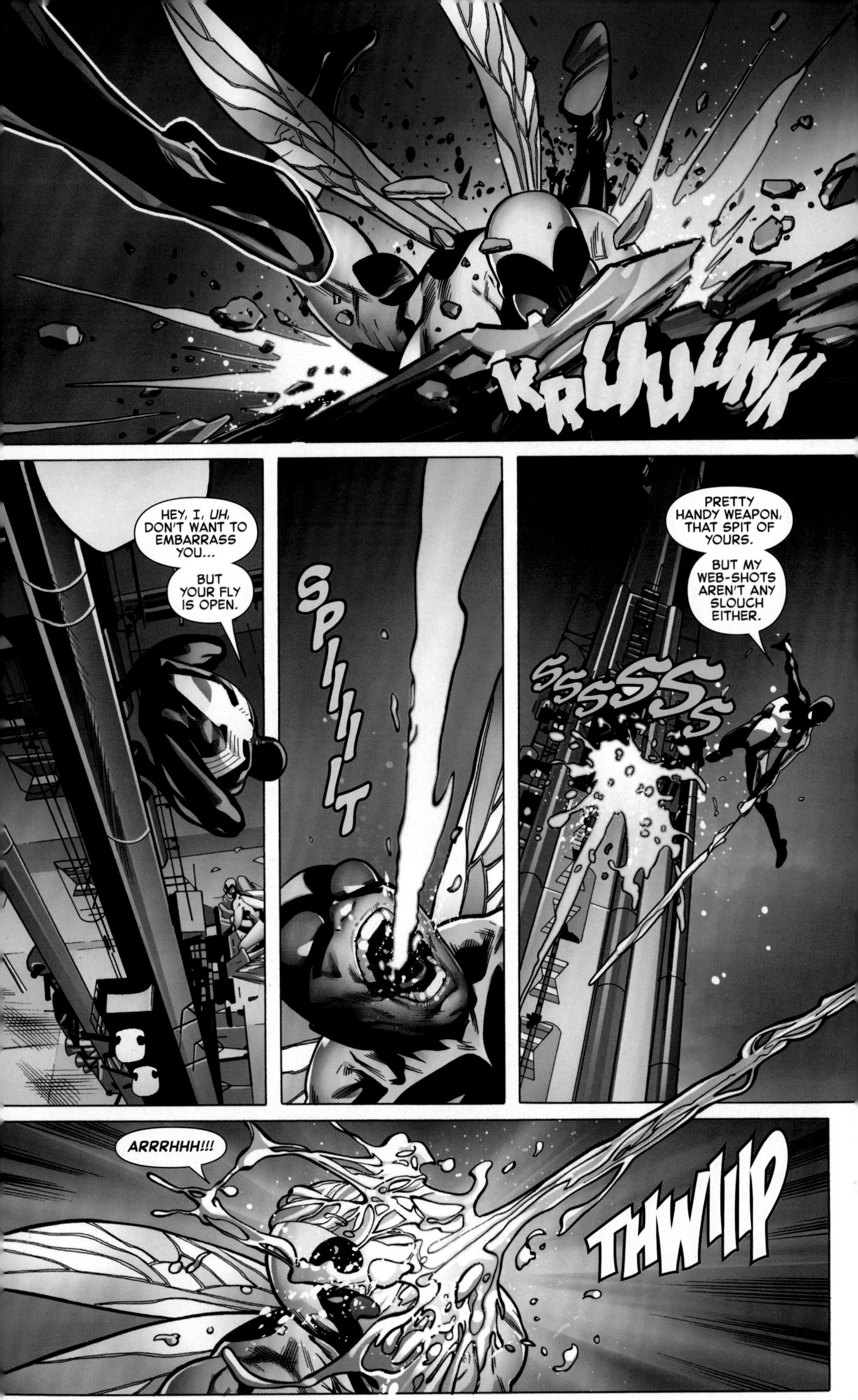
KRUUUNK
HEY, I, UH, DON'T WANT TO EMBARRASS YOU...
BUT YOUR FLY IS OPEN.
SPIIIIT
PRETTY HANDY WEAPON, THAT SPIT OF YOURS.
BUT MY WEB-SHOTS AREN'T ANY SLOUCH EITHER.
SSSSSSS
ARRRHHH!!!
THWIIIP

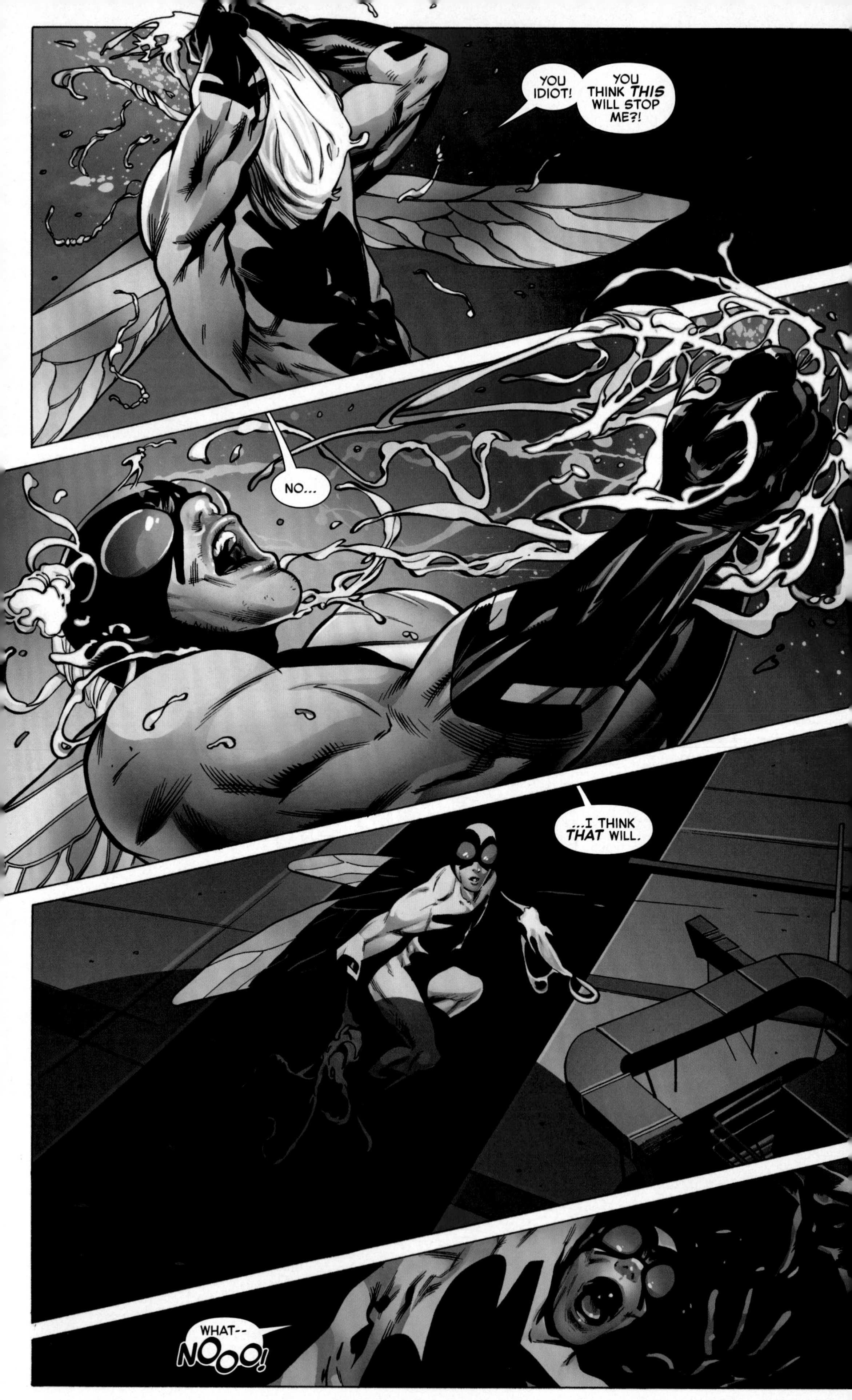
YOU IDIOT!
YOU THINK THIS WILL STOP ME?!
NO...
...I THINK THAT WILL.
WHAT--
NOOO!

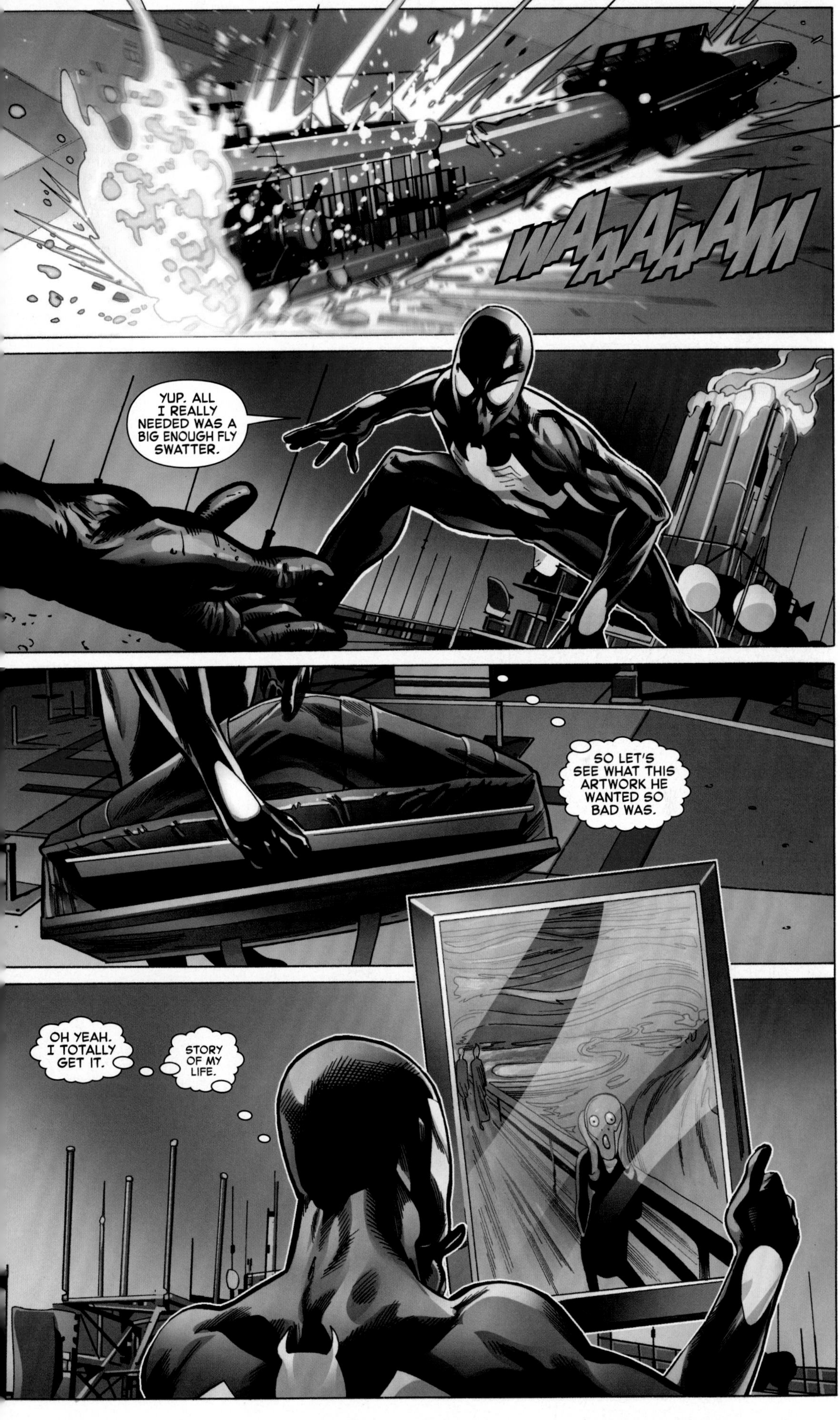
WAAAAAAM
YUP. ALL I REALLY NEEDED WAS A BIG ENOUGH FLY SWATTER.
SO LET'S SEE WHAT THIS ARTWORK HE WANTED SO BAD WAS.
OH YEAH. I TOTALLY GET IT.
STORY OF MY LIFE.

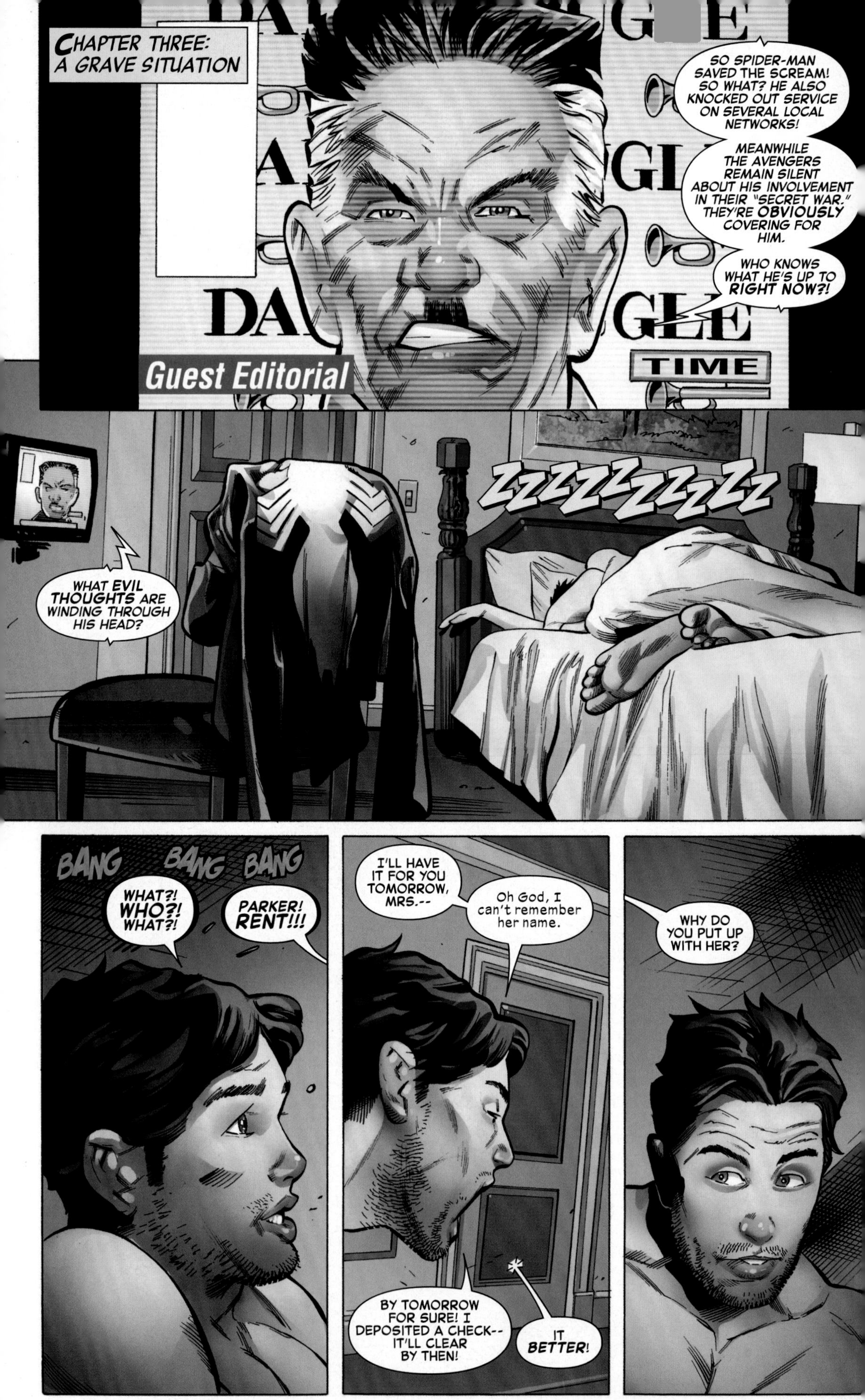
CHAPTER THREE:
A GRAVE SITUATION
SO SPIDER-MAN SAVED THE SCREAM! SO WHAT? HE ALSO KNOCKED OUT SERVICE ON SEVERAL LOCAL NETWORKS!
MEANWHILE THE AVENGERS REMAIN SILENT ABOUT HIS INVOLVEMENT IN THEIR "SECRET WAR." THEY'RE OBVIOUSLY COVERING FOR HIM.
WHO KNOWS WHAT HE'S UP TO RIGHT NOW?!
TIME
Guest Editorial
WHAT EVIL THOUGHTS ARE WINDING THROUGH HIS HEAD?
ZZZZZZZZZZZ
BANG BANG BANG
WHAT?! WHO?! WHAT?!
PARKER! RENT!!!
I'LL HAVE IT FOR YOU TOMORROW, MRS.--
Oh God, I can't remember her name.
BY TOMORROW FOR SURE! I DEPOSITED A CHECK-- IT'LL CLEAR BY THEN!
IT BETTER!
WHY DO YOU PUT UP WITH HER?

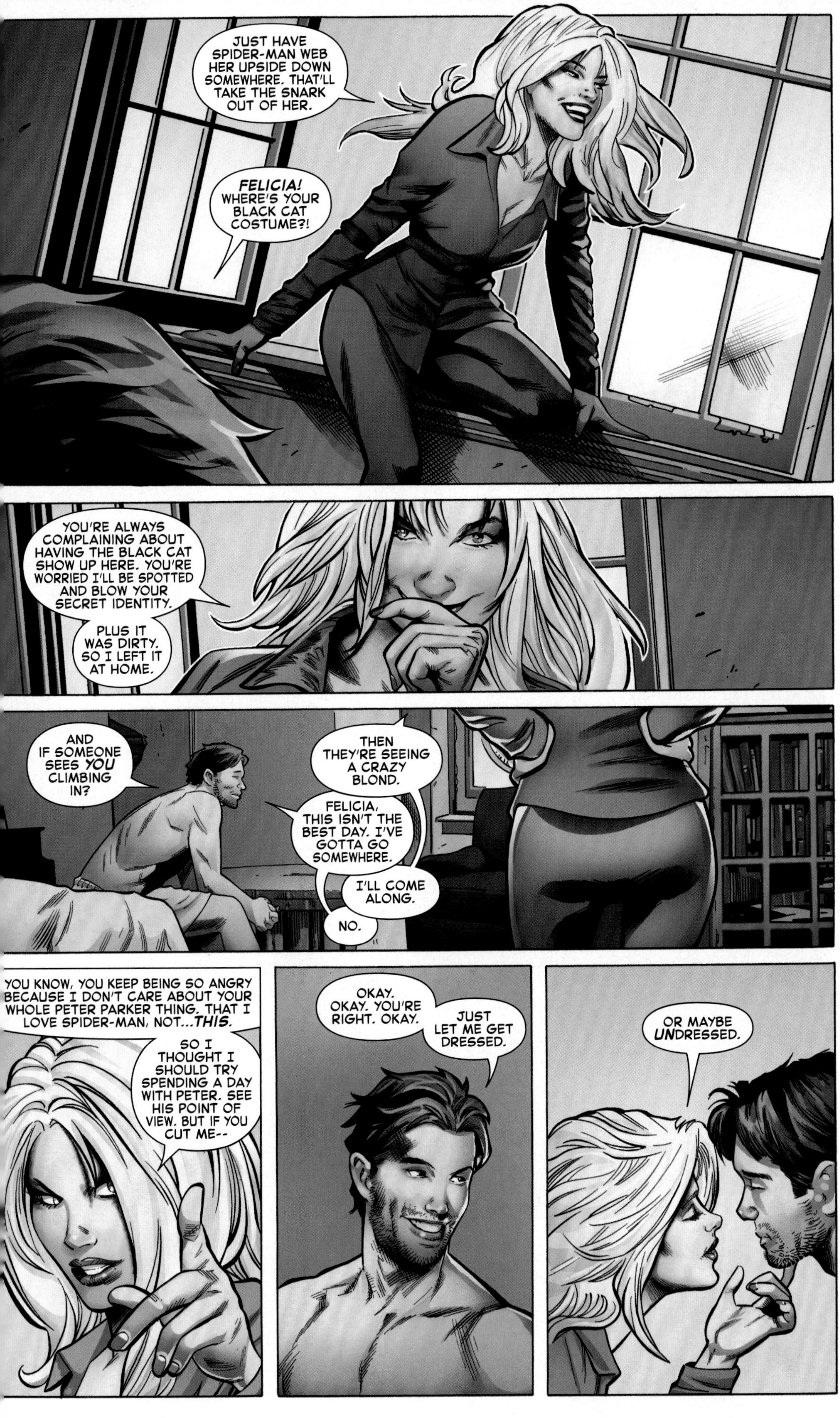
JUST HAVE SPIDER-MAN WEB HER UPSIDE DOWN SOMEWHERE. THAT'LL TAKE THE SNARK OUT OF HER.
FELICIA! WHERE'S YOUR BLACK CAT COSTUME?!
YOU'RE ALWAYS COMPLAINING ABOUT HAVING THE BLACK CAT SHOW UP HERE. YOU'RE WORRIED I'LL BE SPOTTED AND BLOW YOUR SECRET IDENTITY.
PLUS IT WAS DIRTY. SO I LEFT IT AT HOME.
AND IF SOMEONE SEES YOU CLIMBING IN?
THEN THEY'RE SEEING A CRAZY BLOND.
FELICIA, THIS ISN'T THE BEST DAY. I'VE GOTTA GO SOMEWHERE.
I'LL COME ALONG.
NO.
YOU KNOW, YOU KEEP BEING SO ANGRY BECAUSE I DON'T CARE ABOUT YOUR WHOLE PETER PARKER THING. THAT I LOVE SPIDER-MAN, NOT...THIS.
SO I THOUGHT I SHOULD TRY SPENDING A DAY WITH PETER. SEE HIS POINT OF VIEW. BUT IF YOU CUT ME--
OKAY. OKAY. YOU'RE RIGHT. OKAY.
JUST LET ME GET DRESSED.
OR MAYBE UNDRESSED.

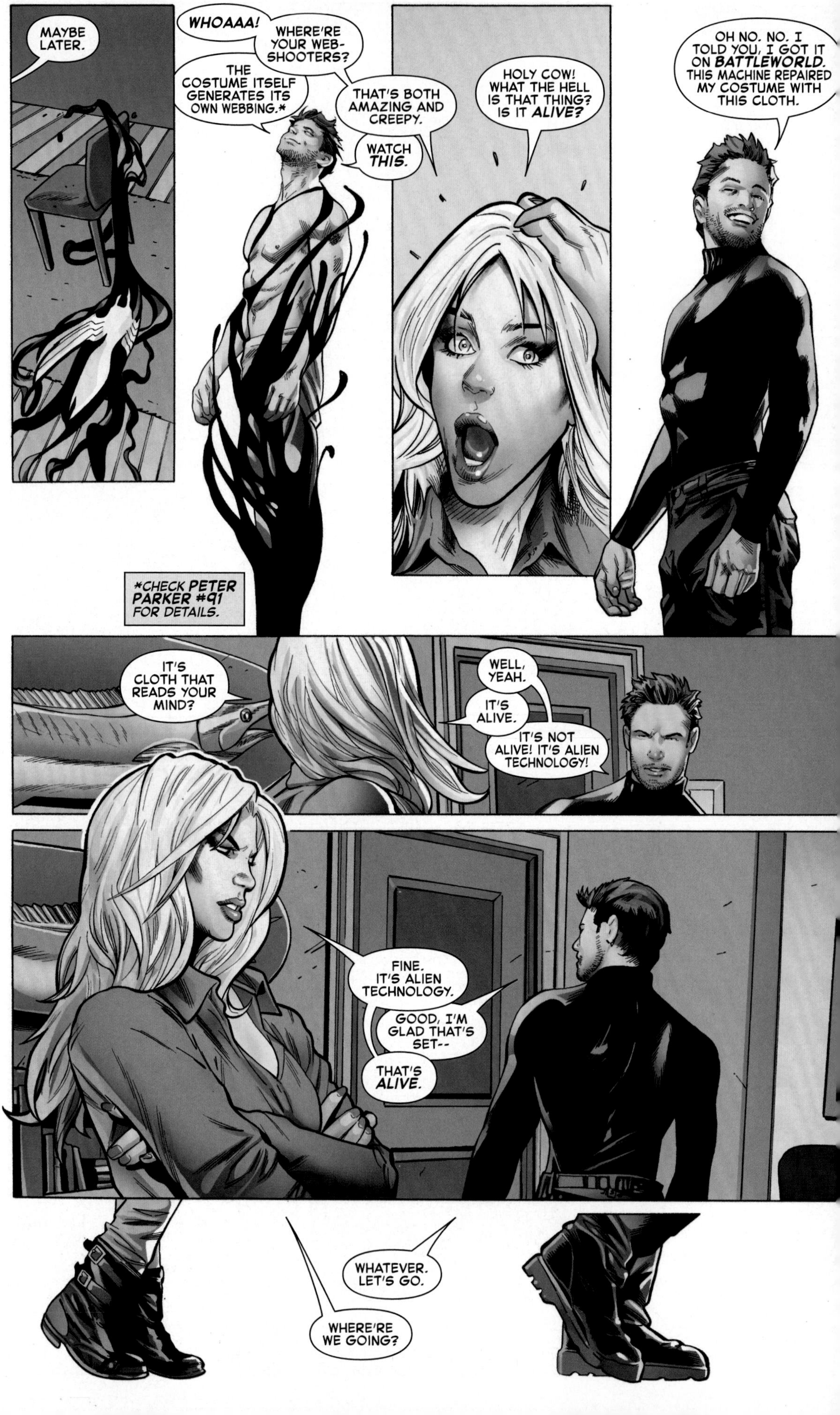
MAYBE LATER.
WHOAAA!
WHERE'RE YOUR WEB-SHOOTERS?
THE COSTUME ITSELF GENERATES ITS OWN WEBBING.*
THAT'S BOTH AMAZING AND CREEPY.
WATCH THIS.
HOLY COW! WHAT THE HELL IS THAT THING? IS IT ALIVE?
OH NO. NO. I TOLD YOU, I GOT IT ON BATTLEWORLD. THIS MACHINE REPAIRED MY COSTUME WITH THIS CLOTH.
*CHECK PETER PARKER #91 FOR DETAILS.
IT'S CLOTH THAT READS YOUR MIND?
WELL, YEAH.
IT'S ALIVE.
IT'S NOT ALIVE! IT'S ALIEN TECHNOLOGY!
FINE. IT'S ALIEN TECHNOLOGY.
GOOD, I'M GLAD THAT'S SET--
THAT'S ALIVE.
WHATEVER. LET'S GO.
WHERE'RE WE GOING?

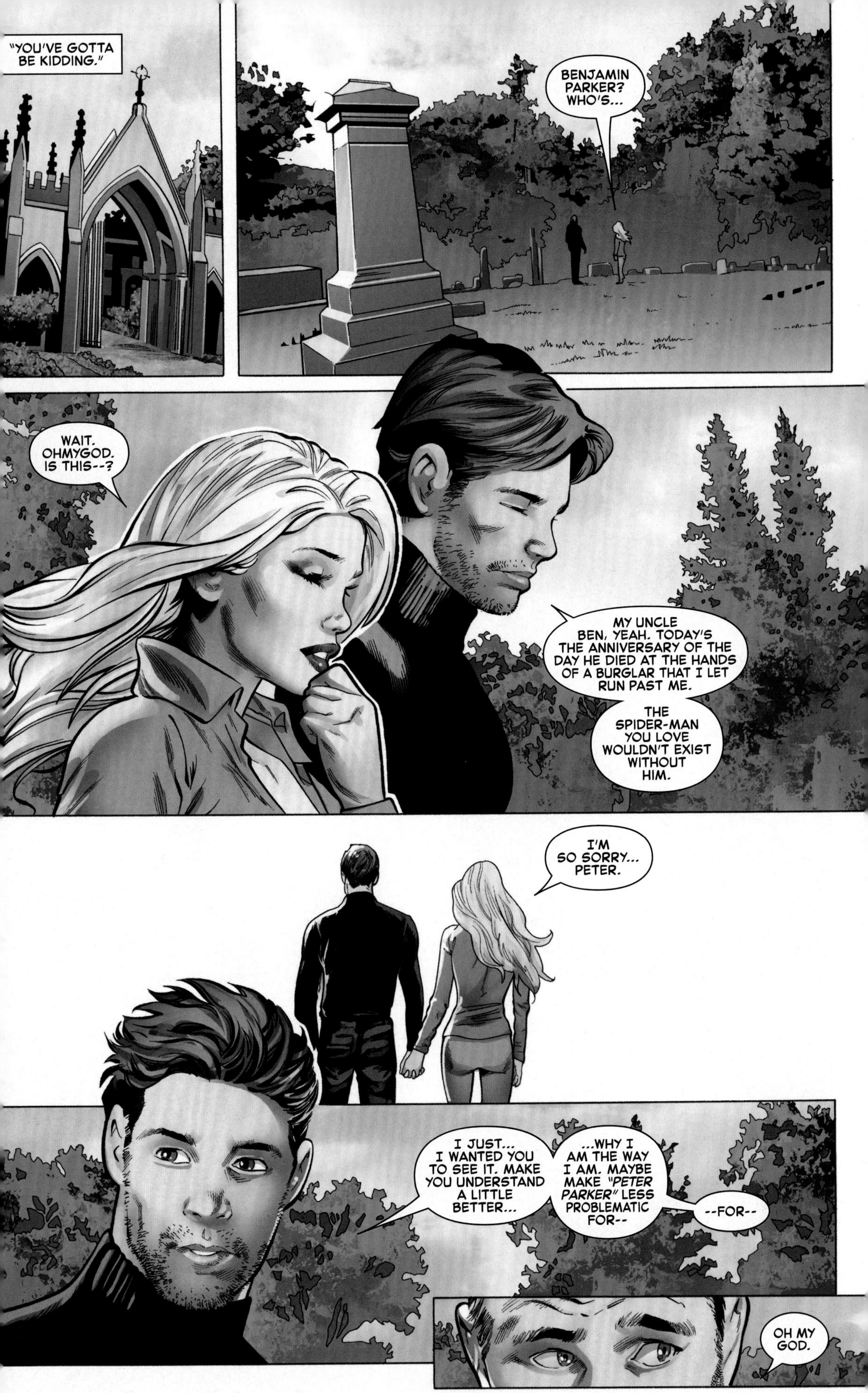
"YOU'VE GOTTA BE KIDDING."
BENJAMIN PARKER? WHO'S...
WAIT. OHMYGOD. IS THIS--?
MY UNCLE BEN, YEAH. TODAY'S THE ANNIVERSARY OF THE DAY HE DIED AT THE HANDS OF A BURGLAR THAT I LET RUN PAST ME.
THE SPIDER-MAN YOU LOVE WOULDN'T EXIST WITHOUT HIM.
I'M SO SORRY... PETER.
I JUST... I WANTED YOU TO SEE IT. MAKE YOU UNDERSTAND A LITTLE BETTER...
...WHY I AM THE WAY I AM. MAYBE MAKE "PETER PARKER" LESS PROBLEMATIC FOR--
--FOR--
OH MY GOD.

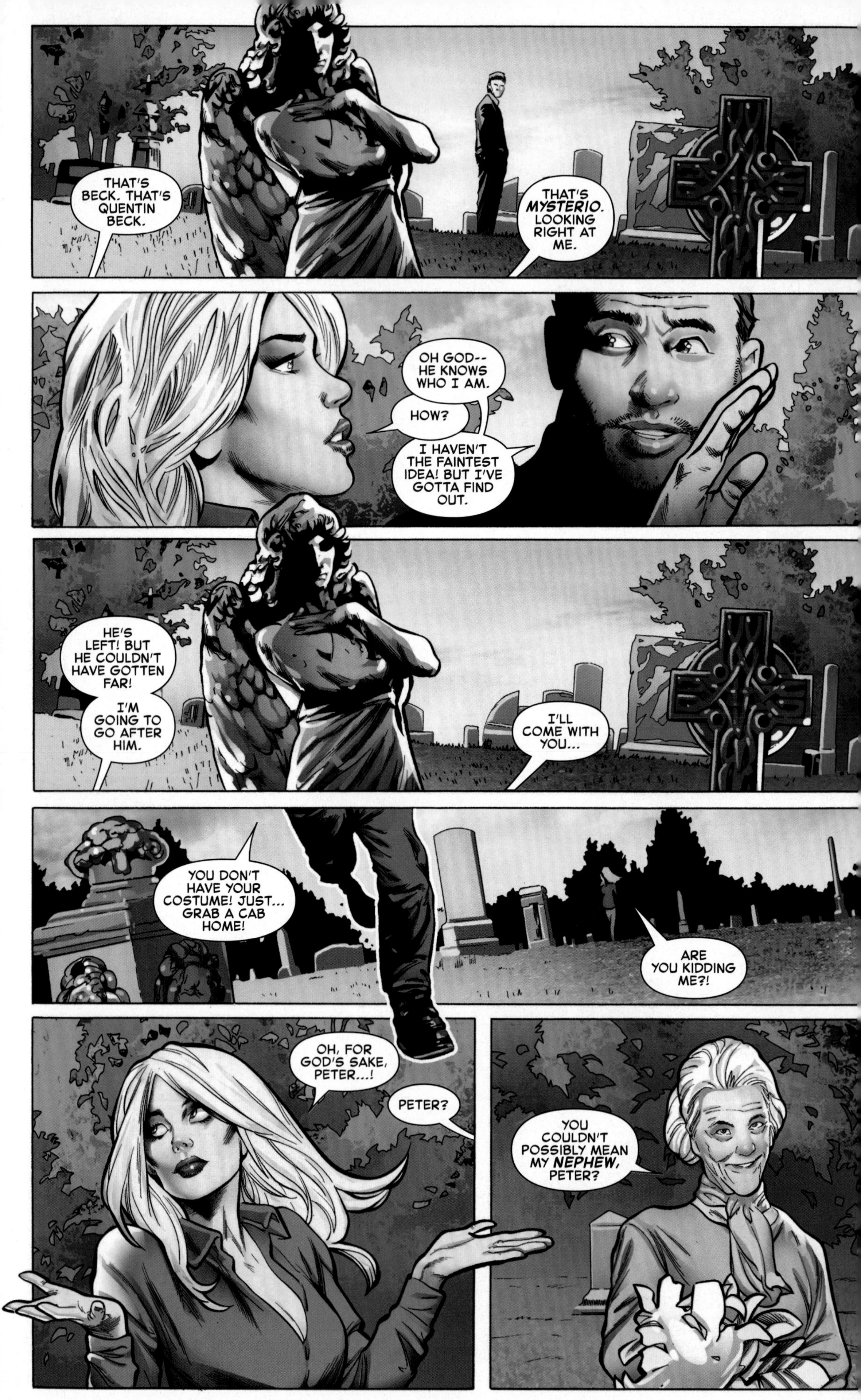
THAT'S BECK. THAT'S QUENTIN BECK.
THAT'S MYSTERIO. LOOKING RIGHT AT ME.
OH GOD-- HE KNOWS WHO I AM.
HOW?
I HAVEN'T THE FAINTEST IDEA! BUT I'VE GOTTA FIND OUT.
HE'S LEFT! BUT HE COULDN'T HAVE GOTTEN FAR!
I'M GOING TO GO AFTER HIM.
I'LL COME WITH YOU...
YOU DON'T HAVE YOUR COSTUME! JUST... GRAB A CAB HOME!
ARE YOU KIDDING ME?!
OH, FOR GOD'S SAKE, PETER...!
PETER?
YOU COULDN'T POSSIBLY MEAN MY NEPHEW, PETER?

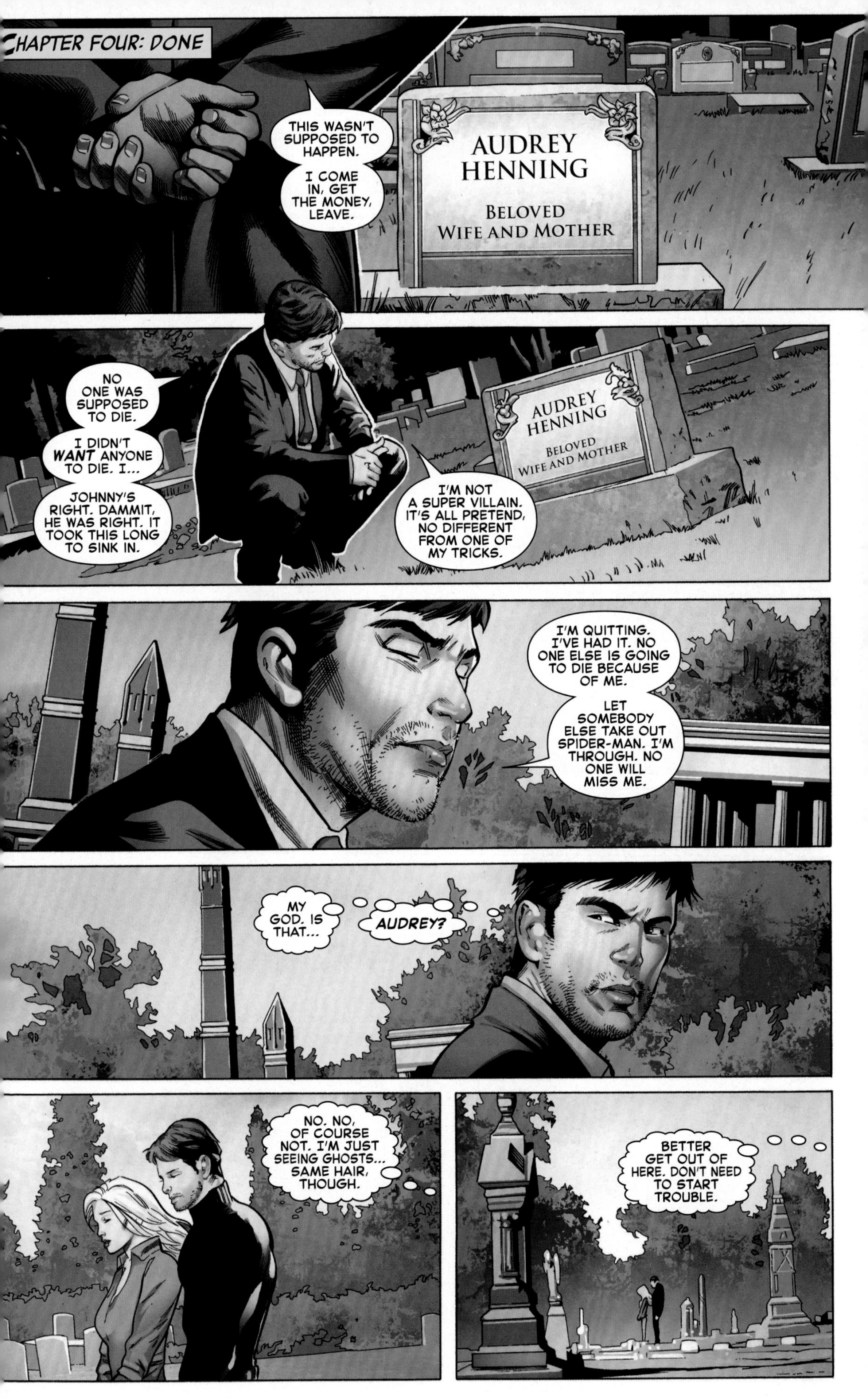
CHAPTER FOUR: DONE
THIS WASN'T SUPPOSED TO HAPPEN.
I COME IN, GET THE MONEY, LEAVE.
AUDREY HENNING
BELOVED WIFE AND MOTHER
NO ONE WAS SUPPOSED TO DIE.
I DIDN'T WANT ANYONE TO DIE. I...
JOHNNY'S RIGHT. DAMMIT, HE WAS RIGHT. IT TOOK THIS LONG TO SINK IN.
I'M NOT A SUPER VILLAIN. IT'S ALL PRETEND, NO DIFFERENT FROM ONE OF MY TRICKS.
AUDREY HENNING
BELOVED WIFE AND MOTHER
I'M QUITTING. I'VE HAD IT. NO ONE ELSE IS GOING TO DIE BECAUSE OF ME.
LET SOMEBODY ELSE TAKE OUT SPIDER-MAN. I'M THROUGH. NO ONE WILL MISS ME.
MY GOD. IS THAT...
AUDREY?
NO. NO, OF COURSE NOT. I'M JUST SEEING GHOSTS... SAME HAIR, THOUGH.
BETTER GET OUT OF HERE. DON'T NEED TO START TROUBLE.

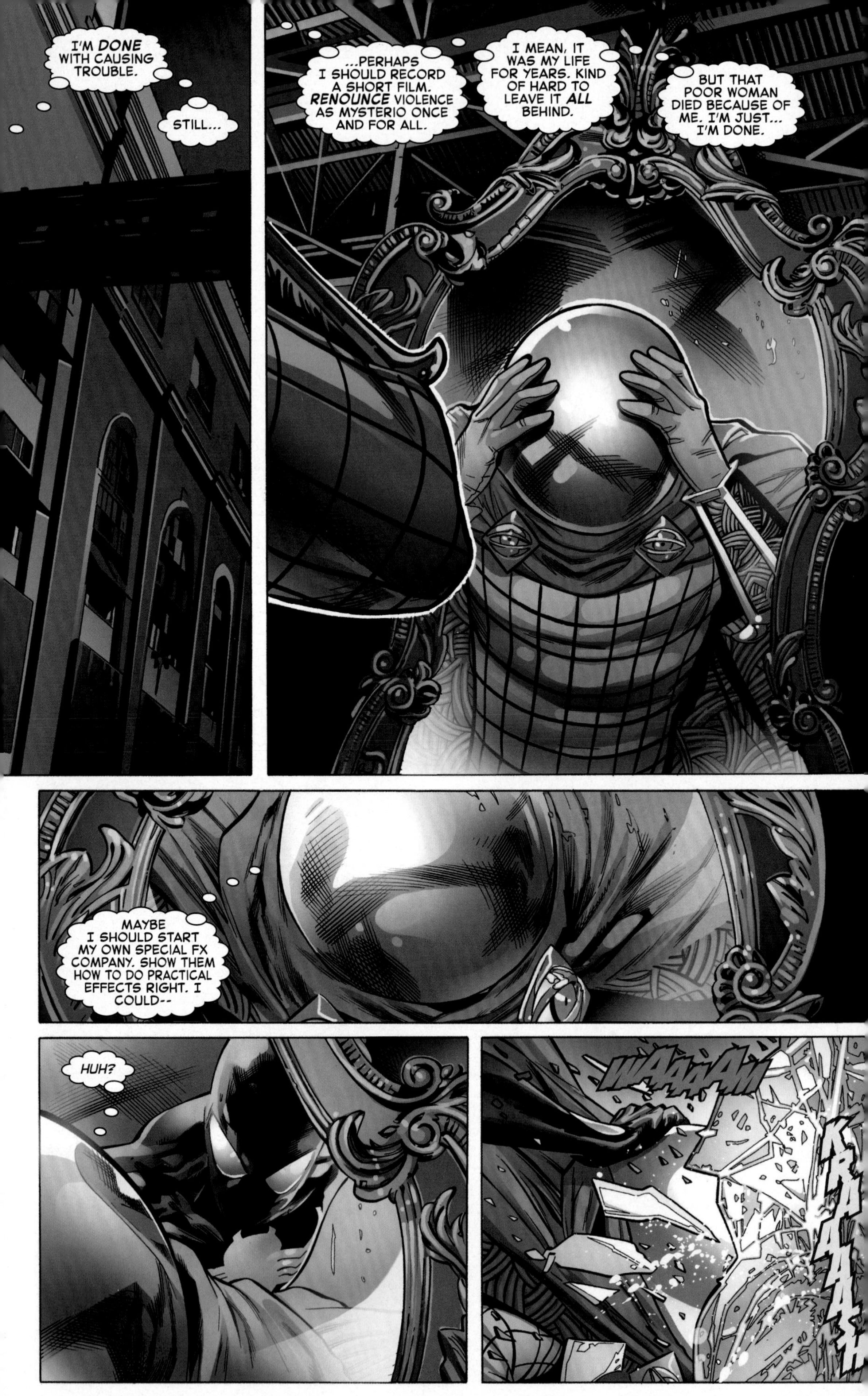

I'M DONE WITH CAUSING TROUBLE.
STILL...
...PERHAPS I SHOULD RECORD A SHORT FILM. RENOUNCE VIOLENCE AS MYSTERIO ONCE AND FOR ALL.
I MEAN, IT WAS MY LIFE FOR YEARS. KIND OF HARD TO LEAVE IT ALL BEHIND.
BUT THAT POOR WOMAN DIED BECAUSE OF ME. I'M JUST... I'M DONE.
MAYBE I SHOULD START MY OWN SPECIAL FX COMPANY. SHOW THEM HOW TO DO PRACTICAL EFFECTS RIGHT. I COULD--
HUH?
WAAAAM
KRAAASH

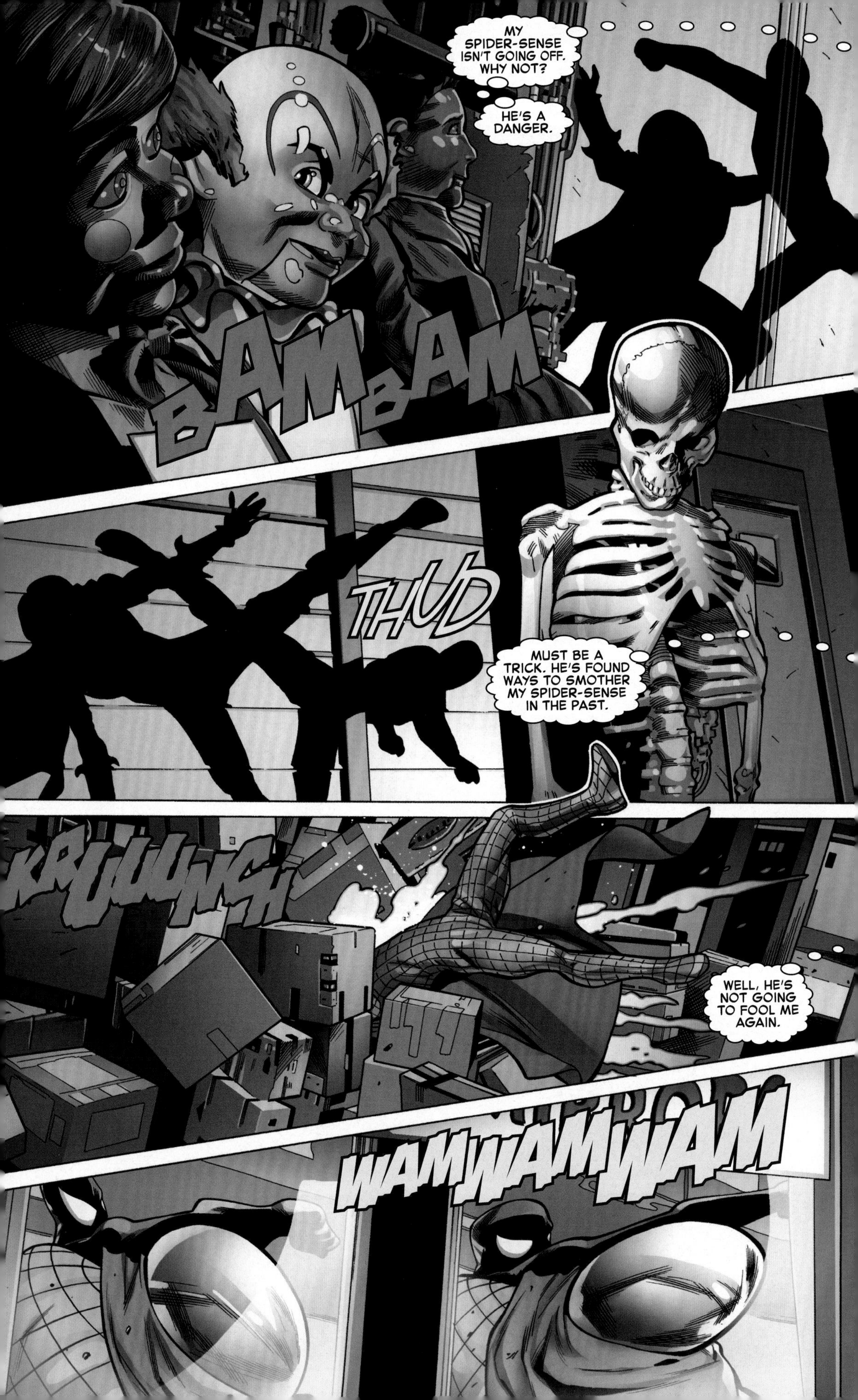
MY SPIDER-SENSE ISN'T GOING OFF. WHY NOT?
HE'S A DANGER.
BAM BAM
THUD
MUST BE A TRICK. HE'S FOUND WAYS TO SMOTHER MY SPIDER-SENSE IN THE PAST.
KRUUUNCH
WELL, HE'S NOT GOING TO FOOL ME AGAIN.
WAM WAM WAM

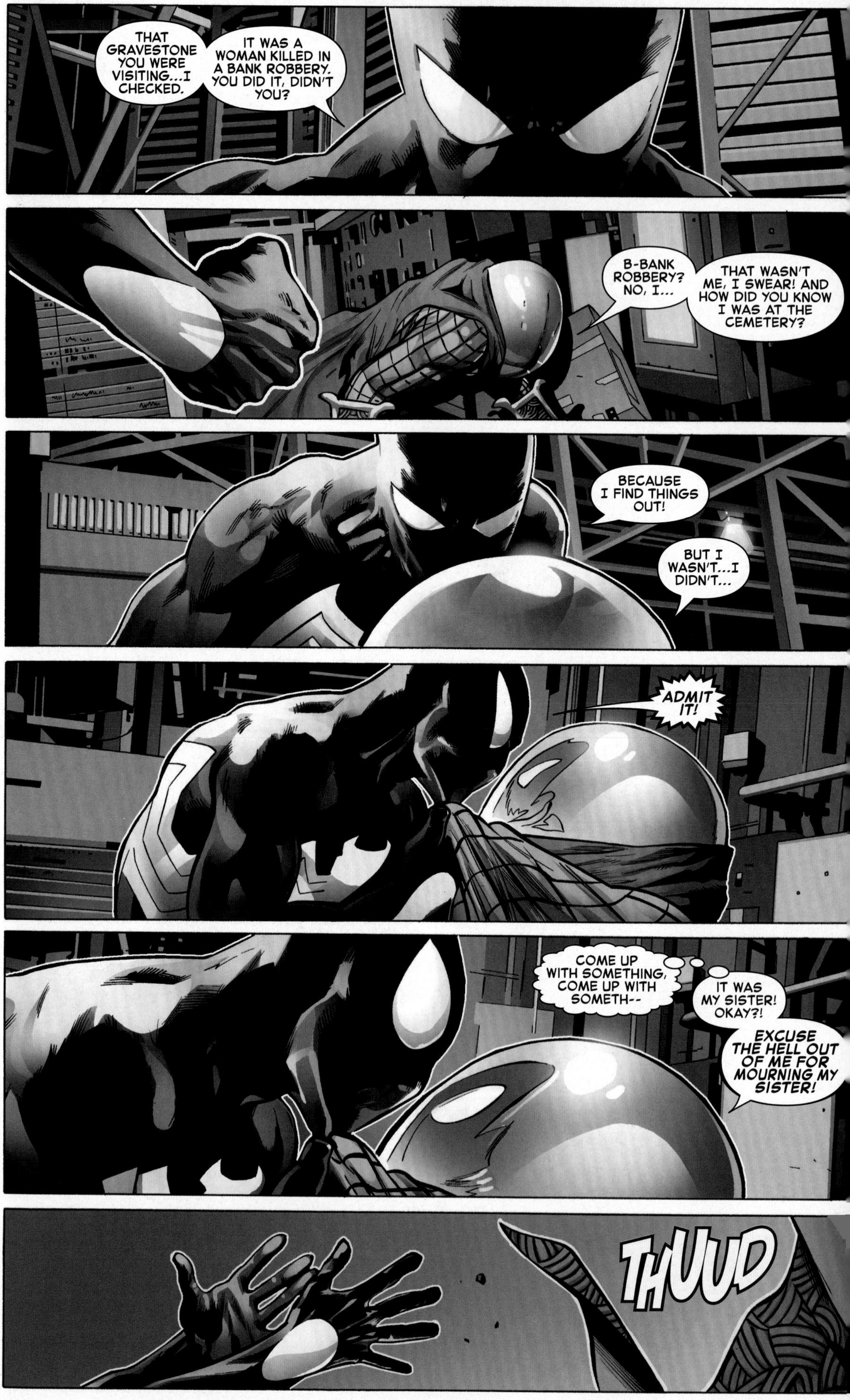
THAT GRAVESTONE YOU WERE VISITING...I CHECKED.
IT WAS A WOMAN KILLED IN A BANK ROBBERY. YOU DID IT, DIDN'T YOU?
B-BANK ROBBERY? NO, I...
THAT WASN'T ME, I SWEAR! AND HOW DID YOU KNOW I WAS AT THE CEMETERY?
BECAUSE I FIND THINGS OUT!
BUT I WASN'T...I DIDN'T...
ADMIT IT!
COME UP WITH SOMETHING, COME UP WITH SOMETH--
IT WAS MY SISTER! OKAY?!
EXCUSE THE HELL OUT OF ME FOR MOURNING MY SISTER!
THUUD

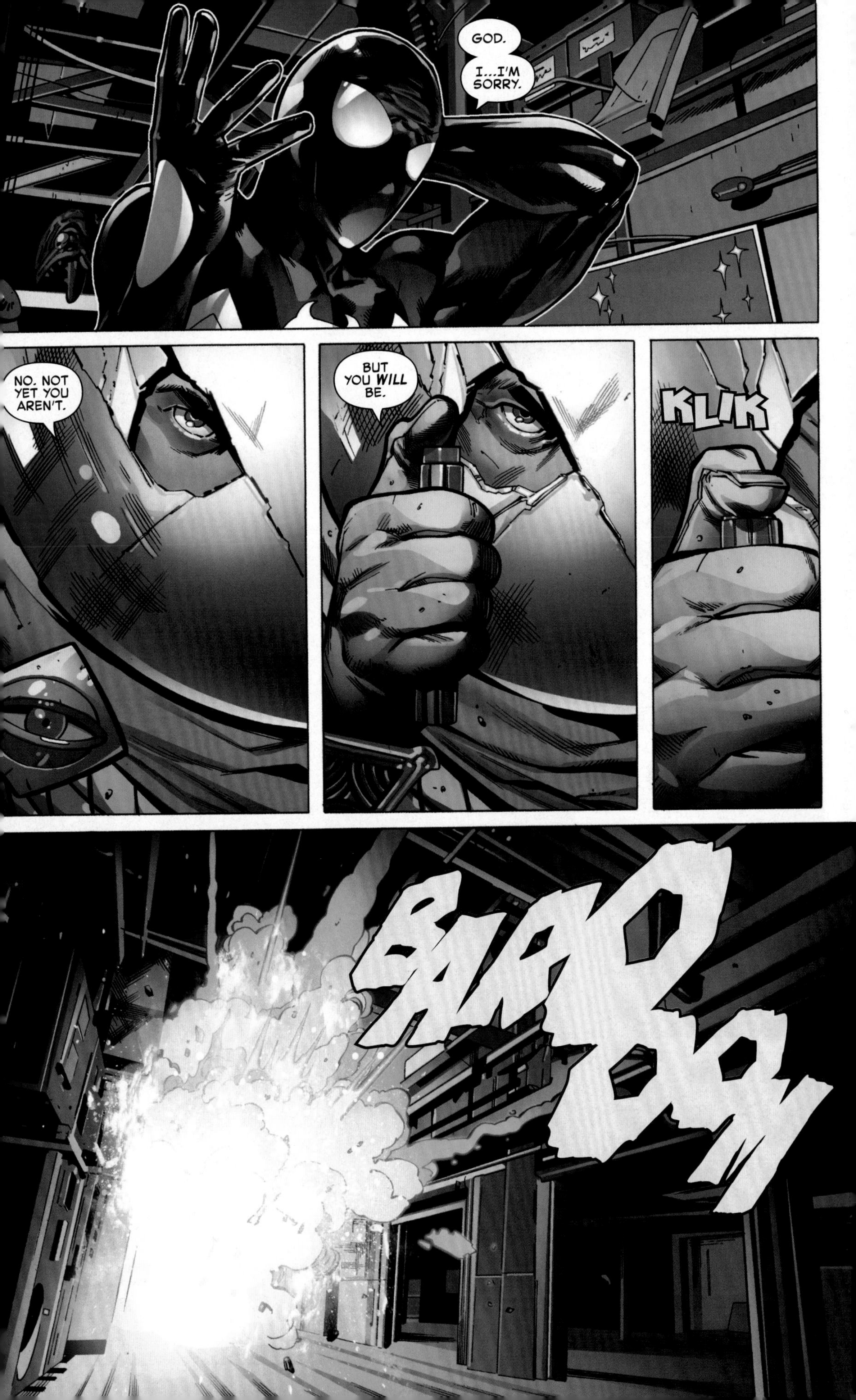
GOD.
I...I'M SORRY.
NO. NOT YET YOU AREN'T.
BUT YOU WILL BE.
KLIK
BADOOM

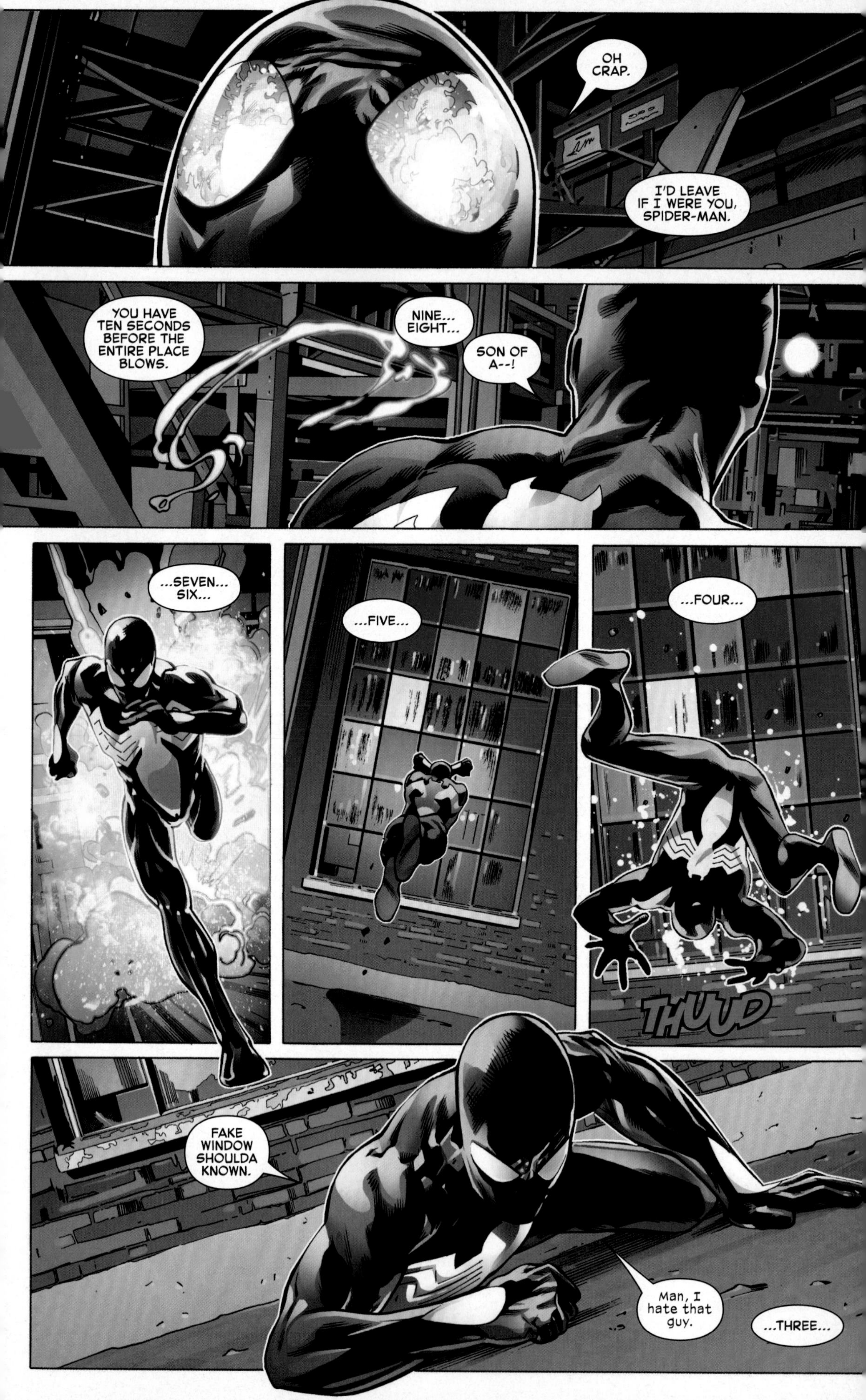
OH CRAP.
I'D LEAVE IF I WERE YOU, SPIDER-MAN.
YOU HAVE TEN SECONDS BEFORE THE ENTIRE PLACE BLOWS.
NINE... EIGHT...
SON OF A--!
...SEVEN... SIX...
...FIVE...
...FOUR...
THUUD
FAKE WINDOW SHOULDA KNOWN.
Man, I hate that guy.
...THREE...

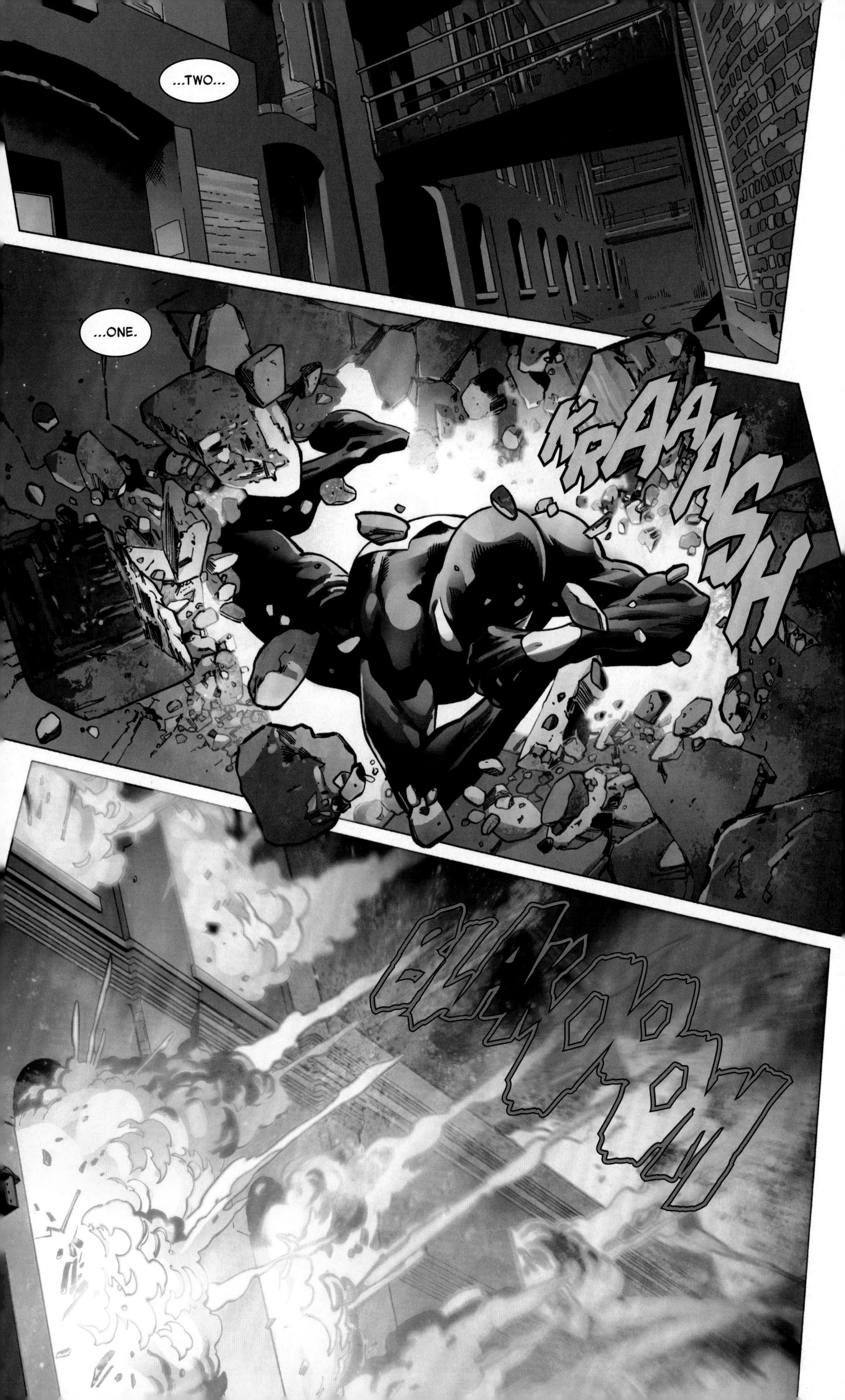
...TWO...
...ONE.
KRAAAASH

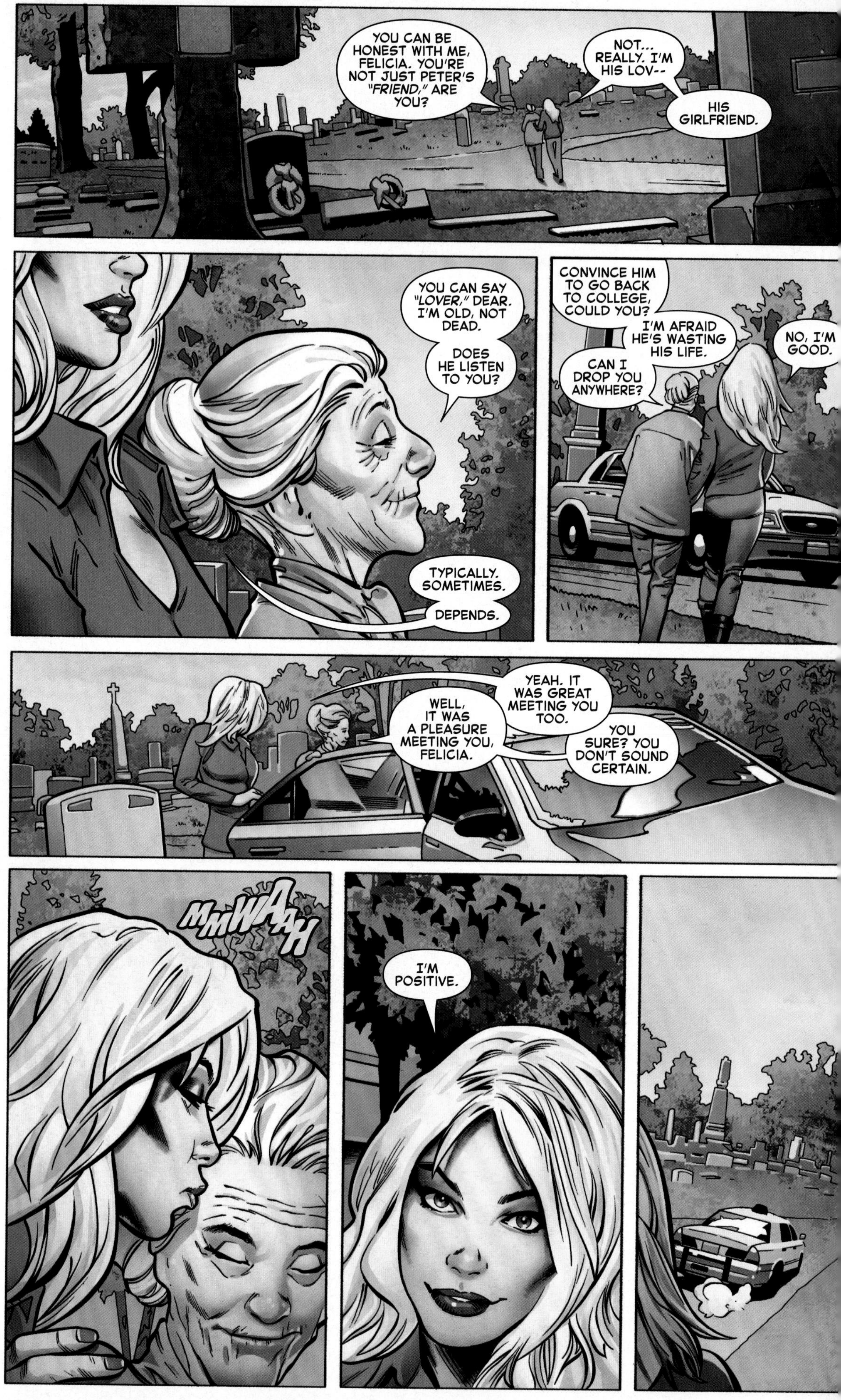

YOU CAN BE HONEST WITH ME, FELICIA. YOU'RE NOT JUST PETER'S "FRIEND," ARE YOU?
NOT... REALLY. I'M HIS LOV--
HIS GIRLFRIEND.
YOU CAN SAY "LOVER," DEAR. I'M OLD, NOT DEAD.
DOES HE LISTEN TO YOU?
TYPICALLY. SOMETIMES.
DEPENDS.
CONVINCE HIM TO GO BACK TO COLLEGE, COULD YOU?
I'M AFRAID HE'S WASTING HIS LIFE.
CAN I DROP YOU ANYWHERE?
NO, I'M GOOD.
WELL, IT WAS A PLEASURE MEETING YOU, FELICIA.
YEAH. IT WAS GREAT MEETING YOU TOO.
YOU SURE? YOU DON'T SOUND CERTAIN.
MMWAAAH
I'M POSITIVE.

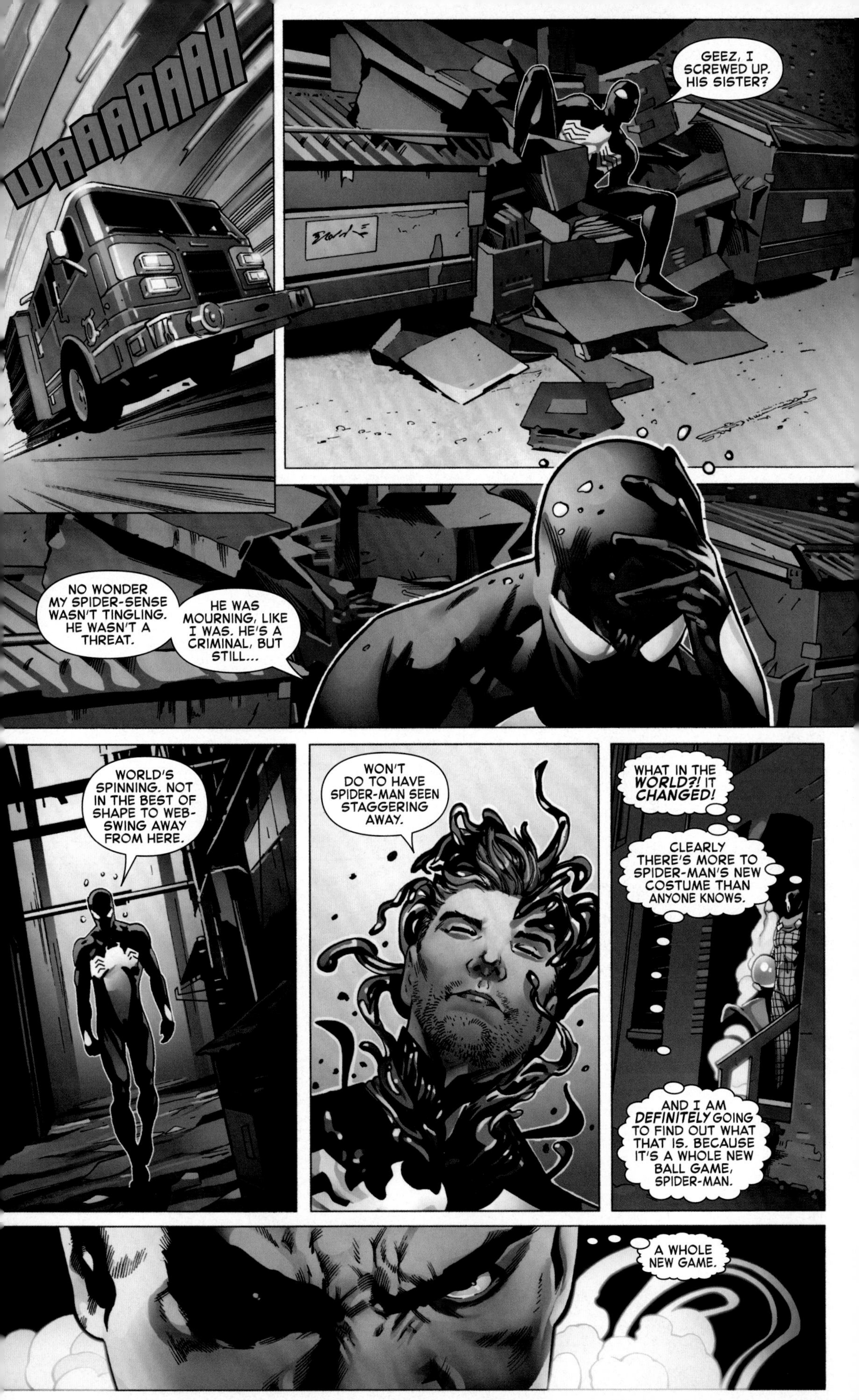
WAAAAAAH
GEEZ, I SCREWED UP. HIS SISTER?
NO WONDER MY SPIDER-SENSE WASN'T TINGLING. HE WASN'T A THREAT.
HE WAS MOURNING, LIKE I WAS. HE'S A CRIMINAL, BUT STILL...
WORLD'S SPINNING. NOT IN THE BEST OF SHAPE TO WEB-SWING AWAY FROM HERE.
WON'T DO TO HAVE SPIDER-MAN SEEN STAGGERING AWAY.
WHAT IN THE *WORLD?!* IT *CHANGED!*
CLEARLY THERE'S MORE TO SPIDER-MAN'S NEW COSTUME THAN ANYONE KNOWS.
AND I AM *DEFINITELY* GOING TO FIND OUT WHAT THAT IS. BECAUSE IT'S A WHOLE NEW BALL GAME, SPIDER-MAN.
A WHOLE NEW GAME.

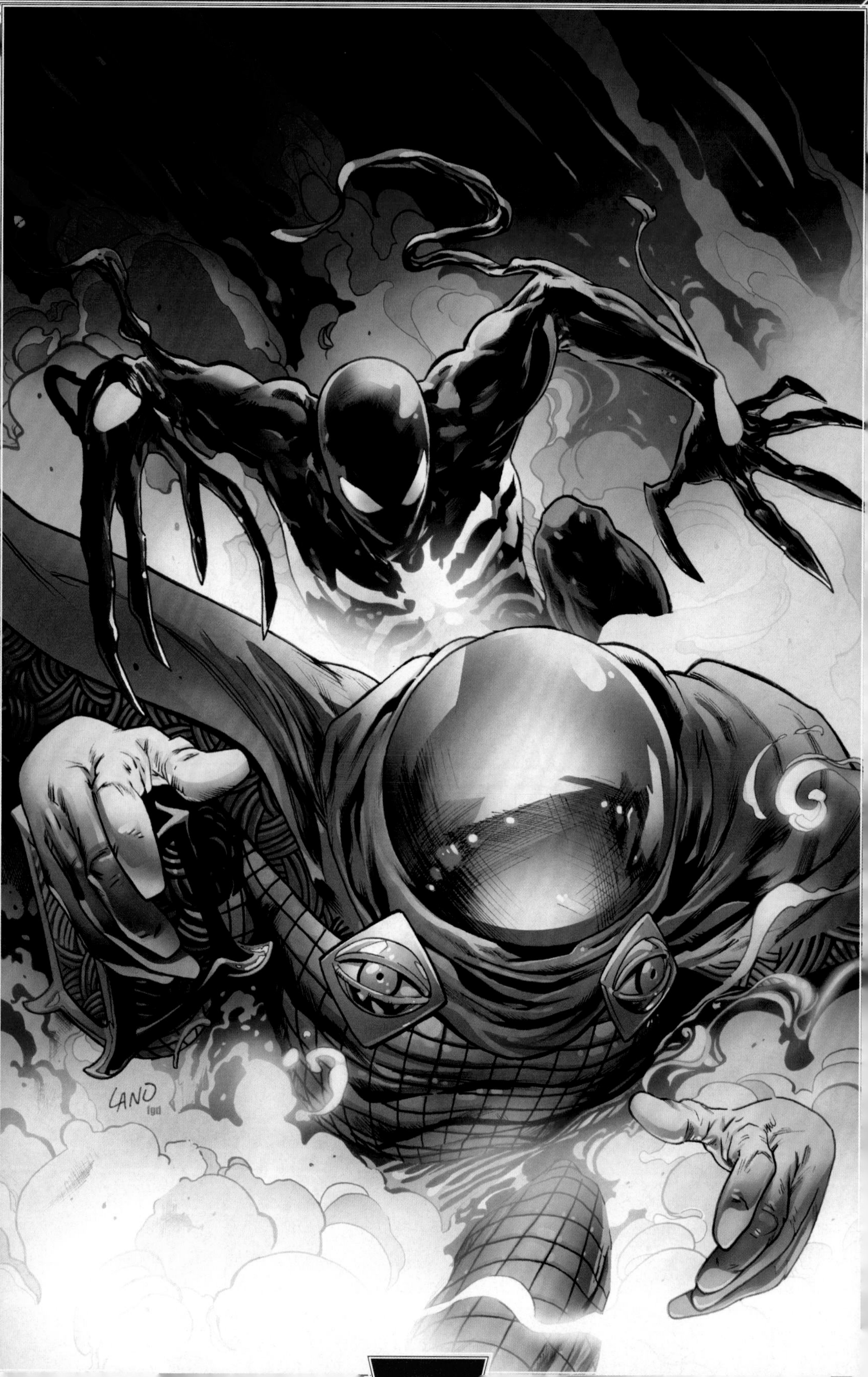
LANO

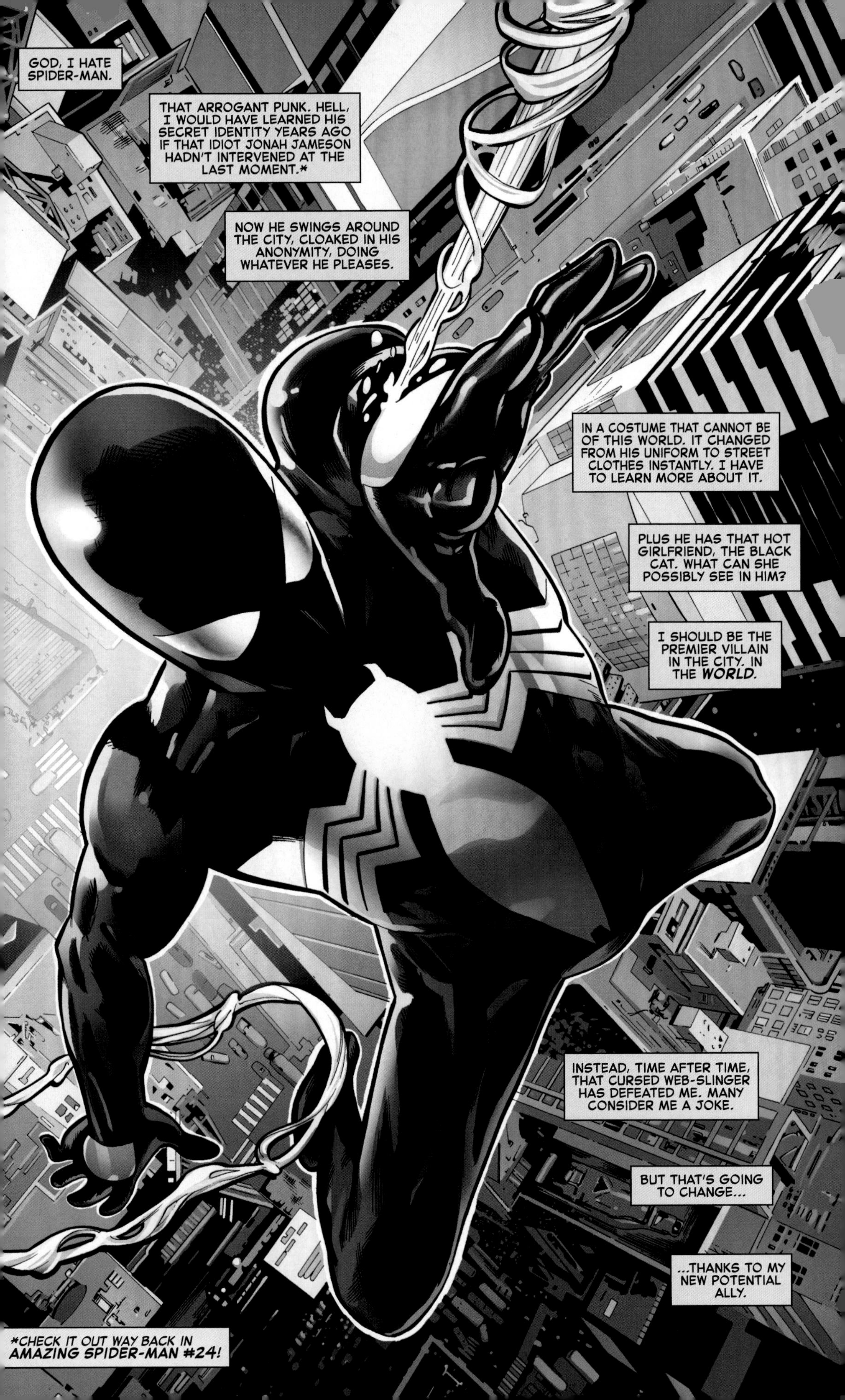
GOD, I HATE SPIDER-MAN.
THAT ARROGANT PUNK. HELL, I WOULD HAVE LEARNED HIS SECRET IDENTITY YEARS AGO IF THAT IDIOT JONAH JAMESON HADN'T INTERVENED AT THE LAST MOMENT.*
NOW HE SWINGS AROUND THE CITY, CLOAKED IN HIS ANONYMITY, DOING WHATEVER HE PLEASES.
IN A COSTUME THAT CANNOT BE OF THIS WORLD. IT CHANGED FROM HIS UNIFORM TO STREET CLOTHES INSTANTLY. I HAVE TO LEARN MORE ABOUT IT.
PLUS HE HAS THAT HOT GIRLFRIEND, THE BLACK CAT. WHAT CAN SHE POSSIBLY SEE IN HIM?
I SHOULD BE THE PREMIER VILLAIN IN THE CITY. IN THE *WORLD.*
INSTEAD, TIME AFTER TIME, THAT CURSED WEB-SLINGER HAS DEFEATED ME. MANY CONSIDER ME A JOKE.
BUT THAT'S GOING TO CHANGE...
...THANKS TO MY NEW POTENTIAL ALLY.
*CHECK IT OUT WAY BACK IN **AMAZING SPIDER-MAN #24!**

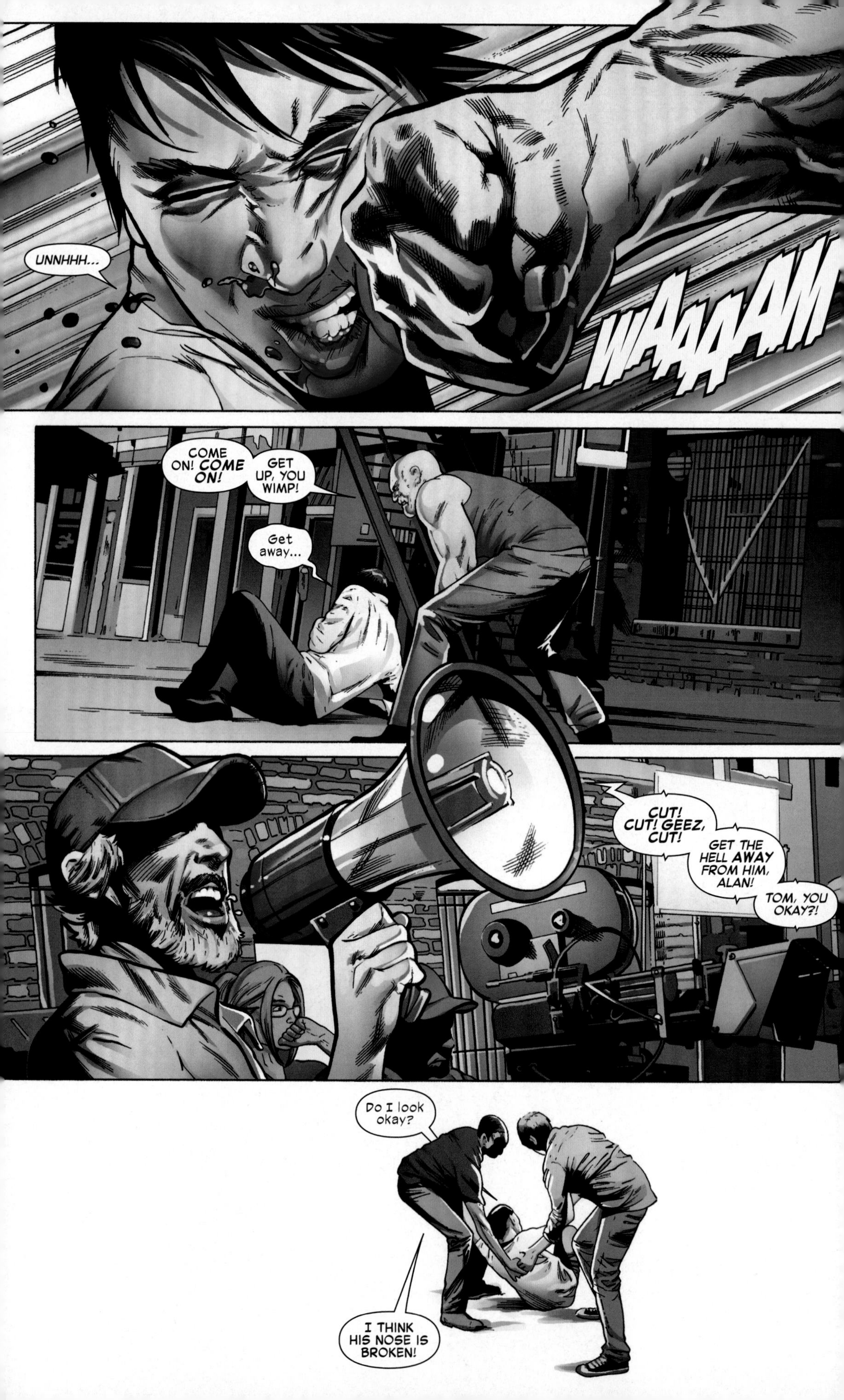
UNNHHH...
WAAAAM
COME ON! COME ON!
GET UP, YOU WIMP!
Get away...
CUT! CUT! GEEZ, CUT!
GET THE HELL AWAY FROM HIM, ALAN!
TOM, YOU OKAY?!
Do I look okay?
I THINK HIS NOSE IS BROKEN!

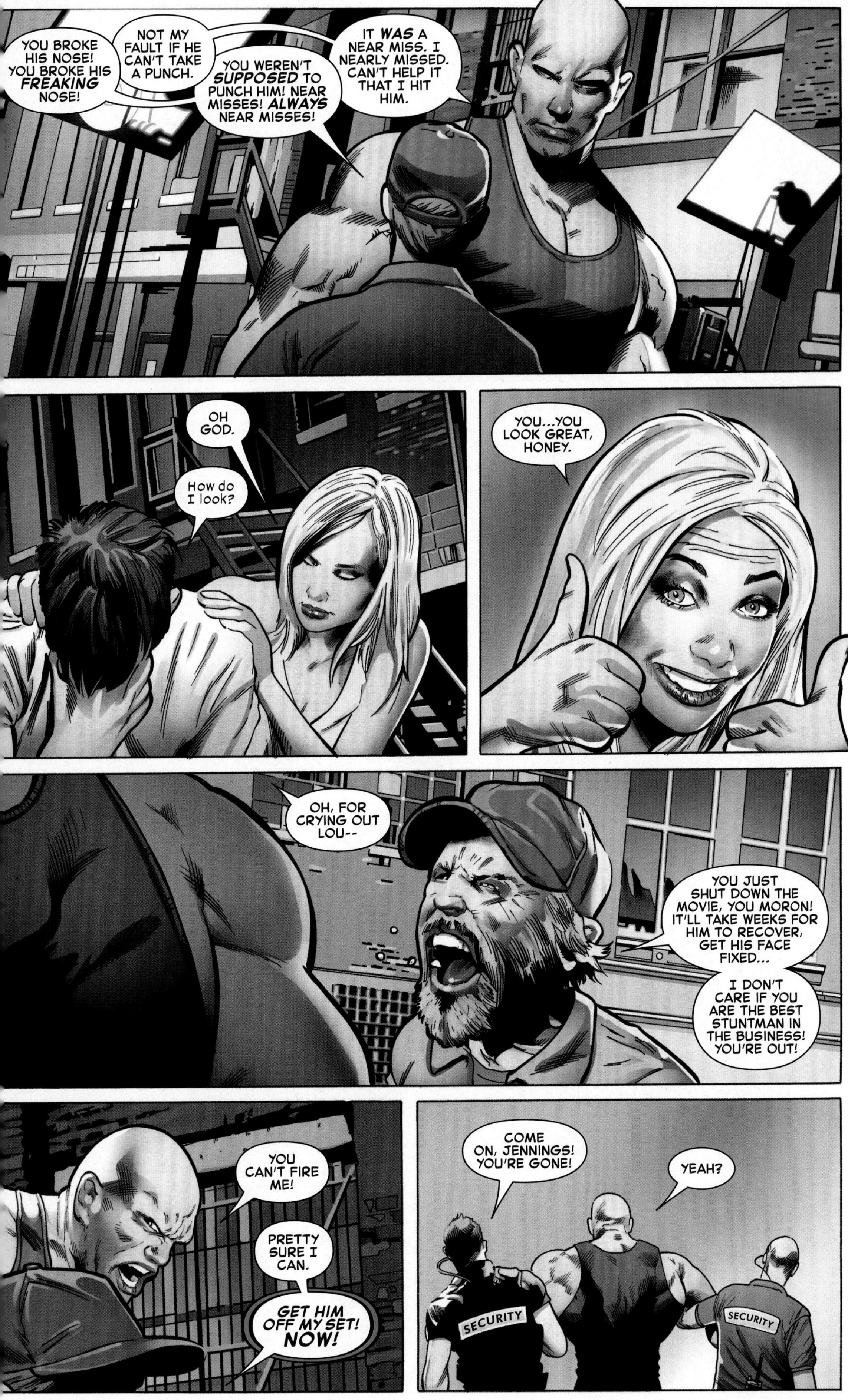

YOU BROKE HIS NOSE! YOU BROKE HIS FREAKING NOSE!
NOT MY FAULT IF HE CAN'T TAKE A PUNCH.
YOU WEREN'T SUPPOSED TO PUNCH HIM! NEAR MISSES! ALWAYS NEAR MISSES!
IT WAS A NEAR MISS. I NEARLY MISSED. CAN'T HELP IT THAT I HIT HIM.
OH GOD.
How do I look?
YOU...YOU LOOK GREAT, HONEY.
OH, FOR CRYING OUT LOU--
YOU JUST SHUT DOWN THE MOVIE, YOU MORON! IT'LL TAKE WEEKS FOR HIM TO RECOVER, GET HIS FACE FIXED...
I DON'T CARE IF YOU ARE THE BEST STUNTMAN IN THE BUSINESS! YOU'RE OUT!
YOU CAN'T FIRE ME!
PRETTY SURE I CAN.
GET HIM OFF MY SET! NOW!
COME ON, JENNINGS! YOU'RE GONE!
YEAH?
SECURITY
SECURITY

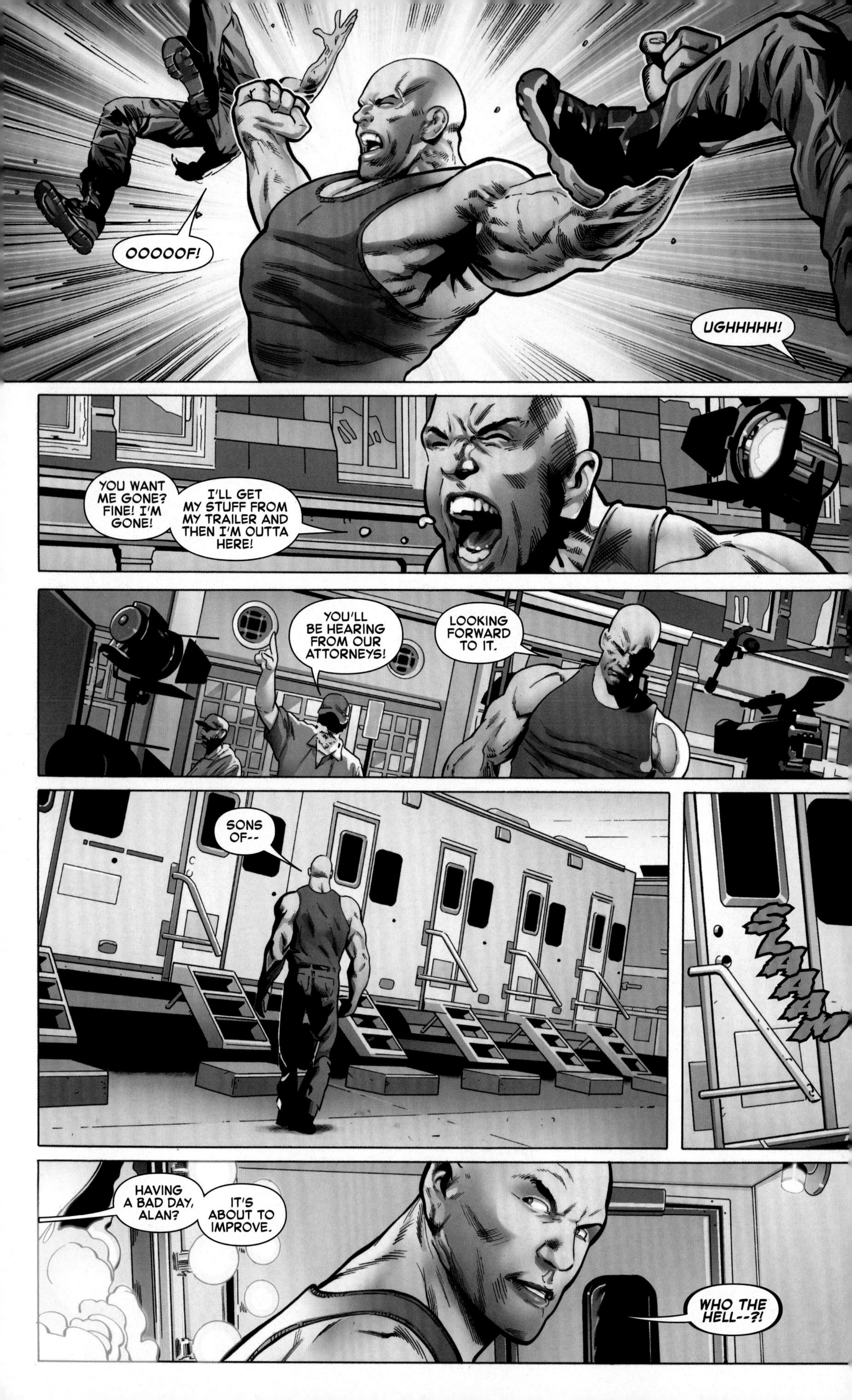
OOOOOF!
UGHHHHH!
YOU WANT ME GONE? FINE! I'M GONE!
I'LL GET MY STUFF FROM MY TRAILER AND THEN I'M OUTTA HERE!
YOU'LL BE HEARING FROM OUR ATTORNEYS!
LOOKING FORWARD TO IT.
SONS OF--
SLAAAM
HAVING A BAD DAY, ALAN?
IT'S ABOUT TO IMPROVE.
WHO THE HELL--?!

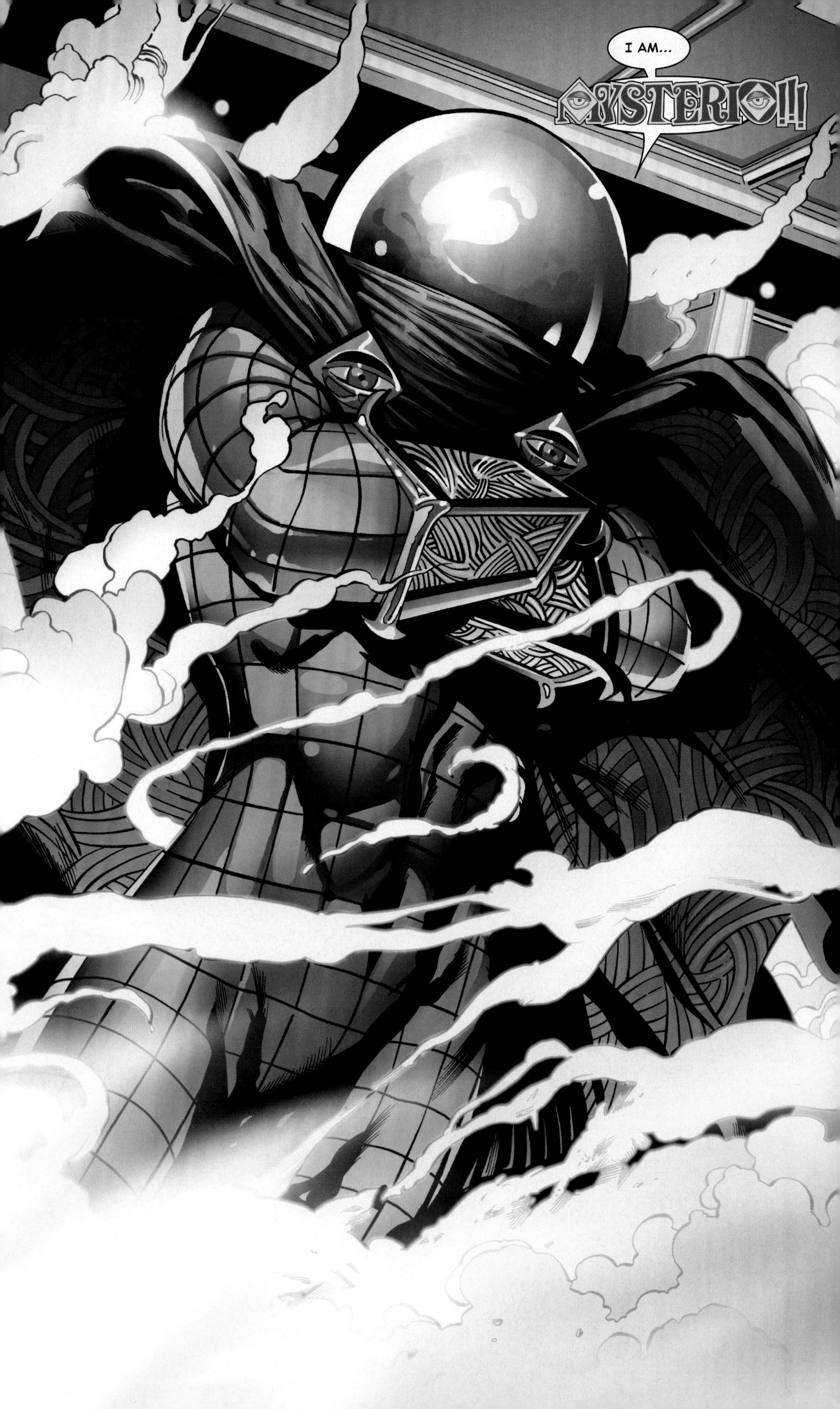
I AM...
MYSTERIO!!!

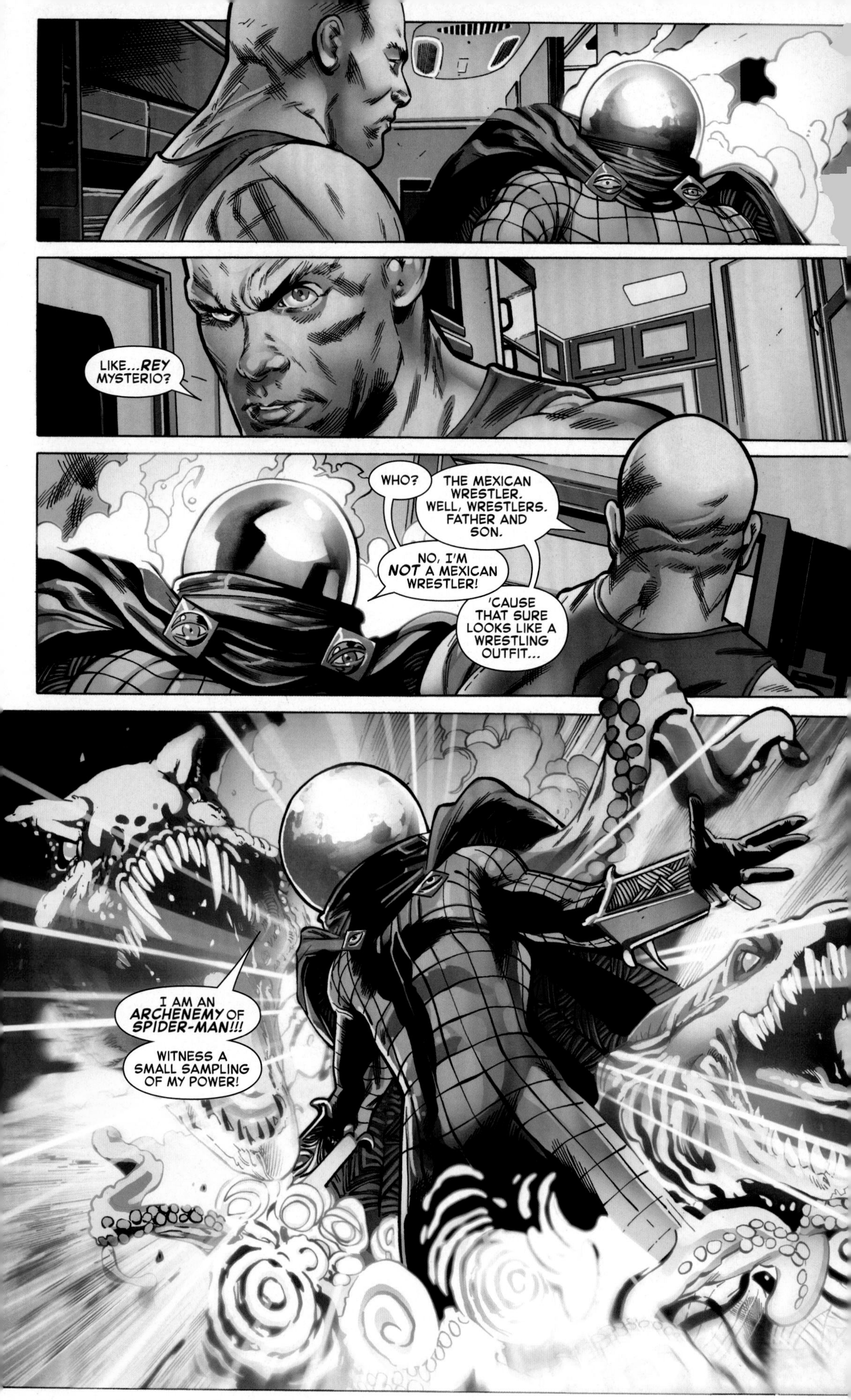
LIKE...REY MYSTERIO?
WHO?
THE MEXICAN WRESTLER. WELL, WRESTLERS. FATHER AND SON.
NO, I'M NOT A MEXICAN WRESTLER!
'CAUSE THAT SURE LOOKS LIKE A WRESTLING OUTFIT...
I AM AN ARCHENEMY OF SPIDER-MAN!!!
WITNESS A SMALL SAMPLING OF MY POWER!

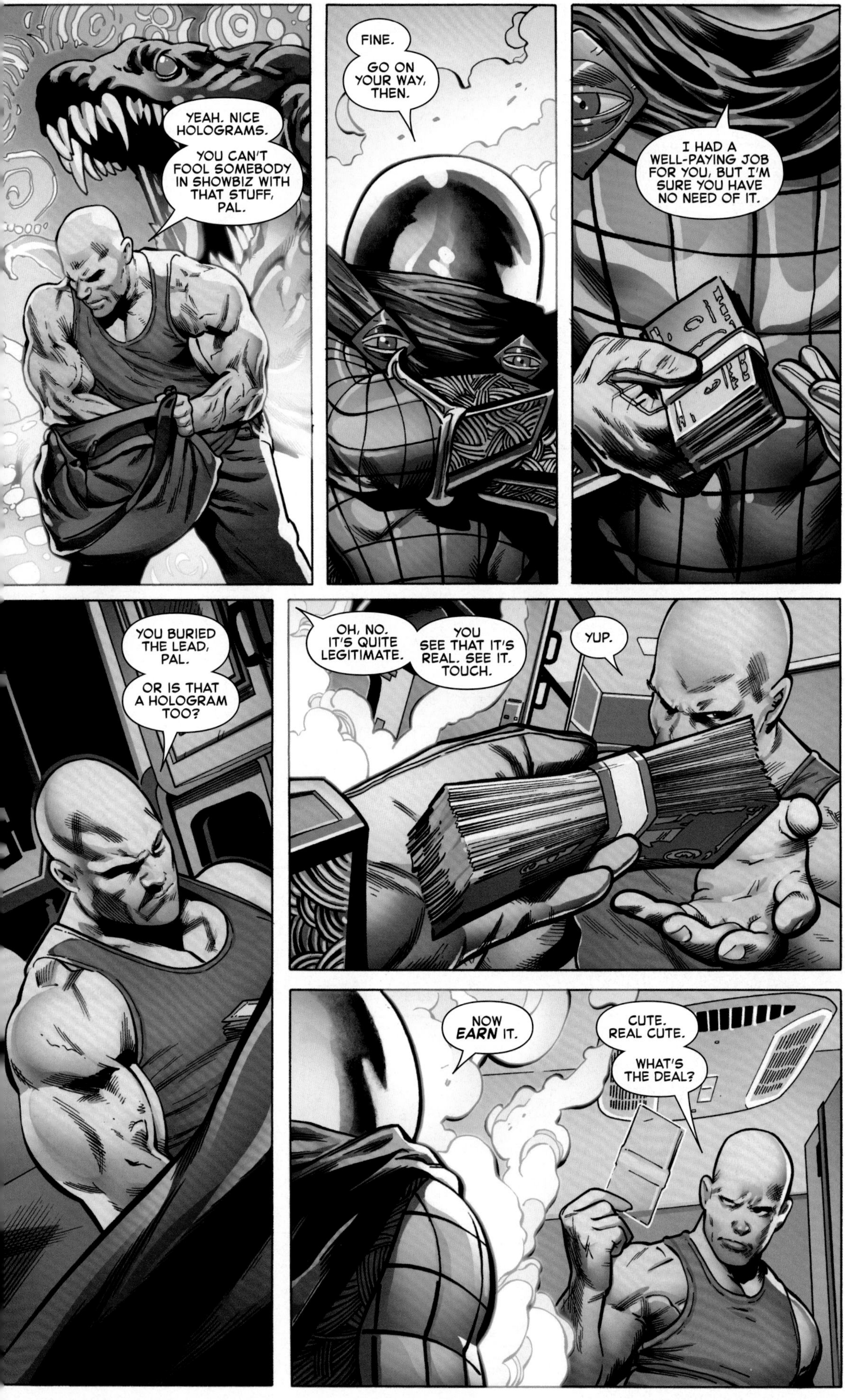
YEAH. NICE HOLOGRAMS.
YOU CAN'T FOOL SOMEBODY IN SHOWBIZ WITH THAT STUFF, PAL.
FINE.
GO ON YOUR WAY, THEN.
I HAD A WELL-PAYING JOB FOR YOU, BUT I'M SURE YOU HAVE NO NEED OF IT.
YOU BURIED THE LEAD, PAL.
OR IS THAT A HOLOGRAM TOO?
OH, NO. IT'S QUITE LEGITIMATE.
YOU SEE THAT IT'S REAL. SEE IT. TOUCH.
YUP.
NOW *EARN* IT.
CUTE. REAL CUTE.
WHAT'S THE DEAL?

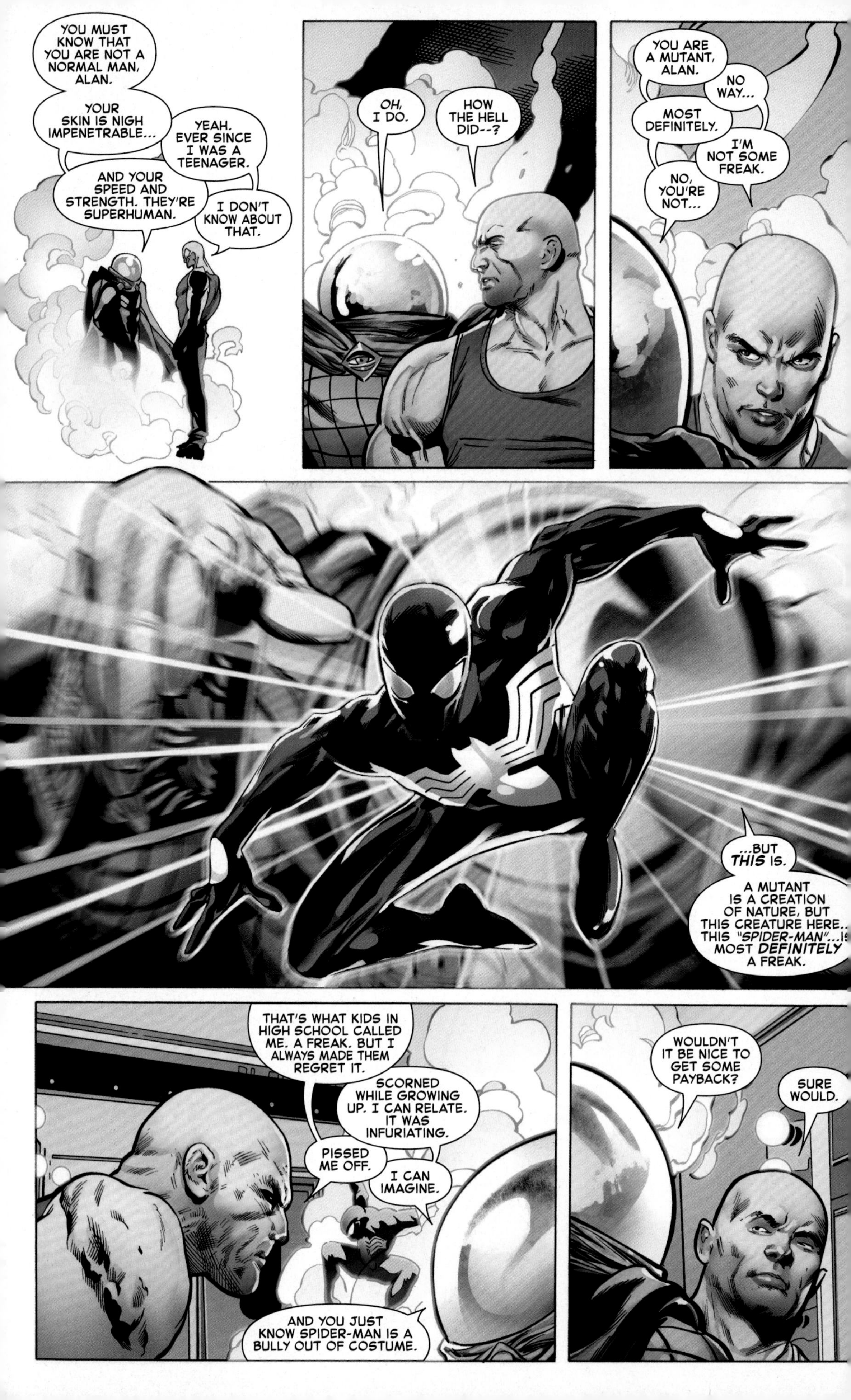

YOU MUST KNOW THAT YOU ARE NOT A NORMAL MAN, ALAN.
YOUR SKIN IS NIGH IMPENETRABLE...
YEAH. EVER SINCE I WAS A TEENAGER.
AND YOUR SPEED AND STRENGTH. THEY'RE SUPERHUMAN.
I DON'T KNOW ABOUT THAT.
OH, I DO.
HOW THE HELL DID--?
YOU ARE A MUTANT, ALAN.
NO WAY...
MOST DEFINITELY.
I'M NOT SOME FREAK.
NO, YOU'RE NOT...
...BUT THIS IS.
A MUTANT IS A CREATION OF NATURE, BUT THIS CREATURE HERE... THIS "SPIDER-MAN"...IS MOST DEFINITELY A FREAK.
THAT'S WHAT KIDS IN HIGH SCHOOL CALLED ME. A FREAK. BUT I ALWAYS MADE THEM REGRET IT.
SCORNED WHILE GROWING UP. I CAN RELATE. IT WAS INFURIATING.
PISSED ME OFF.
I CAN IMAGINE.
AND YOU JUST KNOW SPIDER-MAN IS A BULLY OUT OF COSTUME.
WOULDN'T IT BE NICE TO GET SOME PAYBACK?
SURE WOULD.

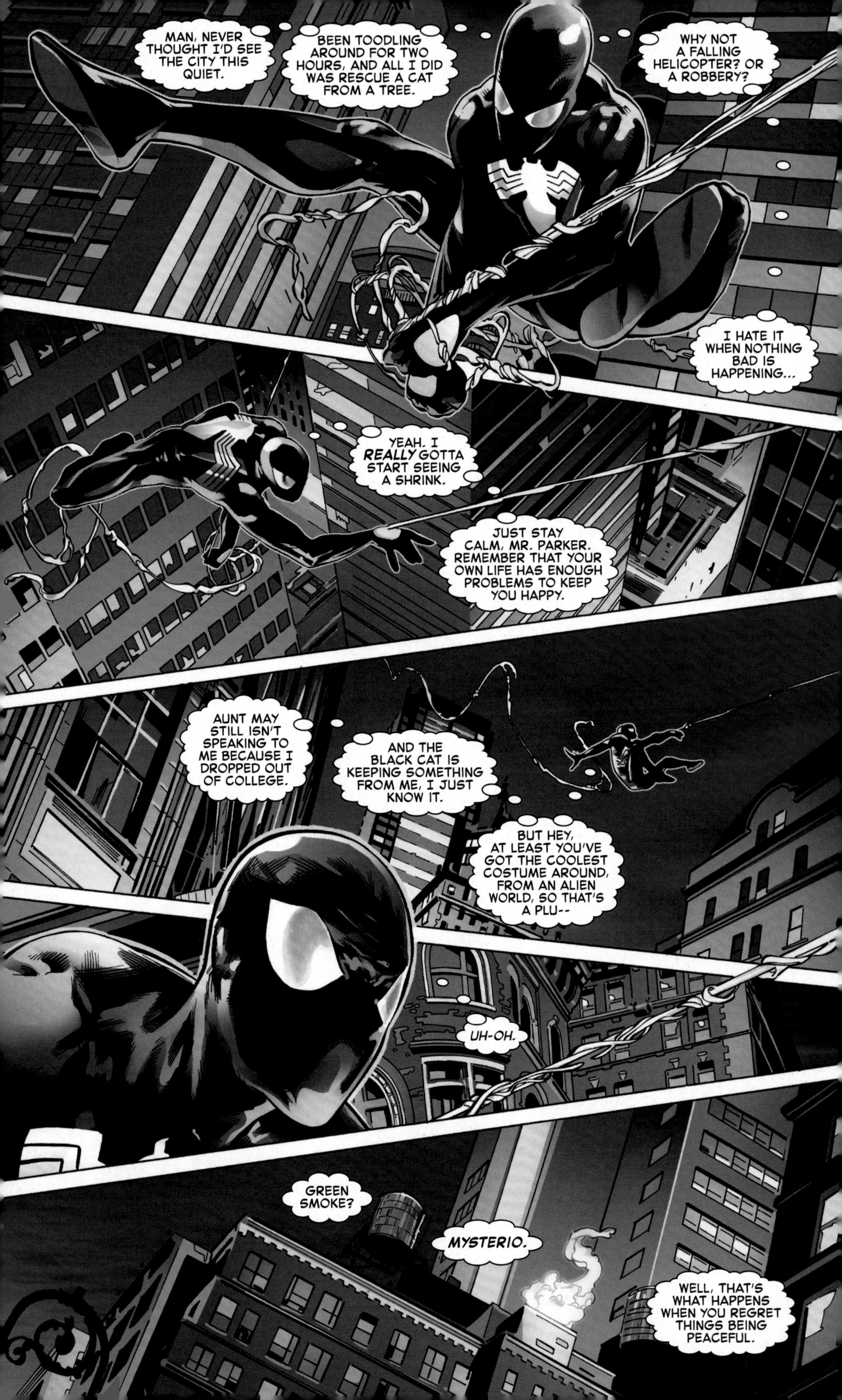
MAN, NEVER THOUGHT I'D SEE THE CITY THIS QUIET.
BEEN TOODLING AROUND FOR TWO HOURS, AND ALL I DID WAS RESCUE A CAT FROM A TREE.
WHY NOT A FALLING HELICOPTER? OR A ROBBERY?
I HATE IT WHEN NOTHING BAD IS HAPPENING...
YEAH. I REALLY GOTTA START SEEING A SHRINK.
JUST STAY CALM, MR. PARKER. REMEMBER THAT YOUR OWN LIFE HAS ENOUGH PROBLEMS TO KEEP YOU HAPPY.
AUNT MAY STILL ISN'T SPEAKING TO ME BECAUSE I DROPPED OUT OF COLLEGE.
AND THE BLACK CAT IS KEEPING SOMETHING FROM ME, I JUST KNOW IT.
BUT HEY, AT LEAST YOU'VE GOT THE COOLEST COSTUME AROUND, FROM AN ALIEN WORLD, SO THAT'S A PLU--
UH-OH.
GREEN SMOKE?
MYSTERIO.
WELL, THAT'S WHAT HAPPENS WHEN YOU REGRET THINGS BEING PEACEFUL.

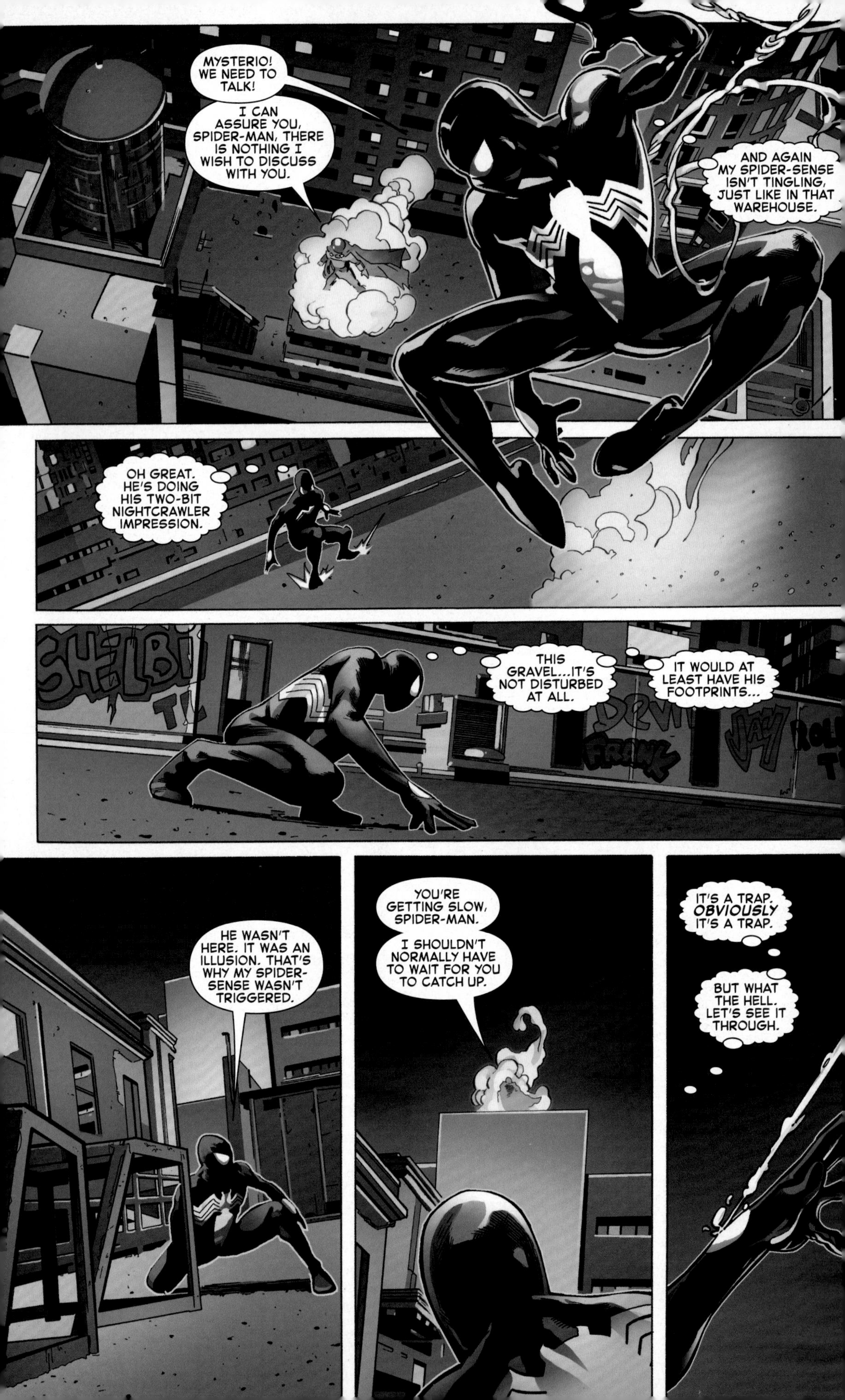
MYSTERIO! WE NEED TO TALK!
I CAN ASSURE YOU, SPIDER-MAN, THERE IS NOTHING I WISH TO DISCUSS WITH YOU.
AND AGAIN MY SPIDER-SENSE ISN'T TINGLING, JUST LIKE IN THAT WAREHOUSE.
OH GREAT. HE'S DOING HIS TWO-BIT NIGHTCRAWLER IMPRESSION.
THIS GRAVEL...IT'S NOT DISTURBED AT ALL.
IT WOULD AT LEAST HAVE HIS FOOTPRINTS...
HE WASN'T HERE. IT WAS AN ILLUSION. THAT'S WHY MY SPIDER-SENSE WASN'T TRIGGERED.
YOU'RE GETTING SLOW, SPIDER-MAN.
I SHOULDN'T NORMALLY HAVE TO WAIT FOR YOU TO CATCH UP.
IT'S A TRAP. *OBVIOUSLY* IT'S A TRAP.
BUT WHAT THE HELL. LET'S SEE IT THROUGH.

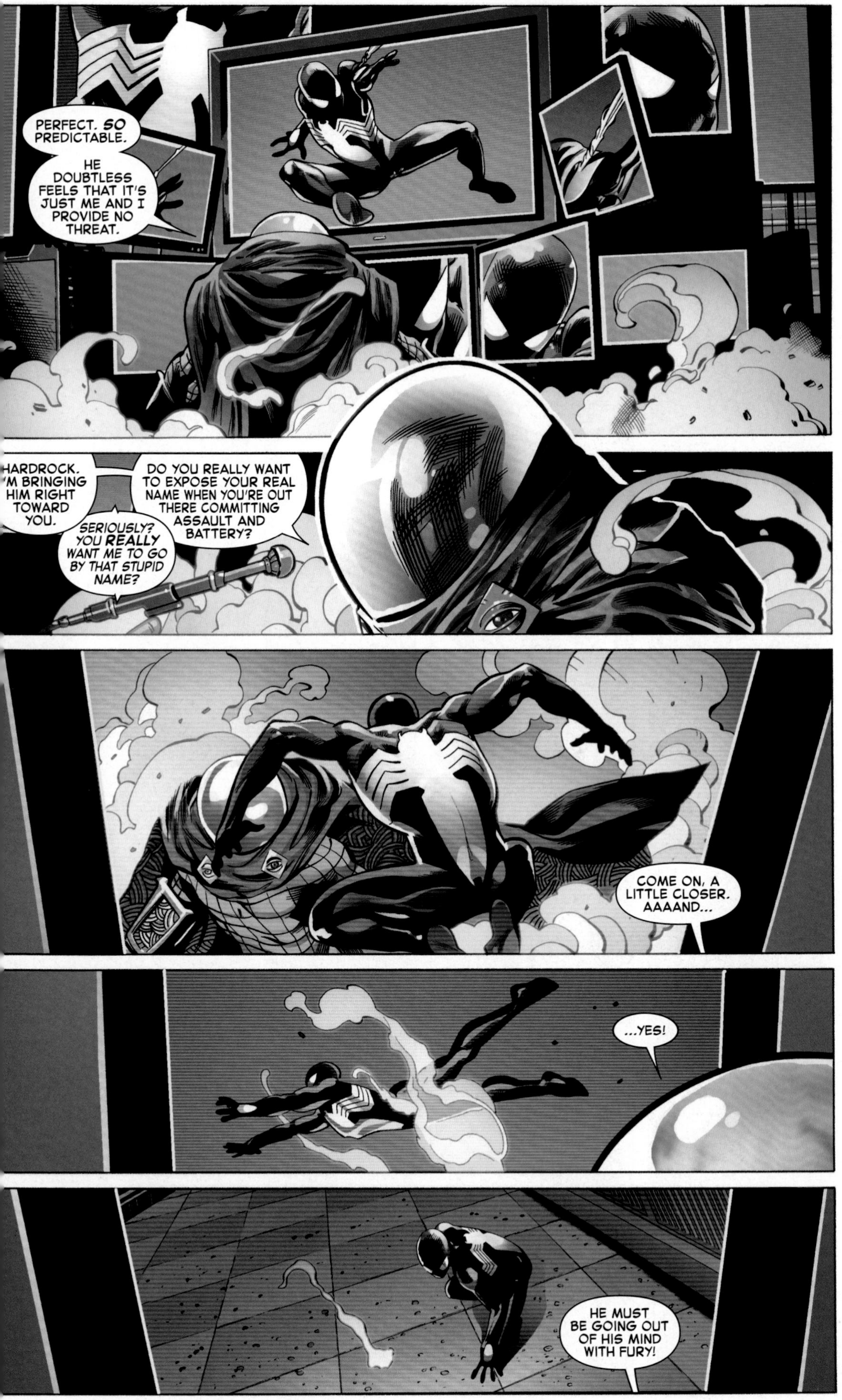
PERFECT. SO PREDICTABLE.
HE DOUBTLESS FEELS THAT IT'S JUST ME AND I PROVIDE NO THREAT.
HARDROCK. I'M BRINGING HIM RIGHT TOWARD YOU.
DO YOU REALLY WANT TO EXPOSE YOUR REAL NAME WHEN YOU'RE OUT THERE COMMITTING ASSAULT AND BATTERY?
SERIOUSLY? YOU REALLY WANT ME TO GO BY THAT STUPID NAME?
COME ON, A LITTLE CLOSER. AAAAND...
...YES!
HE MUST BE GOING OUT OF HIS MIND WITH FURY!

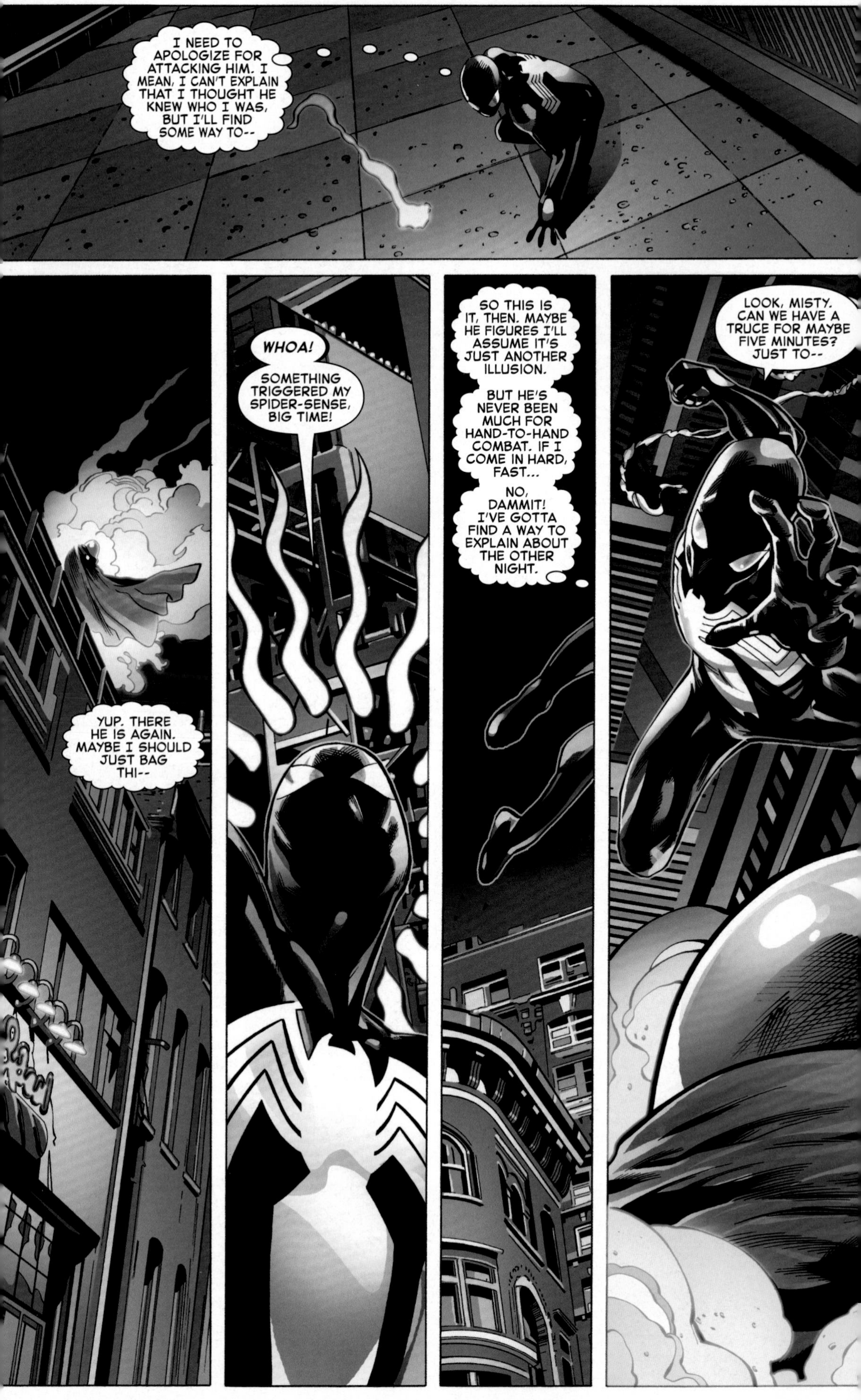

I NEED TO APOLOGIZE FOR ATTACKING HIM. I MEAN, I CAN'T EXPLAIN THAT I THOUGHT HE KNEW WHO I WAS, BUT I'LL FIND SOME WAY TO--
YUP. THERE HE IS AGAIN. MAYBE I SHOULD JUST BAG THI--
WHOA!
SOMETHING TRIGGERED MY SPIDER-SENSE, BIG TIME!
SO THIS IS IT, THEN. MAYBE HE FIGURES I'LL ASSUME IT'S JUST ANOTHER ILLUSION.
BUT HE'S NEVER BEEN MUCH FOR HAND-TO-HAND COMBAT. IF I COME IN HARD, FAST...
NO, DAMMIT! I'VE GOTTA FIND A WAY TO EXPLAIN ABOUT THE OTHER NIGHT.
LOOK, MISTY. CAN WE HAVE A TRUCE FOR MAYBE FIVE MINUTES? JUST TO--

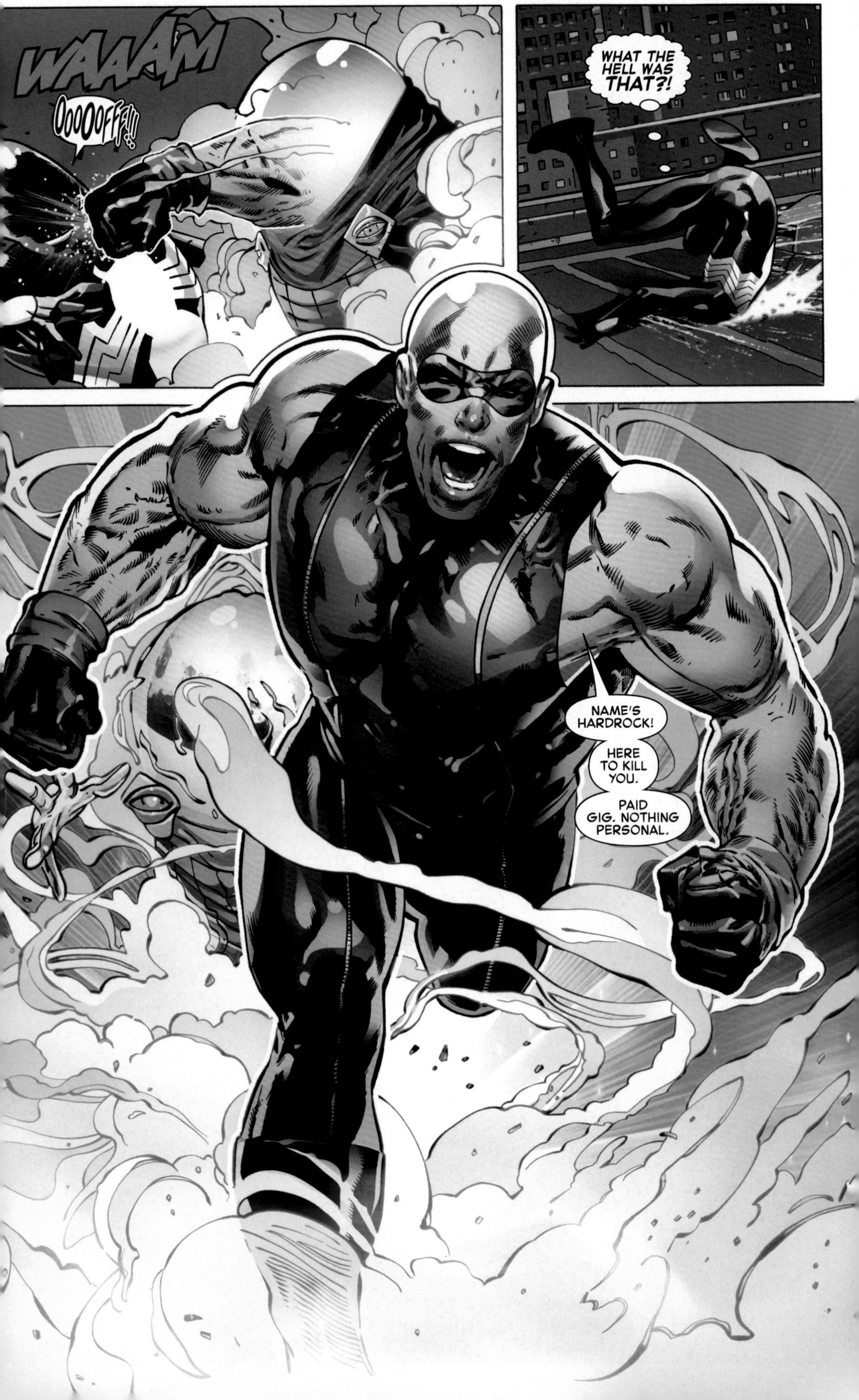
WAAAM
OOOOOFFF!!!
WHAT THE HELL WAS THAT?!
NAME'S HARDROCK!
HERE TO KILL YOU.
PAID GIG. NOTHING PERSONAL.

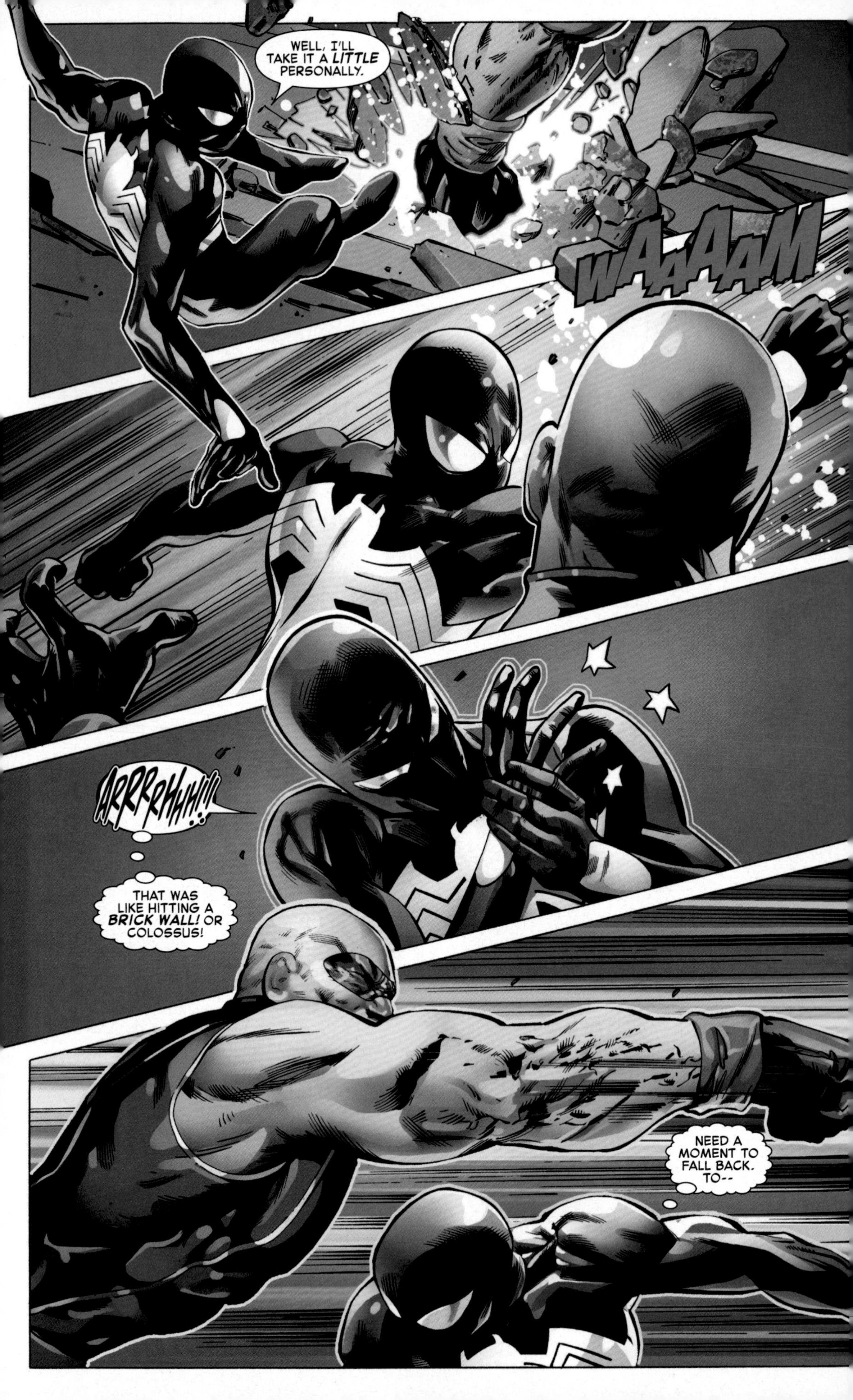
WELL, I'LL TAKE IT A *LITTLE* PERSONALLY.
WAAAAAM
ARRRRKHH!!!
THAT WAS LIKE HITTING A *BRICK WALL!* OR COLOSSUS!
NEED A MOMENT TO FALL BACK. TO--

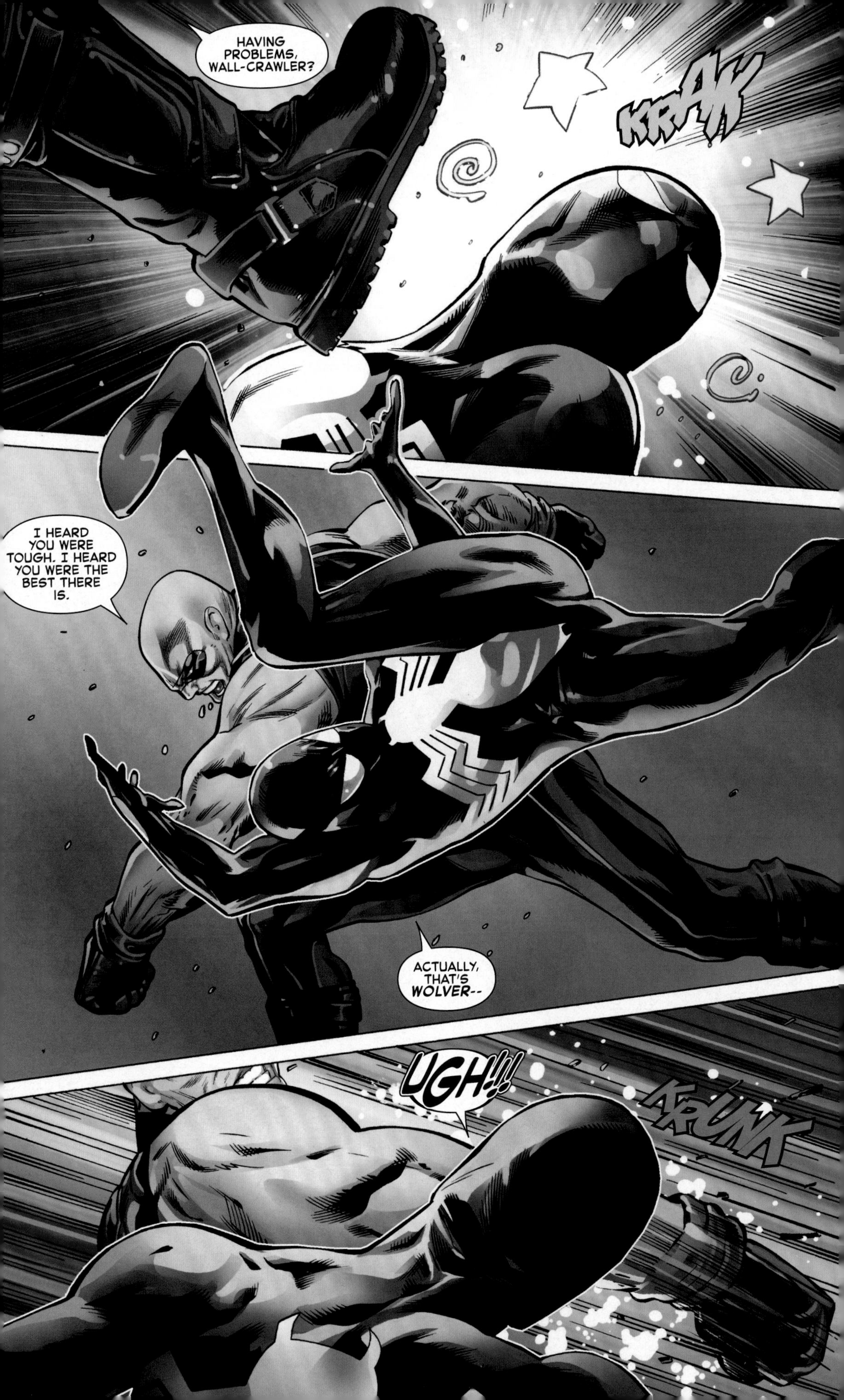

HAVING PROBLEMS, WALL-CRAWLER?
KRAK
I HEARD YOU WERE TOUGH. I HEARD YOU WERE THE BEST THERE IS.
ACTUALLY, THAT'S WOLVER--
UGH!!!
KRUNK

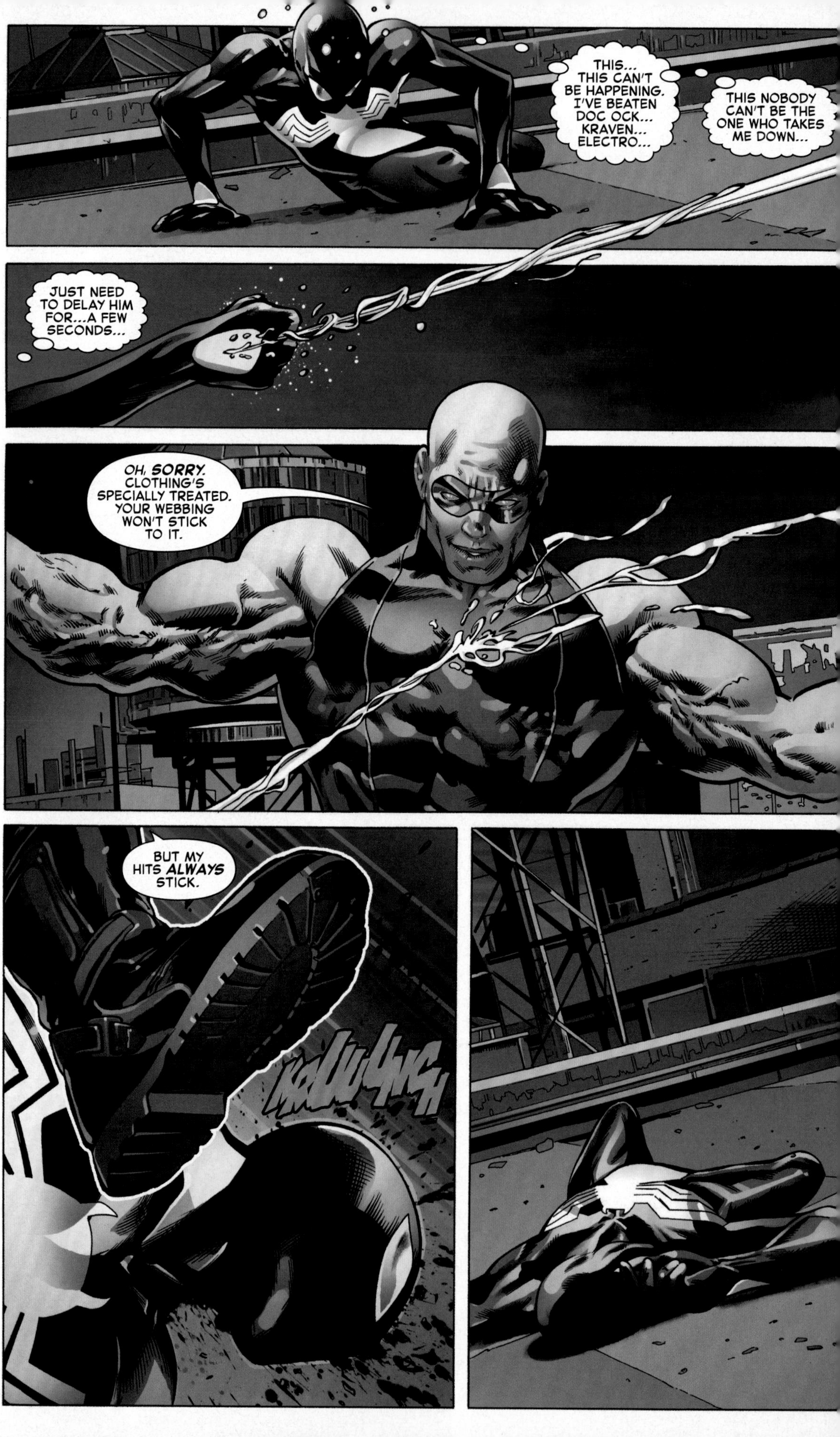
THIS... THIS CAN'T BE HAPPENING. I'VE BEATEN DOC OCK... KRAVEN... ELECTRO...
THIS NOBODY CAN'T BE THE ONE WHO TAKES ME DOWN...
JUST NEED TO DELAY HIM FOR...A FEW SECONDS...
OH, SORRY. CLOTHING'S SPECIALLY TREATED. YOUR WEBBING WON'T STICK TO IT.
BUT MY HITS ALWAYS STICK.
KRUUUNCH

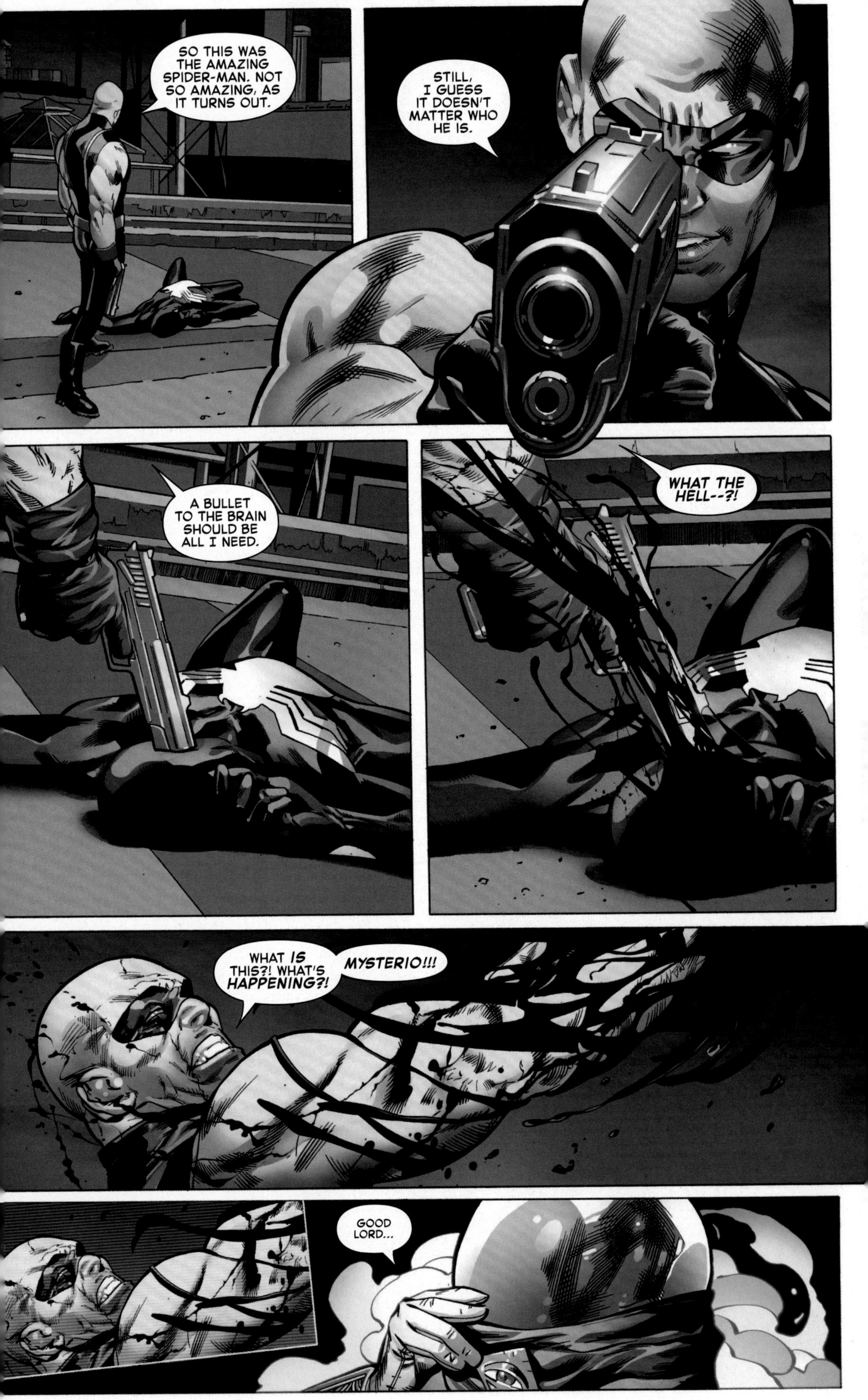

SO THIS WAS THE AMAZING SPIDER-MAN. NOT SO AMAZING, AS IT TURNS OUT.
STILL, I GUESS IT DOESN'T MATTER WHO HE IS.
A BULLET TO THE BRAIN SHOULD BE ALL I NEED.
WHAT THE HELL--?!
WHAT IS THIS?! WHAT'S HAPPENING?!
MYSTERIO!!!
GOOD LORD...

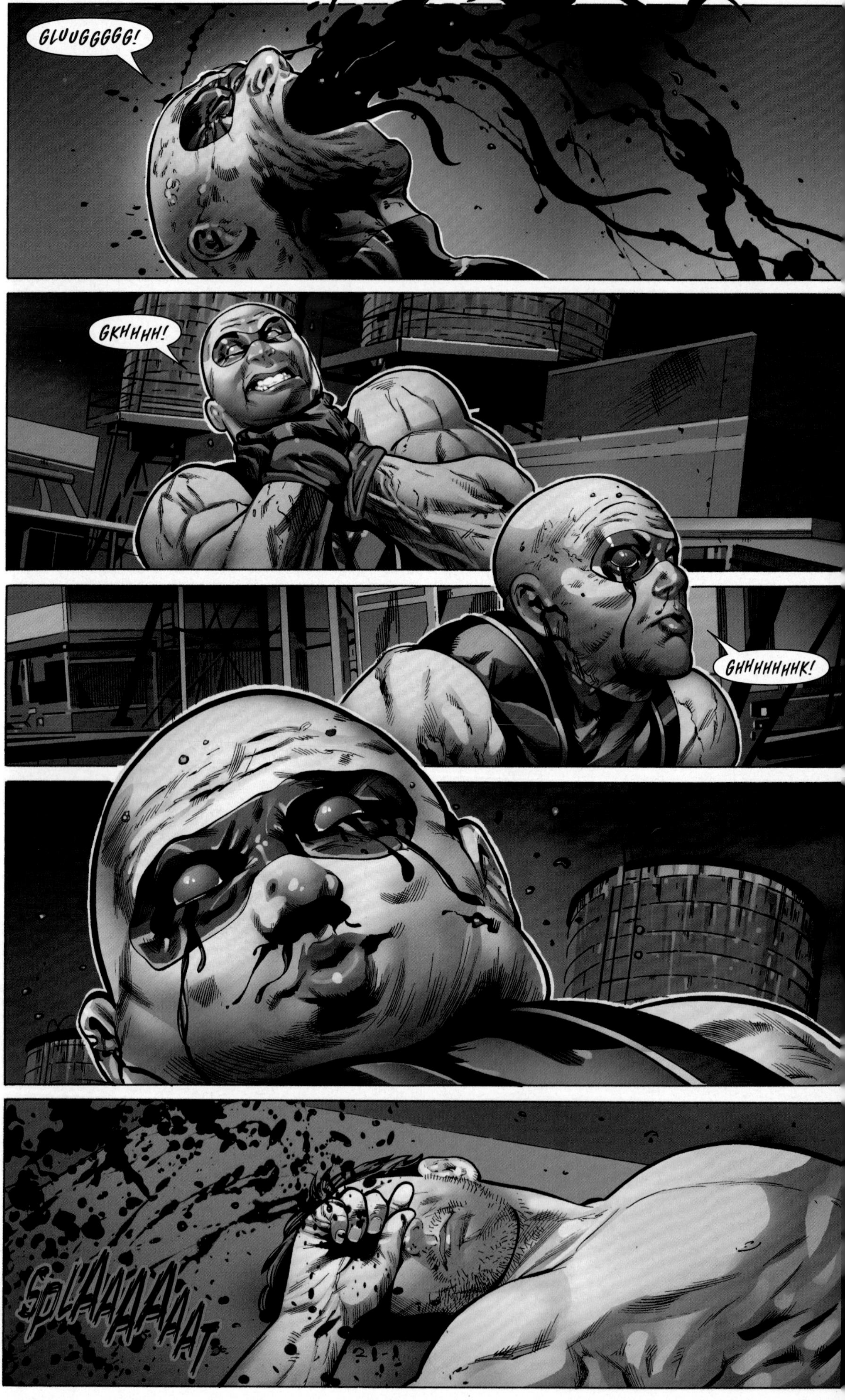
GLUUGGGGG!
GKHHHH!
GHHHHHHHK!
SPLAAAAAAAT

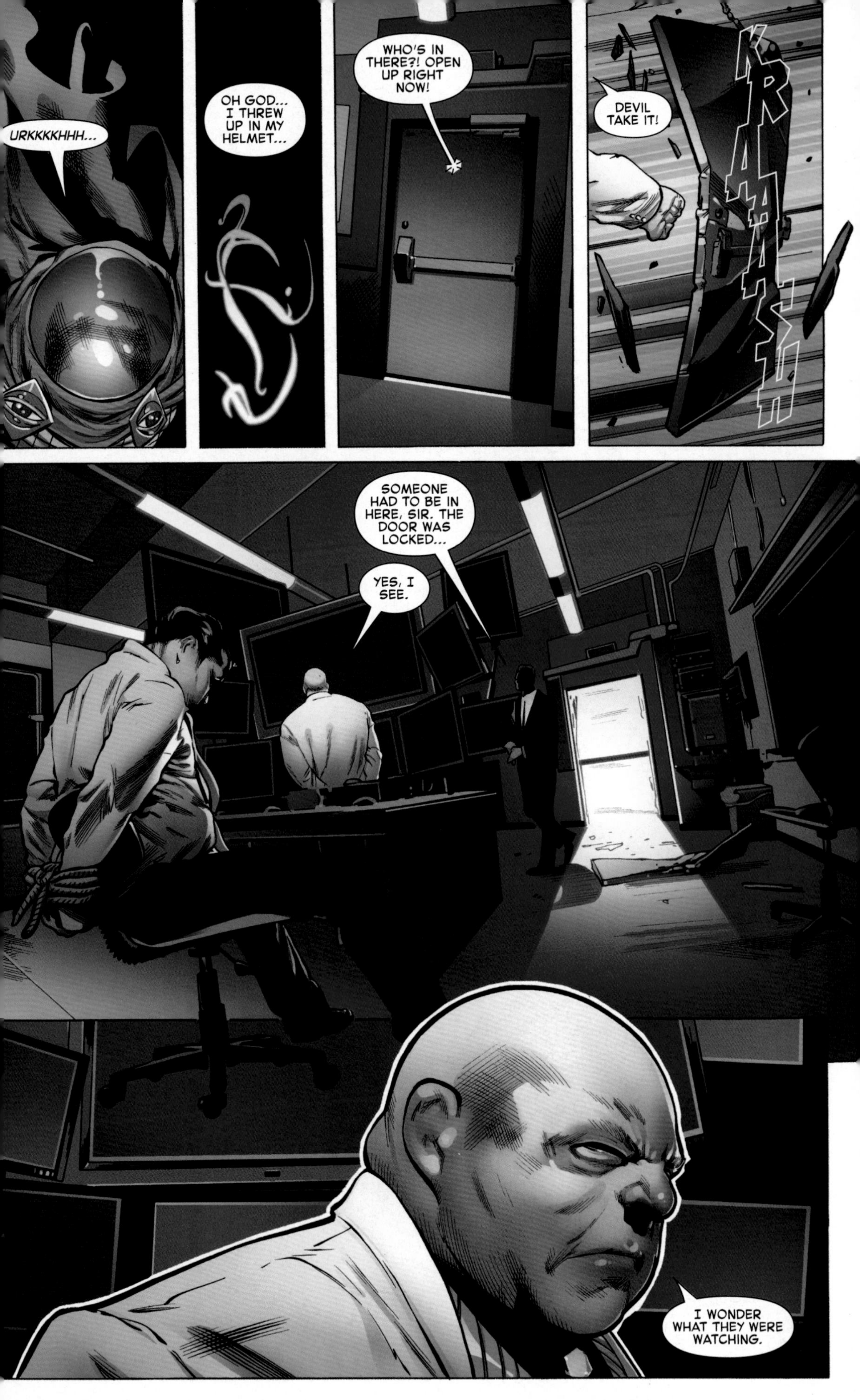
URKKKKHHH...
OH GOD... I THREW UP IN MY HELMET...
WHO'S IN THERE?! OPEN UP RIGHT NOW!
DEVIL TAKE IT!
KRAAASH
SOMEONE HAD TO BE IN HERE, SIR. THE DOOR WAS LOCKED...
YES, I SEE.
I WONDER WHAT THEY WERE WATCHING.

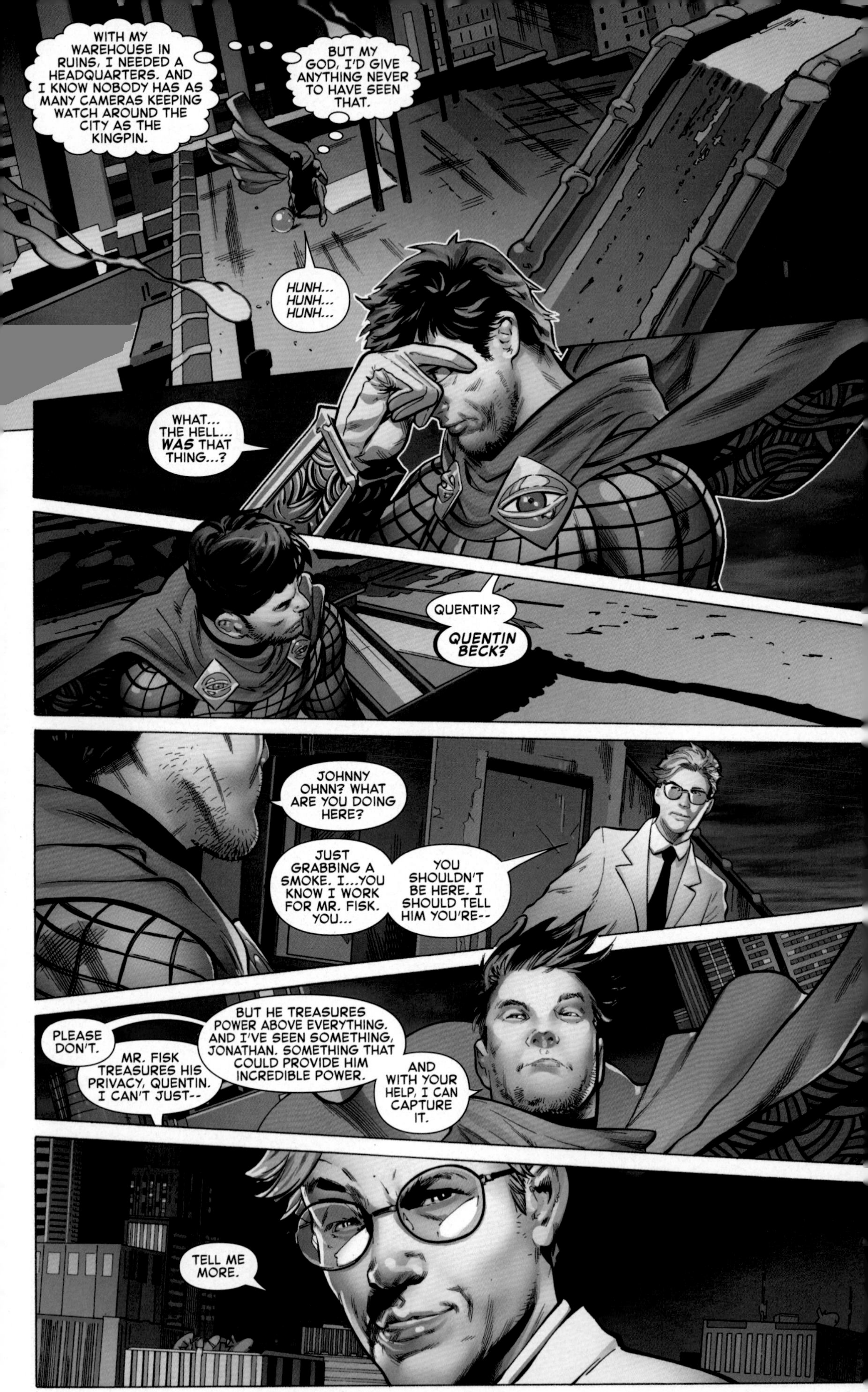
WITH MY WAREHOUSE IN RUINS, I NEEDED A HEADQUARTERS. AND I KNOW NOBODY HAS AS MANY CAMERAS KEEPING WATCH AROUND THE CITY AS THE KINGPIN.
BUT MY GOD, I'D GIVE ANYTHING NEVER TO HAVE SEEN THAT.
HUNH... HUNH... HUNH...
WHAT... THE HELL... WAS THAT THING...?
QUENTIN?
QUENTIN BECK?
JOHNNY OHNN? WHAT ARE YOU DOING HERE?
JUST GRABBING A SMOKE. I...YOU KNOW I WORK FOR MR. FISK. YOU...
YOU SHOULDN'T BE HERE. I SHOULD TELL HIM YOU'RE--
PLEASE DON'T.
MR. FISK TREASURES HIS PRIVACY, QUENTIN. I CAN'T JUST--
BUT HE TREASURES POWER ABOVE EVERYTHING. AND I'VE SEEN SOMETHING, JONATHAN. SOMETHING THAT COULD PROVIDE HIM INCREDIBLE POWER.
AND WITH YOUR HELP, I CAN CAPTURE IT.
TELL ME MORE.

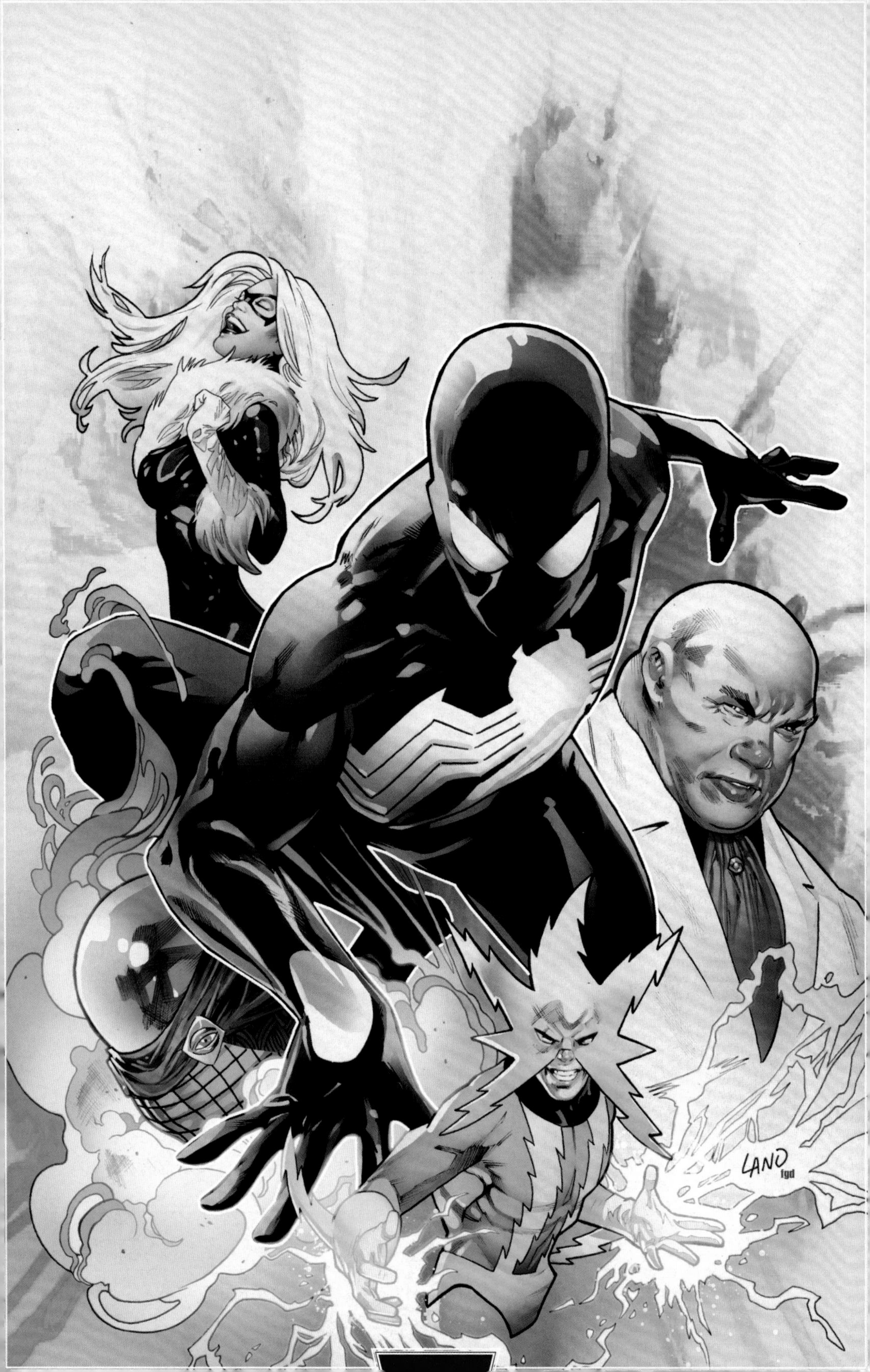
LANO
fgd

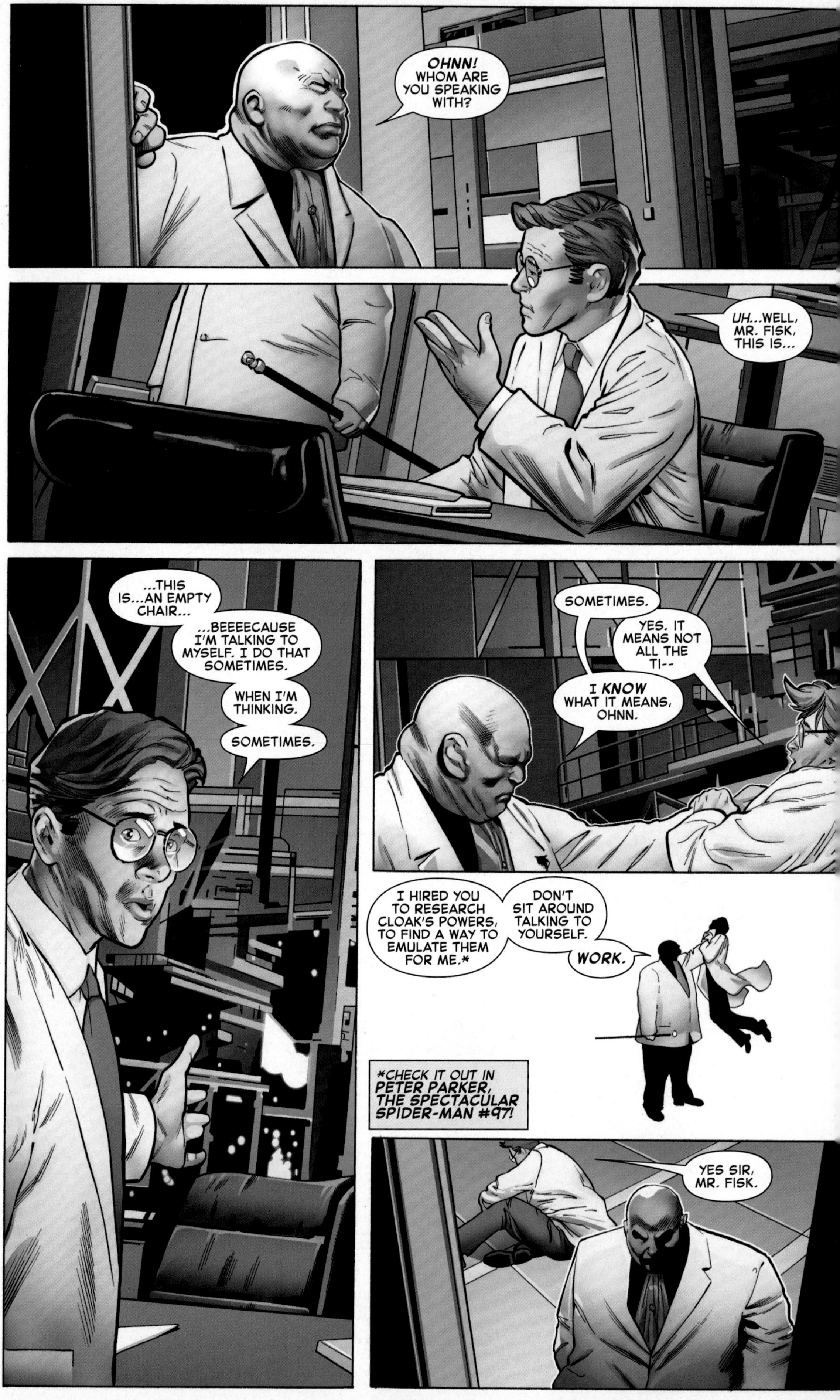
OHNN! WHOM ARE YOU SPEAKING WITH?
UH...WELL, MR. FISK, THIS IS...
...THIS IS...AN EMPTY CHAIR...
...BEEEECAUSE I'M TALKING TO MYSELF. I DO THAT SOMETIMES.
WHEN I'M THINKING.
SOMETIMES.
SOMETIMES.
YES. IT MEANS NOT ALL THE TI--
I KNOW WHAT IT MEANS, OHNN.
I HIRED YOU TO RESEARCH CLOAK'S POWERS, TO FIND A WAY TO EMULATE THEM FOR ME.*
DON'T SIT AROUND TALKING TO YOURSELF.
WORK.
*CHECK IT OUT IN PETER PARKER, THE SPECTACULAR SPIDER-MAN #97!
YES SIR, MR. FISK.

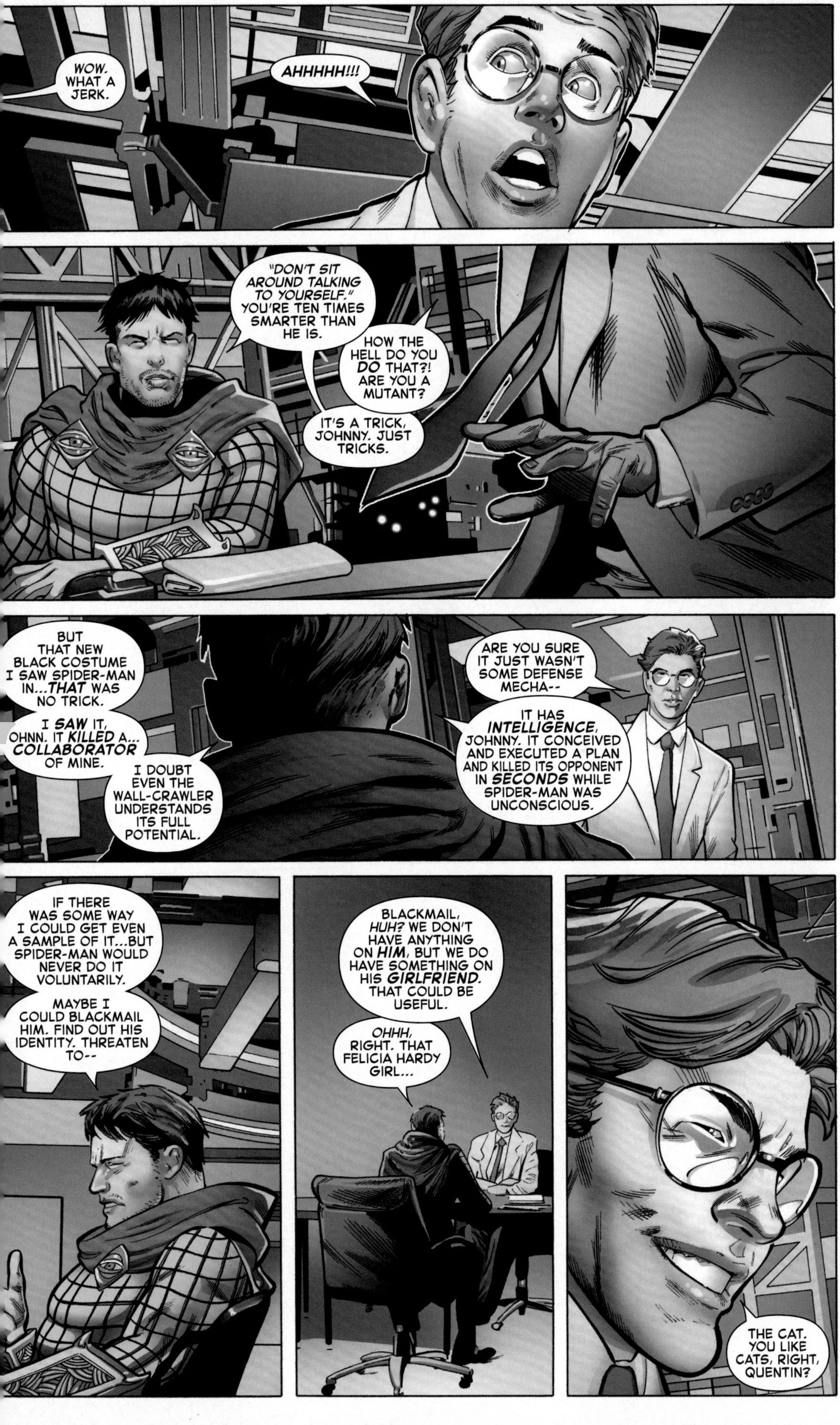
WOW. WHAT A JERK.
AHHHHH!!!
"DON'T SIT AROUND TALKING TO YOURSELF." YOU'RE TEN TIMES SMARTER THAN HE IS.
HOW THE HELL DO YOU DO THAT?! ARE YOU A MUTANT?
IT'S A TRICK, JOHNNY. JUST TRICKS.
BUT THAT NEW BLACK COSTUME I SAW SPIDER-MAN IN...THAT WAS NO TRICK.
I SAW IT, OHNN. IT KILLED A... COLLABORATOR OF MINE.
I DOUBT EVEN THE WALL-CRAWLER UNDERSTANDS ITS FULL POTENTIAL.
ARE YOU SURE IT JUST WASN'T SOME DEFENSE MECHA--
IT HAS INTELLIGENCE, JOHNNY. IT CONCEIVED AND EXECUTED A PLAN AND KILLED ITS OPPONENT IN SECONDS WHILE SPIDER-MAN WAS UNCONSCIOUS.
IF THERE WAS SOME WAY I COULD GET EVEN A SAMPLE OF IT...BUT SPIDER-MAN WOULD NEVER DO IT VOLUNTARILY.
MAYBE I COULD BLACKMAIL HIM. FIND OUT HIS IDENTITY. THREATEN TO--
BLACKMAIL, HUH? WE DON'T HAVE ANYTHING ON HIM, BUT WE DO HAVE SOMETHING ON HIS GIRLFRIEND. THAT COULD BE USEFUL.
OHHH, RIGHT. THAT FELICIA HARDY GIRL...
THE CAT. YOU LIKE CATS, RIGHT, QUENTIN?

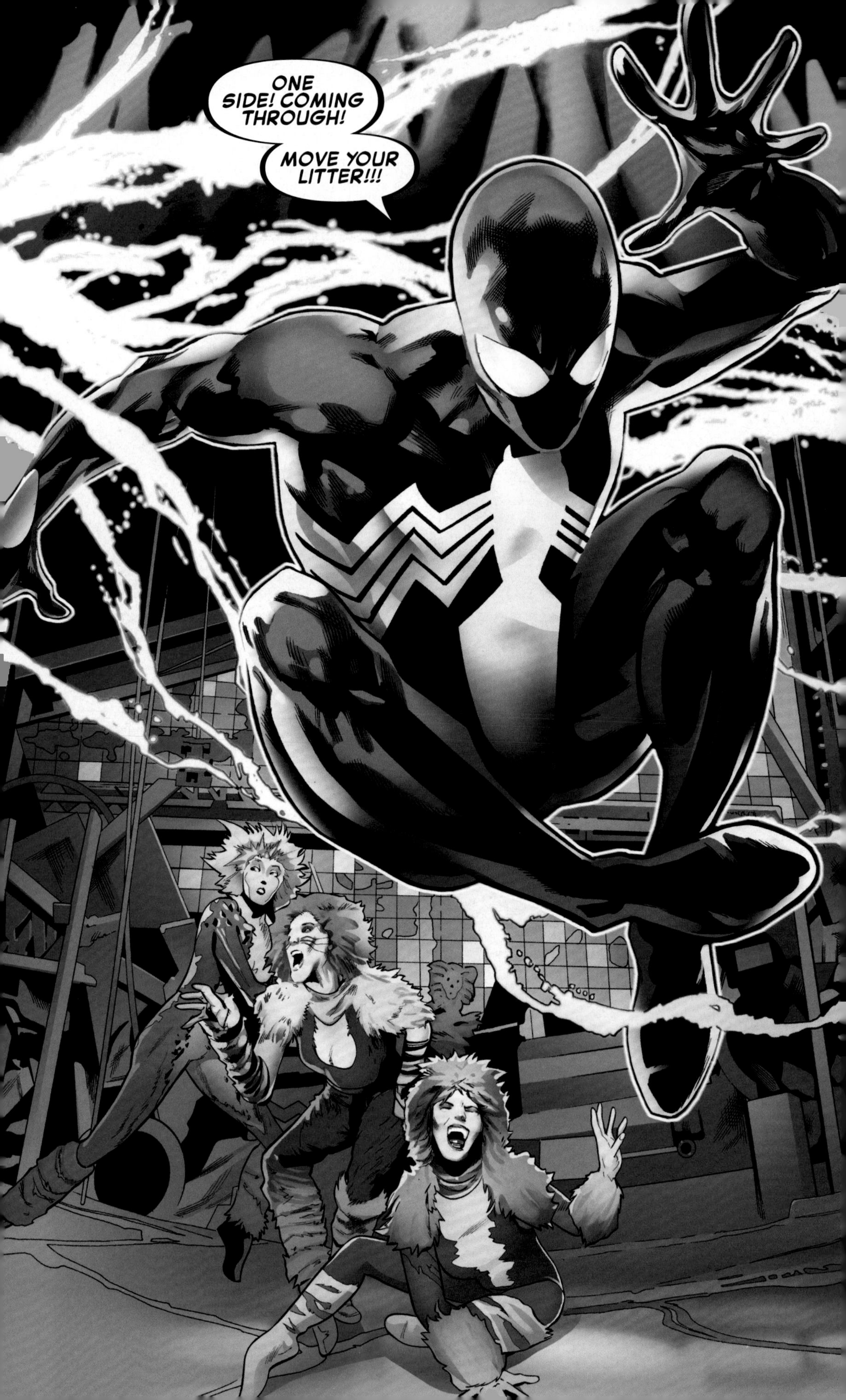
ONE SIDE! COMING THROUGH!
MOVE YOUR LITTER!!!

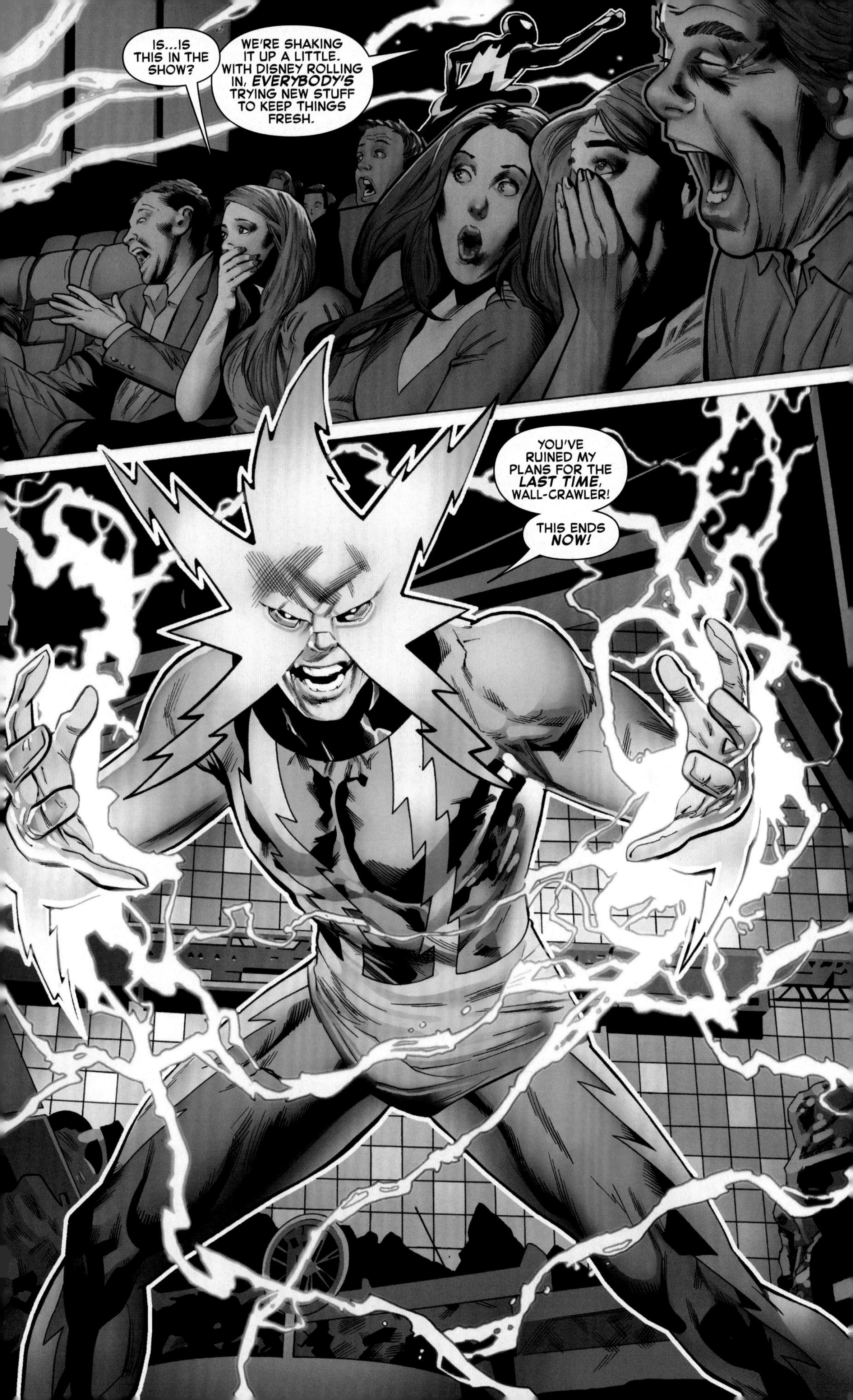
IS...IS THIS IN THE SHOW?
WE'RE SHAKING IT UP A LITTLE. WITH DISNEY ROLLING IN, EVERYBODY'S TRYING NEW STUFF TO KEEP THINGS FRESH.
YOU'VE RUINED MY PLANS FOR THE LAST TIME, WALL-CRAWLER!
THIS ENDS NOW!

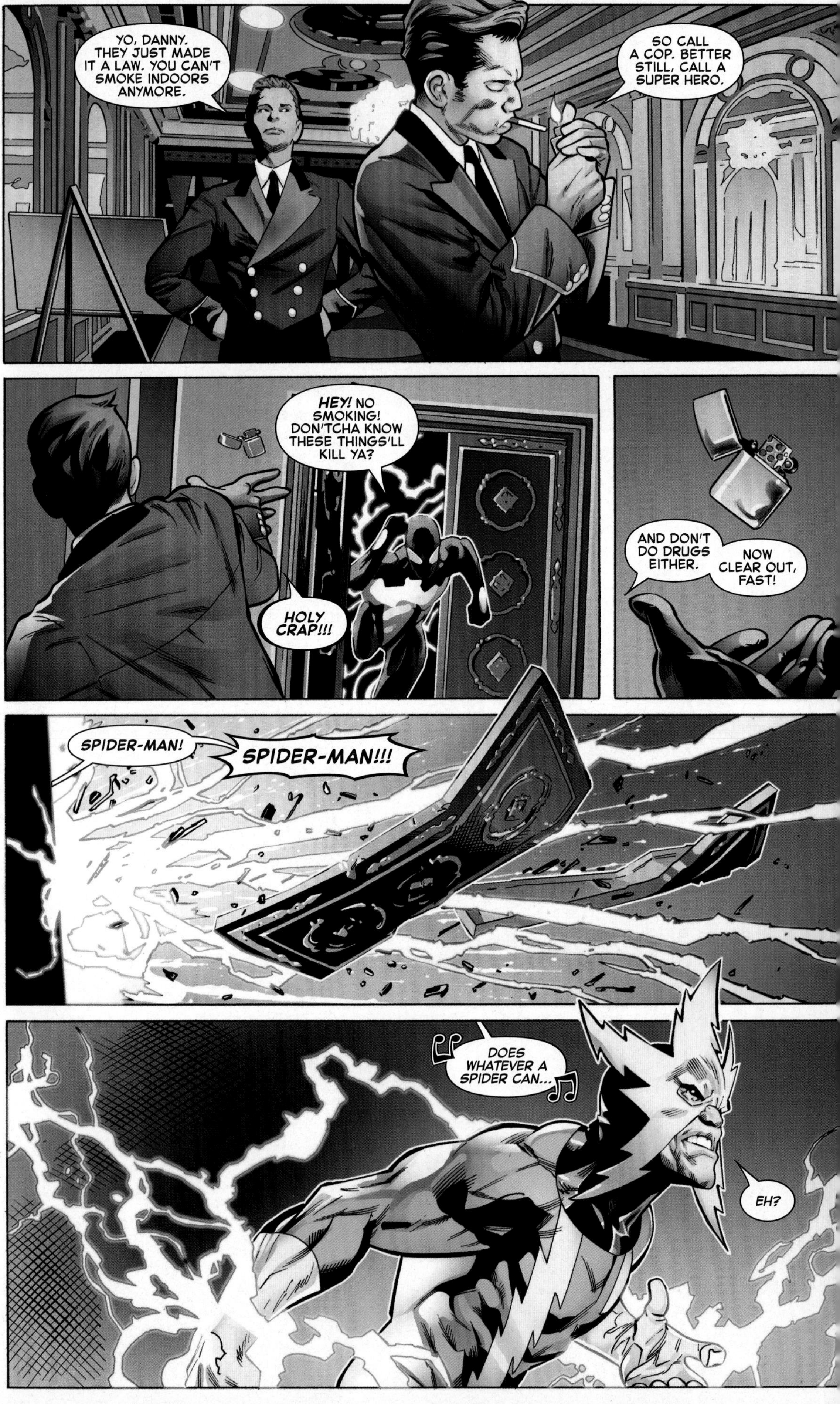
YO, DANNY. THEY JUST MADE IT A LAW. YOU CAN'T SMOKE INDOORS ANYMORE.
SO CALL A COP. BETTER STILL, CALL A SUPER HERO.
HEY! NO SMOKING! DON'TCHA KNOW THESE THINGS'LL KILL YA?
HOLY CRAP!!!
AND DON'T DO DRUGS EITHER.
NOW CLEAR OUT, FAST!
SPIDER-MAN!
SPIDER-MAN!!!
DOES WHATEVER A SPIDER CAN...
EH?

KILLS HIS PREY, EATS THEM WHOLE, WHEN HE IS ON A ROLL... ♪

KLIK

KIDDING.

MAYBE.

SSSSSSSSS

WHAAAAKOWWWW!!

YEEARRRGHH!!

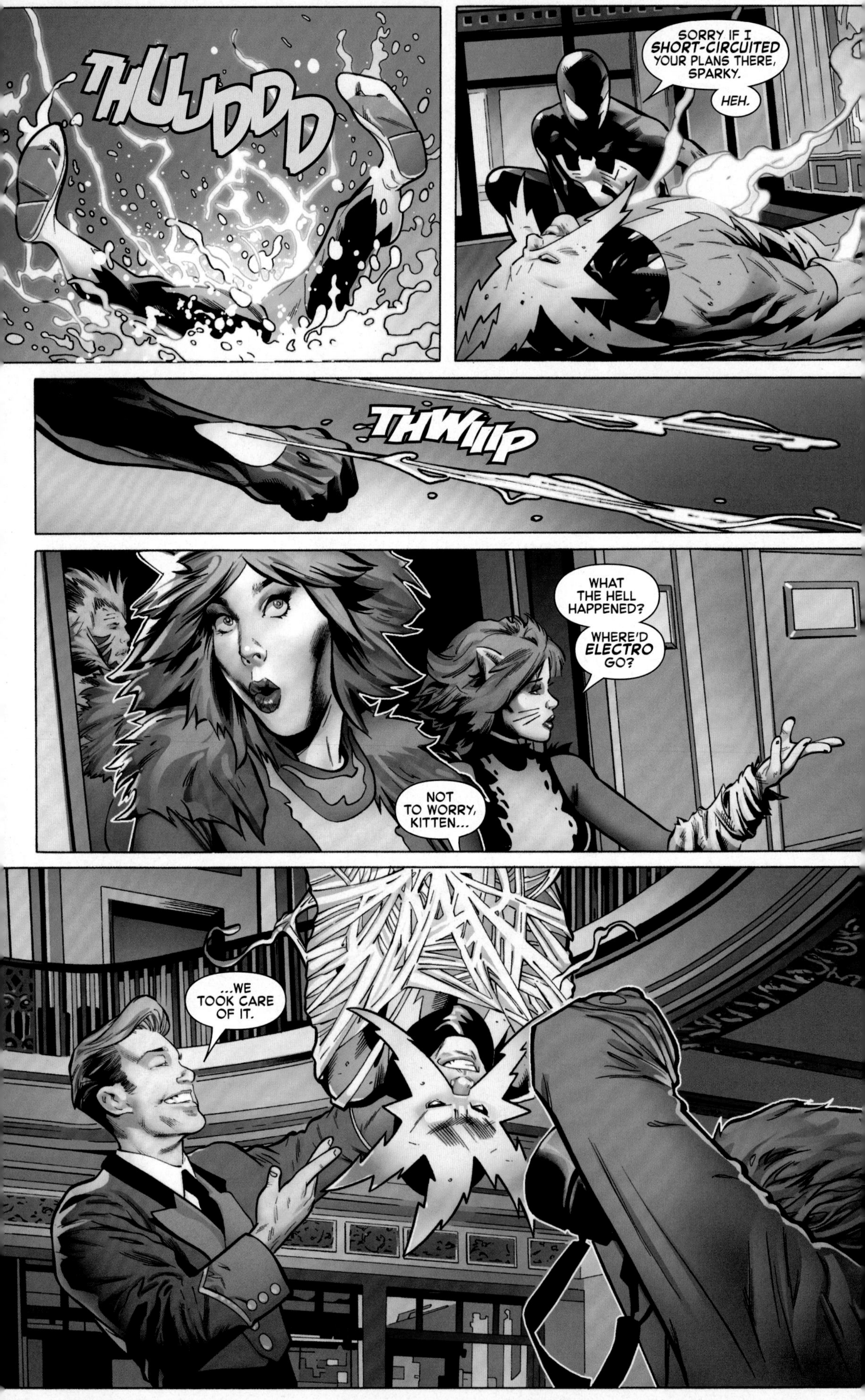
THUUDDD
SORRY IF I SHORT-CIRCUITED YOUR PLANS THERE, SPARKY.
HEH.
THWIIP
WHAT THE HELL HAPPENED?
WHERE'D ELECTRO GO?
NOT TO WORRY, KITTEN...
...WE TOOK CARE OF IT.

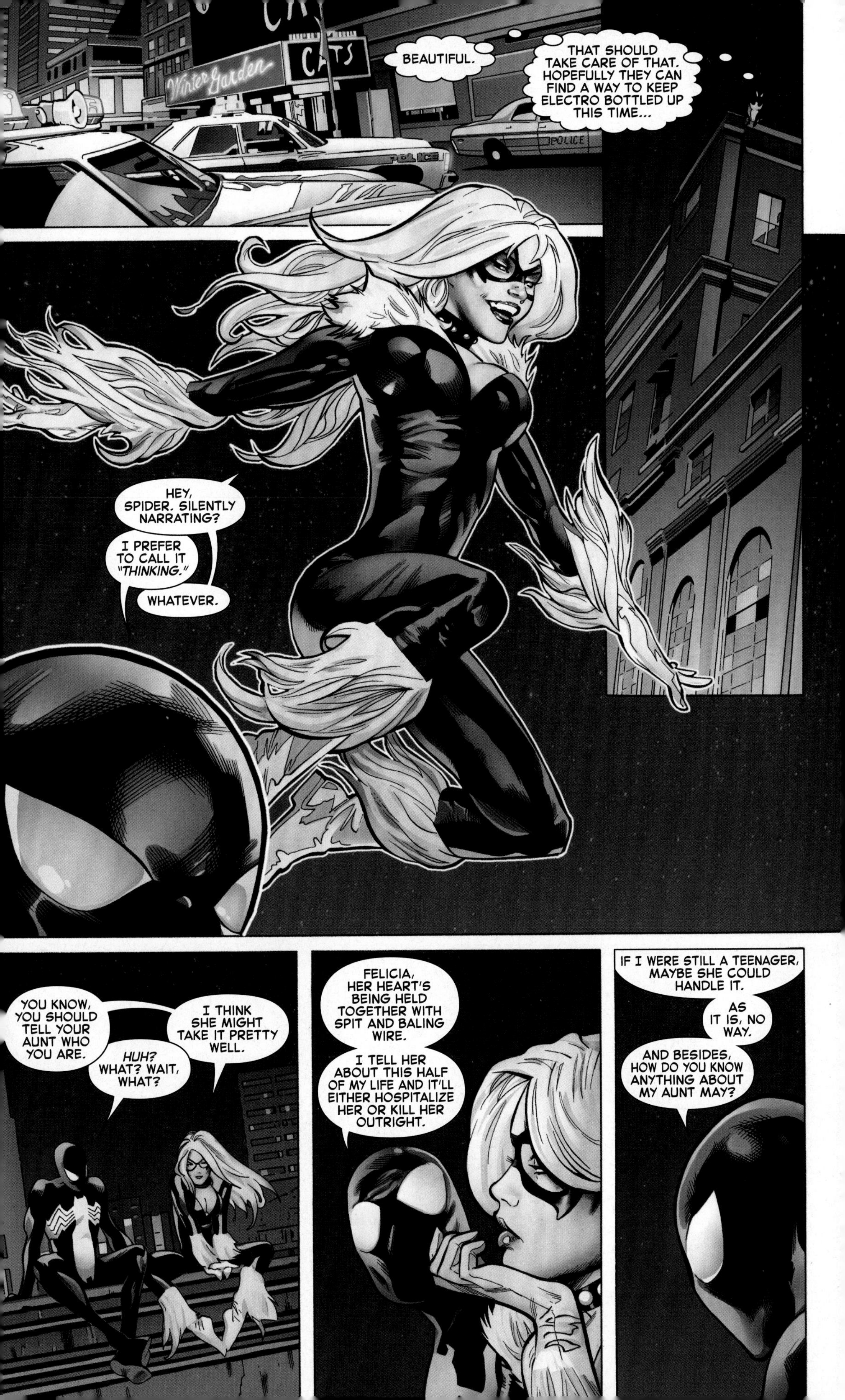

Winter Garden
CATS
POLICE
BEAUTIFUL.
THAT SHOULD TAKE CARE OF THAT. HOPEFULLY THEY CAN FIND A WAY TO KEEP ELECTRO BOTTLED UP THIS TIME...
HEY, SPIDER. SILENTLY NARRATING?
I PREFER TO CALL IT "*THINKING*."
WHATEVER.
YOU KNOW, YOU SHOULD TELL YOUR AUNT WHO YOU ARE.
HUH? WHAT? WAIT, WHAT?
I THINK SHE MIGHT TAKE IT PRETTY WELL.
FELICIA, HER HEART'S BEING HELD TOGETHER WITH SPIT AND BALING WIRE.
I TELL HER ABOUT THIS HALF OF MY LIFE AND IT'LL EITHER HOSPITALIZE HER OR KILL HER OUTRIGHT.
IF I WERE STILL A TEENAGER, MAYBE SHE COULD HANDLE IT.
AS IT IS, NO WAY.
AND BESIDES, HOW DO YOU KNOW ANYTHING ABOUT MY AUNT MAY?

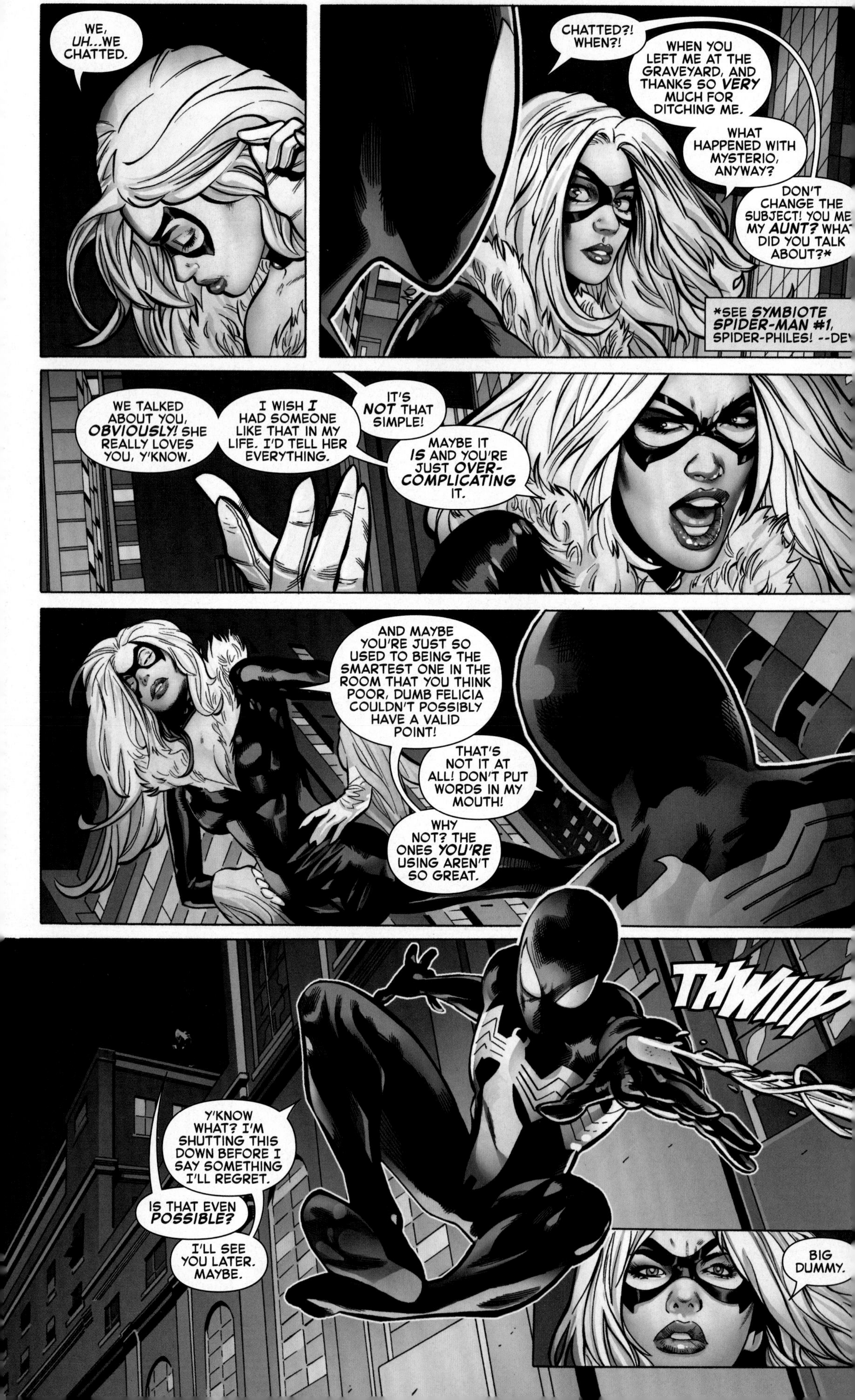
WE, UH...WE CHATTED.
CHATTED?! WHEN?!
WHEN YOU LEFT ME AT THE GRAVEYARD, AND THANKS SO VERY MUCH FOR DITCHING ME.
WHAT HAPPENED WITH MYSTERIO, ANYWAY?
DON'T CHANGE THE SUBJECT! YOU ME MY AUNT? WHA DID YOU TALK ABOUT?*
*SEE SYMBIOTE SPIDER-MAN #1, SPIDER-PHILES! --DEV
WE TALKED ABOUT YOU, OBVIOUSLY! SHE REALLY LOVES YOU, Y'KNOW.
I WISH I HAD SOMEONE LIKE THAT IN MY LIFE. I'D TELL HER EVERYTHING.
IT'S NOT THAT SIMPLE!
MAYBE IT IS AND YOU'RE JUST OVER-COMPLICATING IT.
AND MAYBE YOU'RE JUST SO USED TO BEING THE SMARTEST ONE IN THE ROOM THAT YOU THINK POOR, DUMB FELICIA COULDN'T POSSIBLY HAVE A VALID POINT!
THAT'S NOT IT AT ALL! DON'T PUT WORDS IN MY MOUTH!
WHY NOT? THE ONES YOU'RE USING AREN'T SO GREAT.
THWIIP
Y'KNOW WHAT? I'M SHUTTING THIS DOWN BEFORE I SAY SOMETHING I'LL REGRET.
IS THAT EVEN POSSIBLE?
I'LL SEE YOU LATER. MAYBE.
BIG DUMMY.

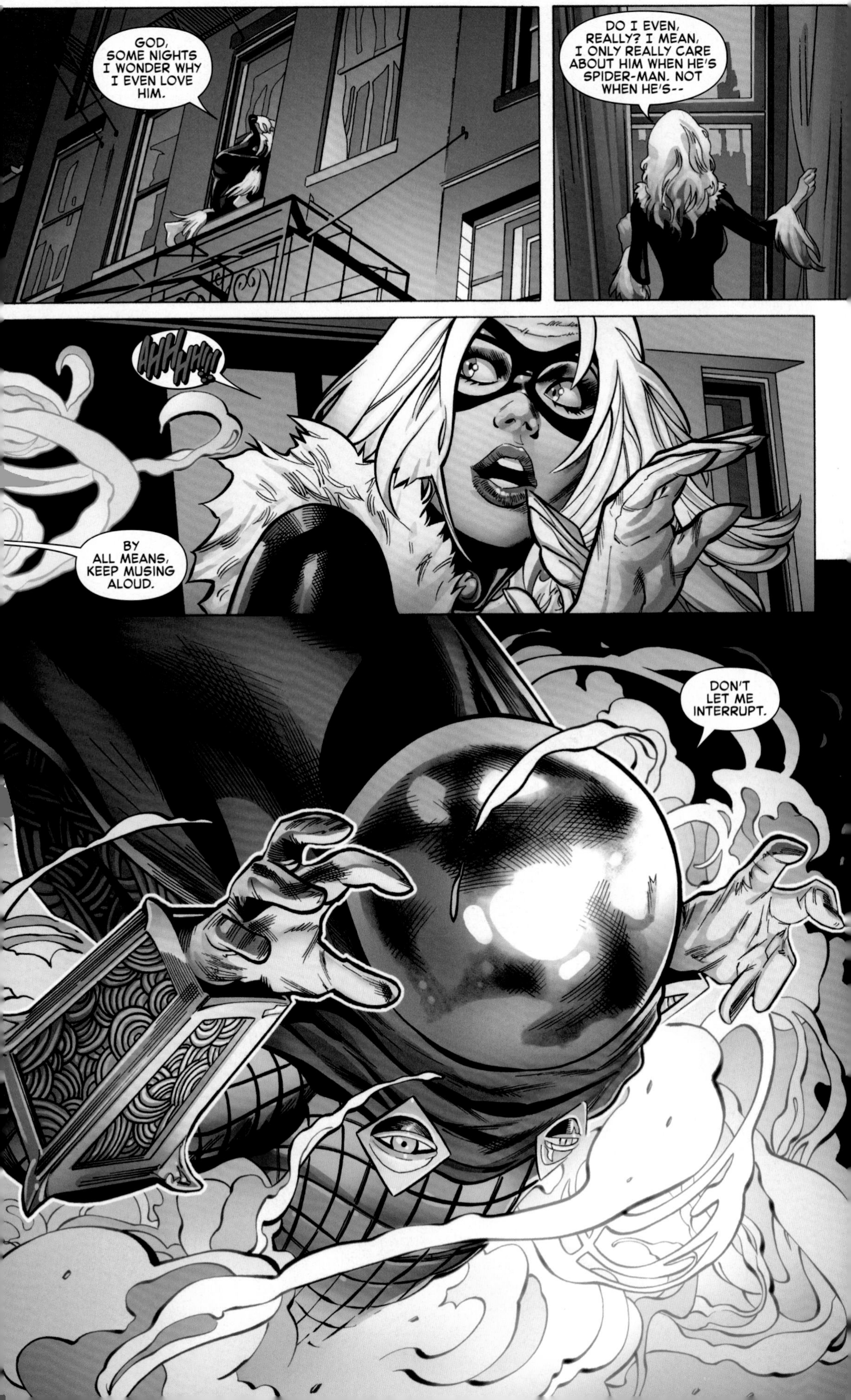
GOD, SOME NIGHTS I WONDER WHY I EVEN LOVE HIM.
DO I EVEN, REALLY? I MEAN, I ONLY REALLY CARE ABOUT HIM WHEN HE'S SPIDER-MAN. NOT WHEN HE'S--
AHHHHH!!!
BY ALL MEANS, KEEP MUSING ALOUD.
DON'T LET ME INTERRUPT.

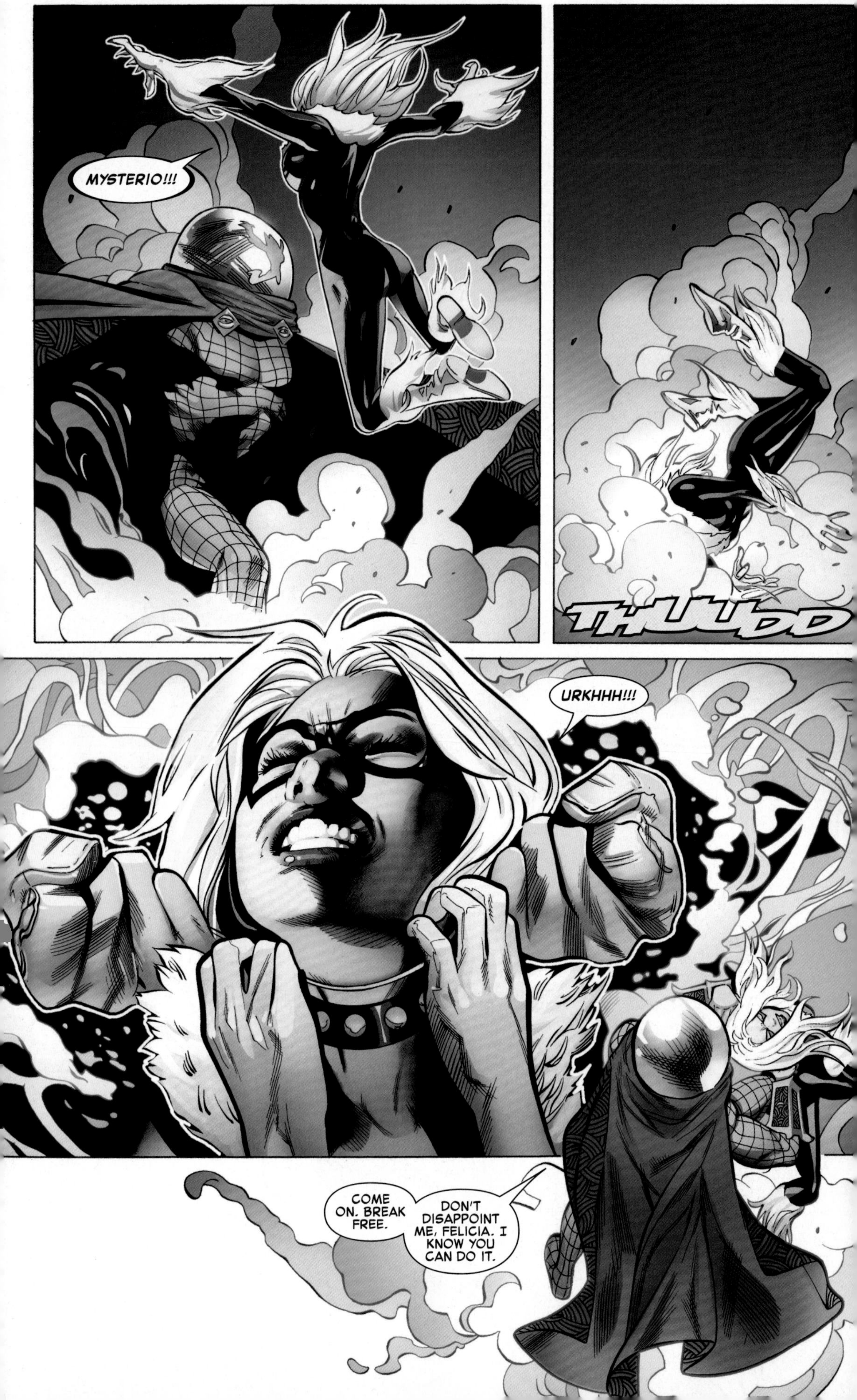
MYSTERIO!!!
THUUDD
URKHHH!!!
COME ON. BREAK FREE.
DON'T DISAPPOINT ME, FELICIA. I KNOW YOU CAN DO IT.

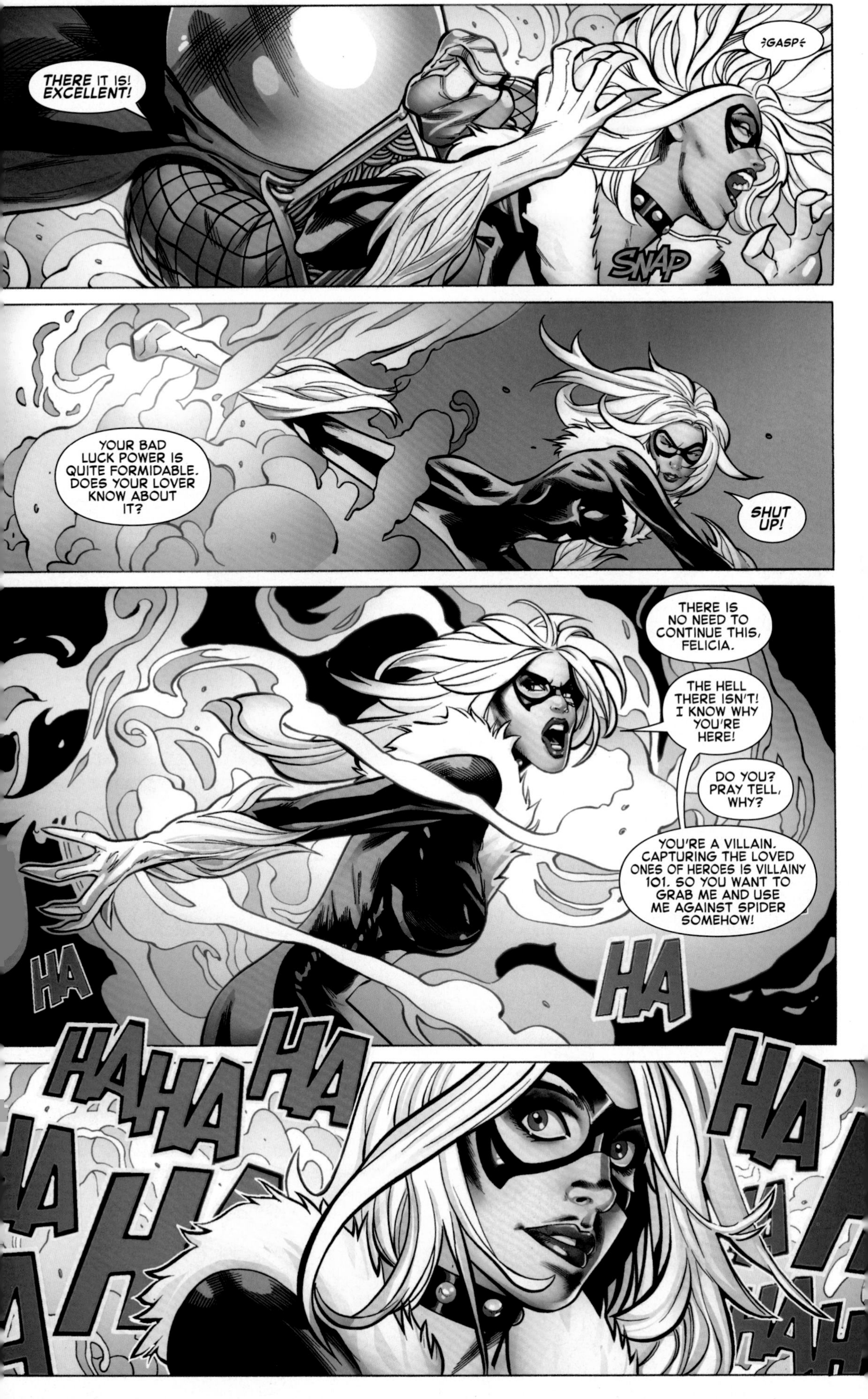
THERE IT IS! EXCELLENT!
GASP
SNAP
YOUR BAD LUCK POWER IS QUITE FORMIDABLE. DOES YOUR LOVER KNOW ABOUT IT?
SHUT UP!
THERE IS NO NEED TO CONTINUE THIS, FELICIA.
THE HELL THERE ISN'T! I KNOW WHY YOU'RE HERE!
DO YOU? PRAY TELL, WHY?
YOU'RE A VILLAIN. CAPTURING THE LOVED ONES OF HEROES IS VILLAINY 101. SO YOU WANT TO GRAB ME AND USE ME AGAINST SPIDER SOMEHOW!
HA
HA
HAHAHA
HA

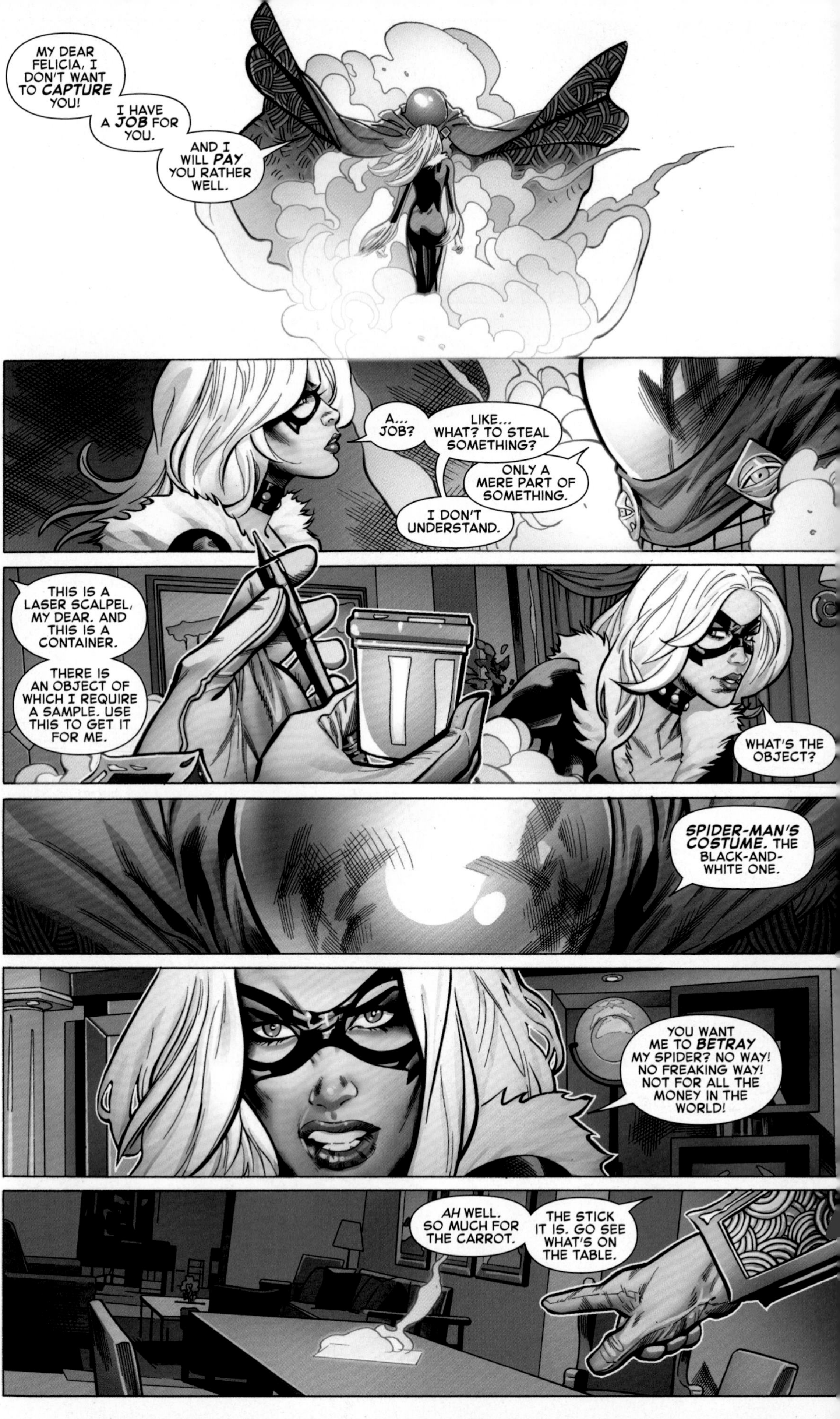
MY DEAR FELICIA, I DON'T WANT TO CAPTURE YOU!
I HAVE A JOB FOR YOU.
AND I WILL PAY YOU RATHER WELL.
A... JOB?
LIKE... WHAT? TO STEAL SOMETHING?
ONLY A MERE PART OF SOMETHING.
I DON'T UNDERSTAND.
THIS IS A LASER SCALPEL, MY DEAR. AND THIS IS A CONTAINER.
THERE IS AN OBJECT OF WHICH I REQUIRE A SAMPLE. USE THIS TO GET IT FOR ME.
WHAT'S THE OBJECT?
SPIDER-MAN'S COSTUME. THE BLACK-AND-WHITE ONE.
YOU WANT ME TO BETRAY MY SPIDER? NO WAY! NO FREAKING WAY! NOT FOR ALL THE MONEY IN THE WORLD!
AH WELL. SO MUCH FOR THE CARROT.
THE STICK IT IS. GO SEE WHAT'S ON THE TABLE.

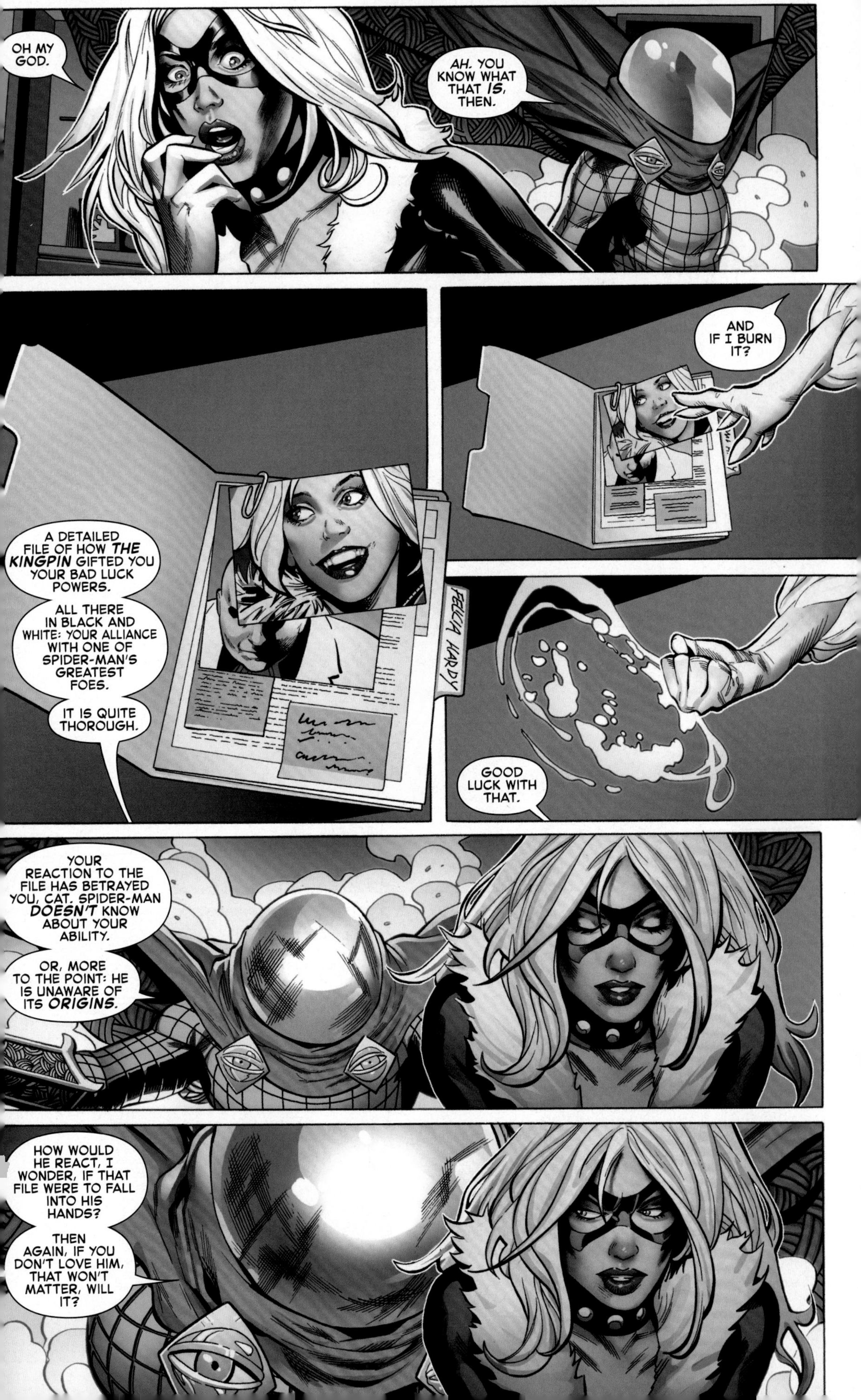
OH MY GOD.
AH. YOU KNOW WHAT THAT IS, THEN.
A DETAILED FILE OF HOW THE KINGPIN GIFTED YOU YOUR BAD LUCK POWERS.
ALL THERE IN BLACK AND WHITE: YOUR ALLIANCE WITH ONE OF SPIDER-MAN'S GREATEST FOES.
IT IS QUITE THOROUGH.
FELICIA HARDY
AND IF I BURN IT?
GOOD LUCK WITH THAT.
YOUR REACTION TO THE FILE HAS BETRAYED YOU, CAT. SPIDER-MAN DOESN'T KNOW ABOUT YOUR ABILITY.
OR, MORE TO THE POINT: HE IS UNAWARE OF ITS ORIGINS.
HOW WOULD HE REACT, I WONDER, IF THAT FILE WERE TO FALL INTO HIS HANDS?
THEN AGAIN, IF YOU DON'T LOVE HIM, THAT WON'T MATTER, WILL IT?

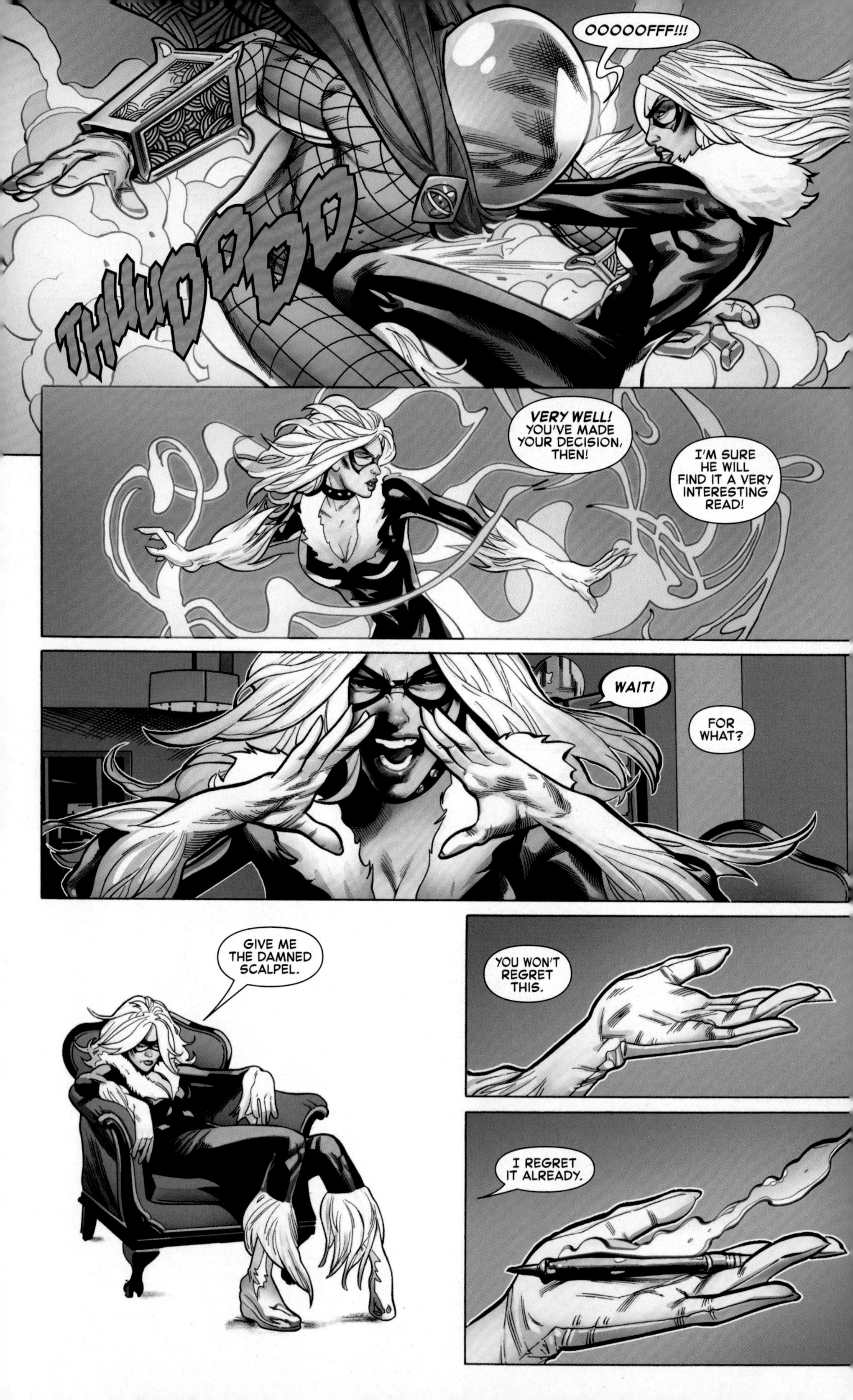
OOOOOFFF!!!
THUDDDD
VERY WELL! YOU'VE MADE YOUR DECISION, THEN!
I'M SURE HE WILL FIND IT A VERY INTERESTING READ!
WAIT!
FOR WHAT?
GIVE ME THE DAMNED SCALPEL.
YOU WON'T REGRET THIS.
I REGRET IT ALREADY.

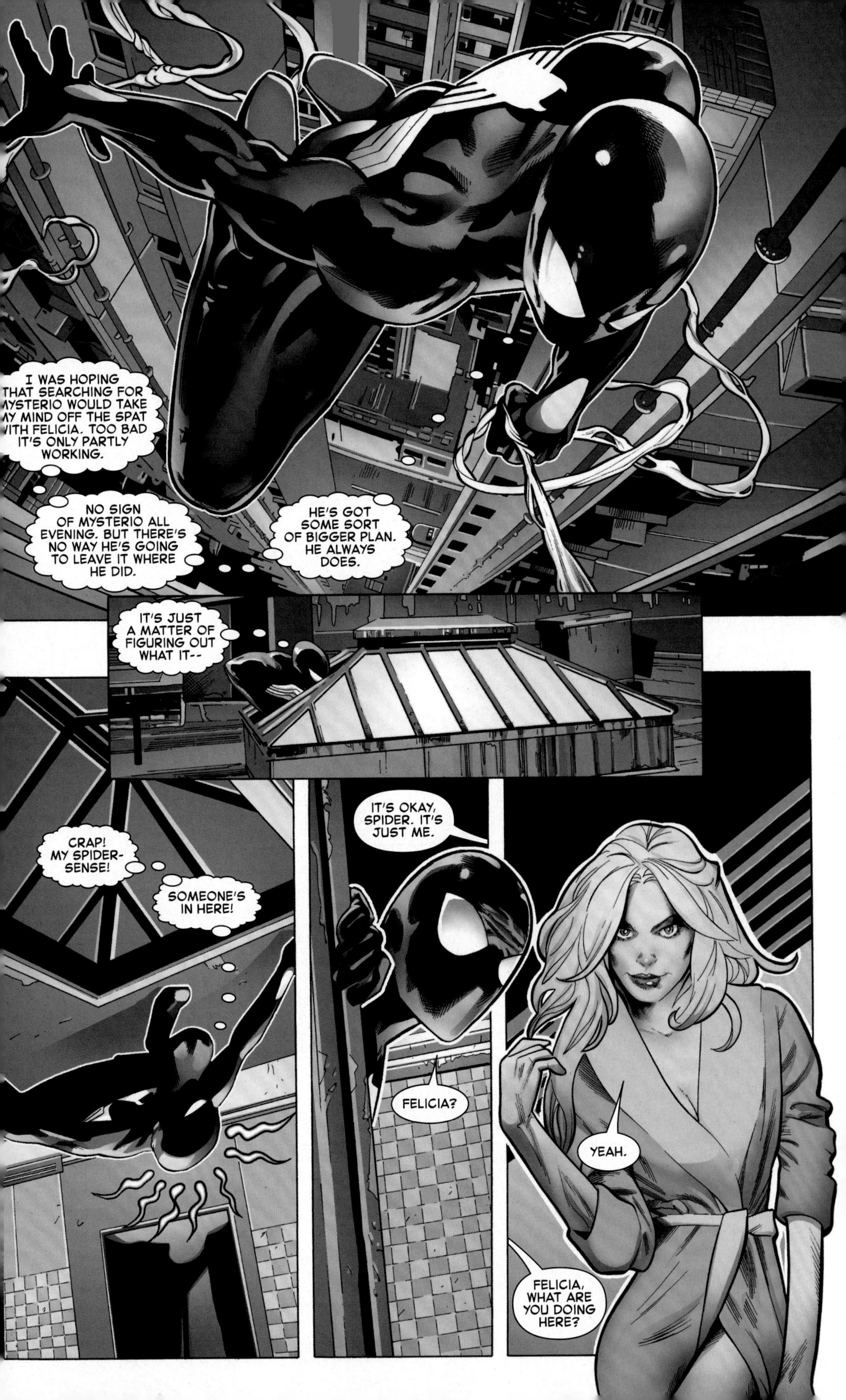

I WAS HOPING THAT SEARCHING FOR MYSTERIO WOULD TAKE MY MIND OFF THE SPAT WITH FELICIA. TOO BAD IT'S ONLY PARTLY WORKING.
NO SIGN OF MYSTERIO ALL EVENING. BUT THERE'S NO WAY HE'S GOING TO LEAVE IT WHERE HE DID.
HE'S GOT SOME SORT OF BIGGER PLAN. HE ALWAYS DOES.
IT'S JUST A MATTER OF FIGURING OUT WHAT IT--
CRAP! MY SPIDER-SENSE!
SOMEONE'S IN HERE!
IT'S OKAY, SPIDER. IT'S JUST ME.
FELICIA?
YEAH.
FELICIA, WHAT ARE YOU DOING HERE?

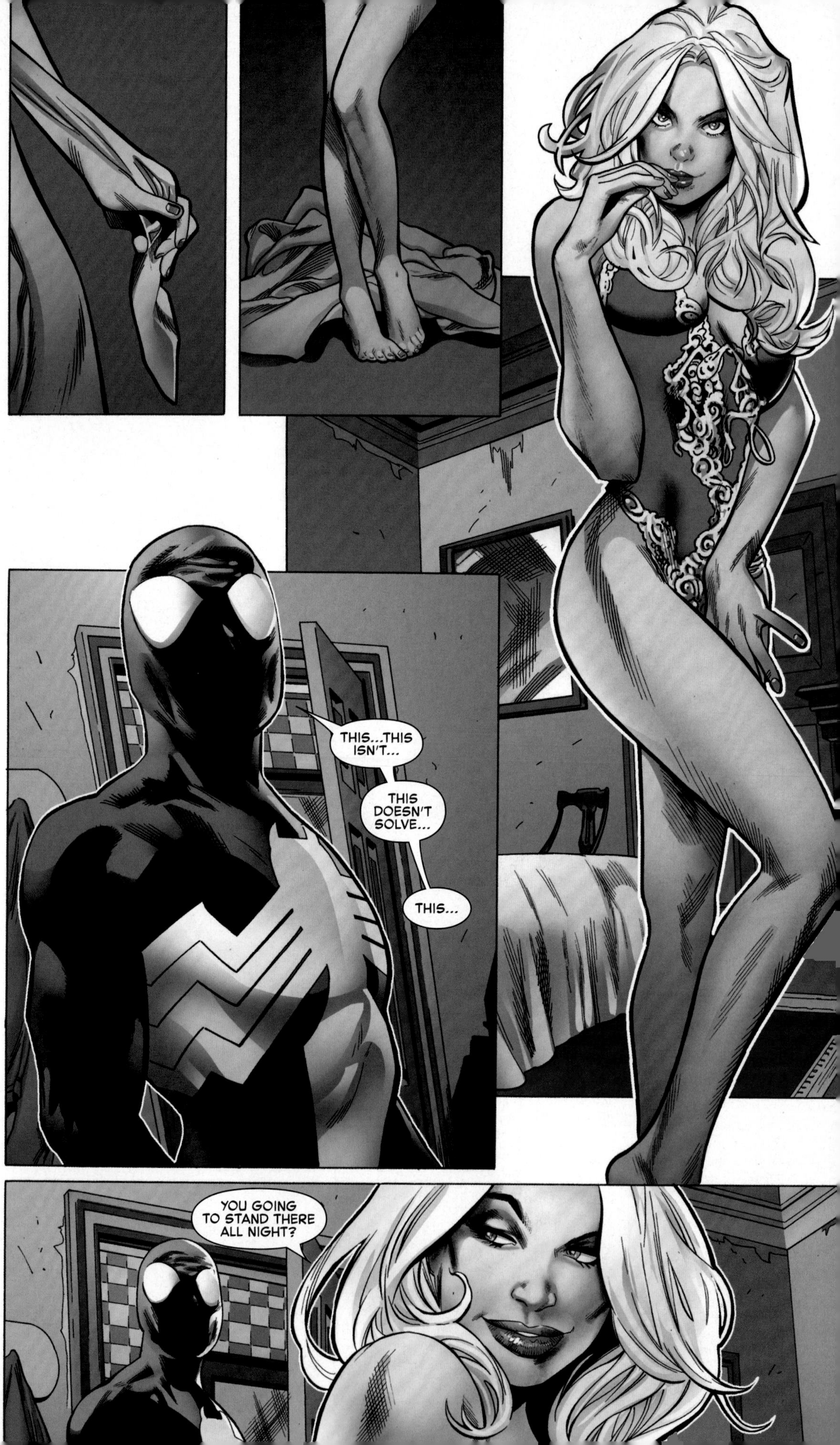

THIS...THIS ISN'T...
THIS DOESN'T SOLVE...
THIS...
YOU GOING TO STAND THERE ALL NIGHT?

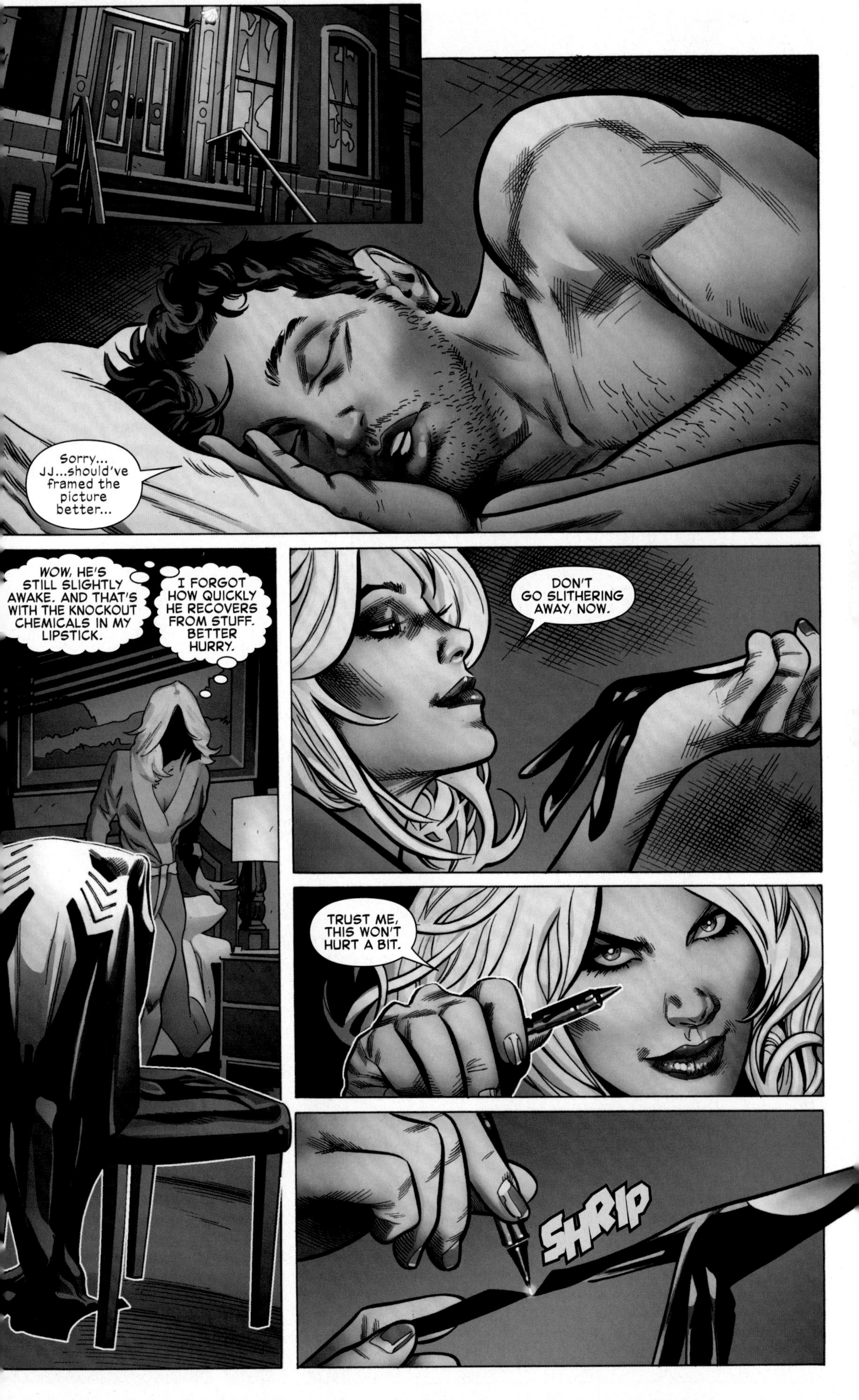
Sorry... JJ...should've framed the picture better...
WOW, HE'S STILL SLIGHTLY AWAKE. AND THAT'S WITH THE KNOCKOUT CHEMICALS IN MY LIPSTICK.
I FORGOT HOW QUICKLY HE RECOVERS FROM STUFF. BETTER HURRY.
DON'T GO SLITHERING AWAY, NOW.
TRUST ME, THIS WON'T HURT A BIT.
SHRIP

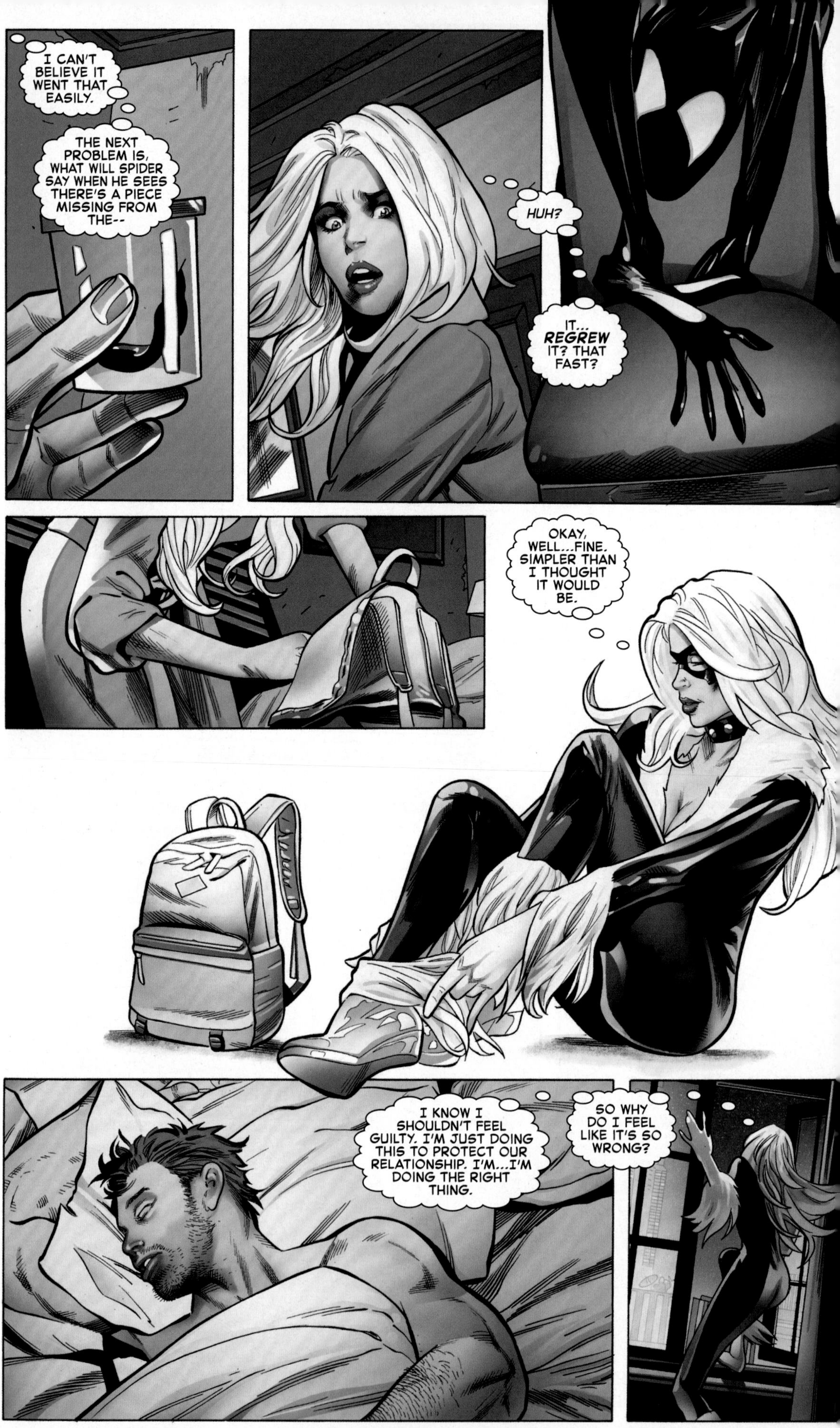
I CAN'T BELIEVE IT WENT THAT EASILY.
THE NEXT PROBLEM IS, WHAT WILL SPIDER SAY WHEN HE SEES THERE'S A PIECE MISSING FROM THE--
HUH?
IT... REGREW IT? THAT FAST?
OKAY, WELL...FINE. SIMPLER THAN I THOUGHT IT WOULD BE.
I KNOW I SHOULDN'T FEEL GUILTY. I'M JUST DOING THIS TO PROTECT OUR RELATIONSHIP. I'M...I'M DOING THE RIGHT THING.
SO WHY DO I FEEL LIKE IT'S SO WRONG?

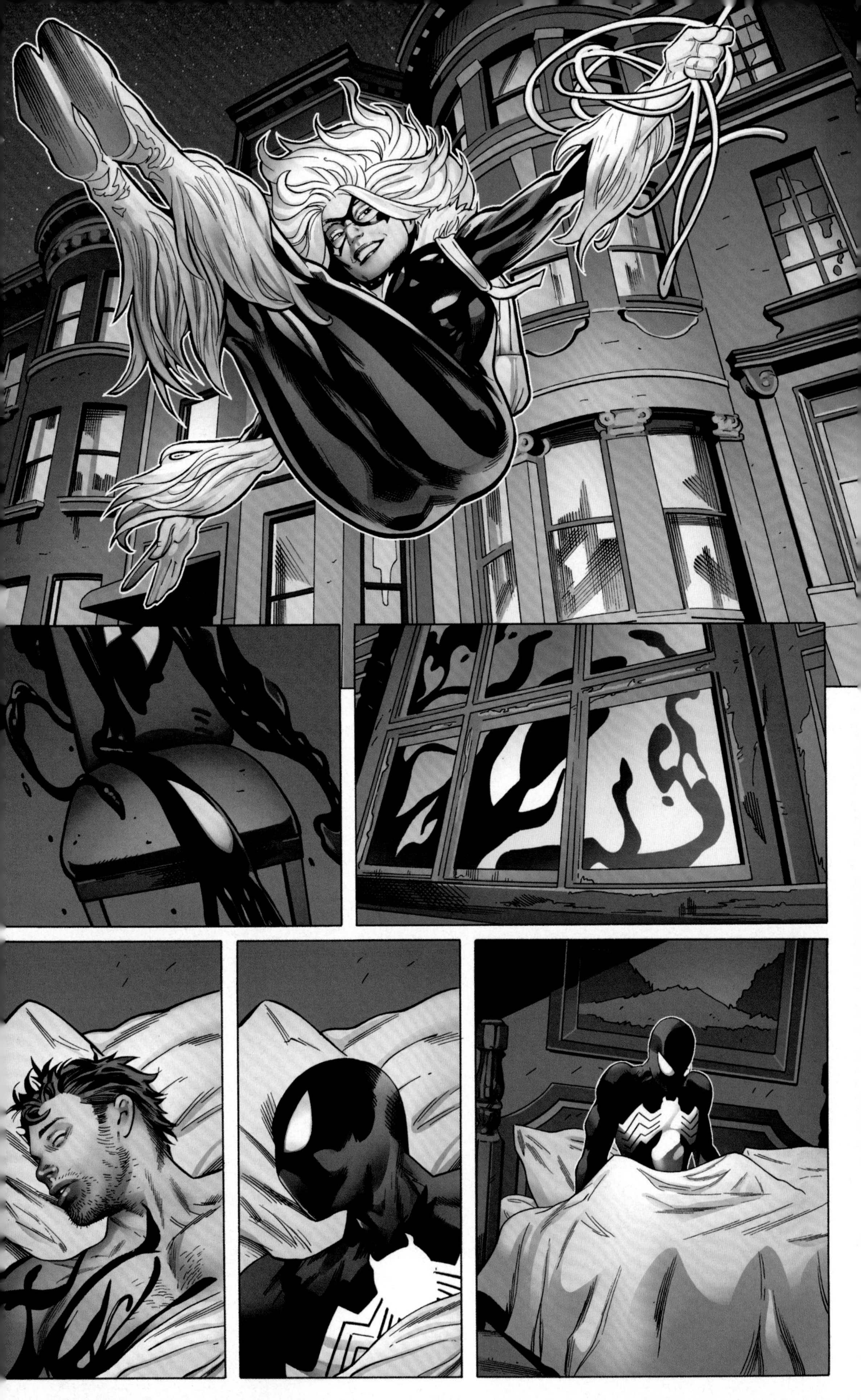

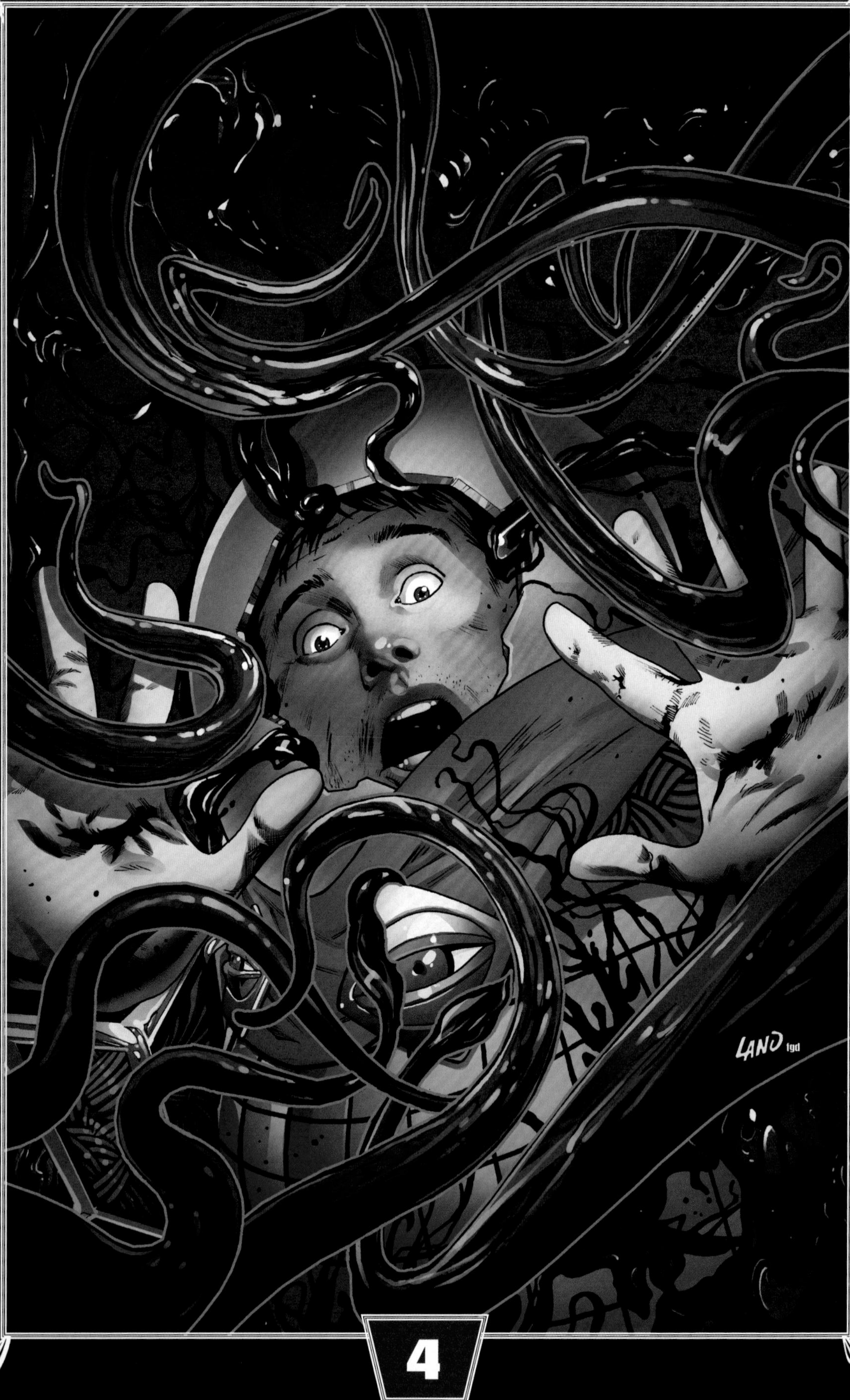
LAND lgd

4

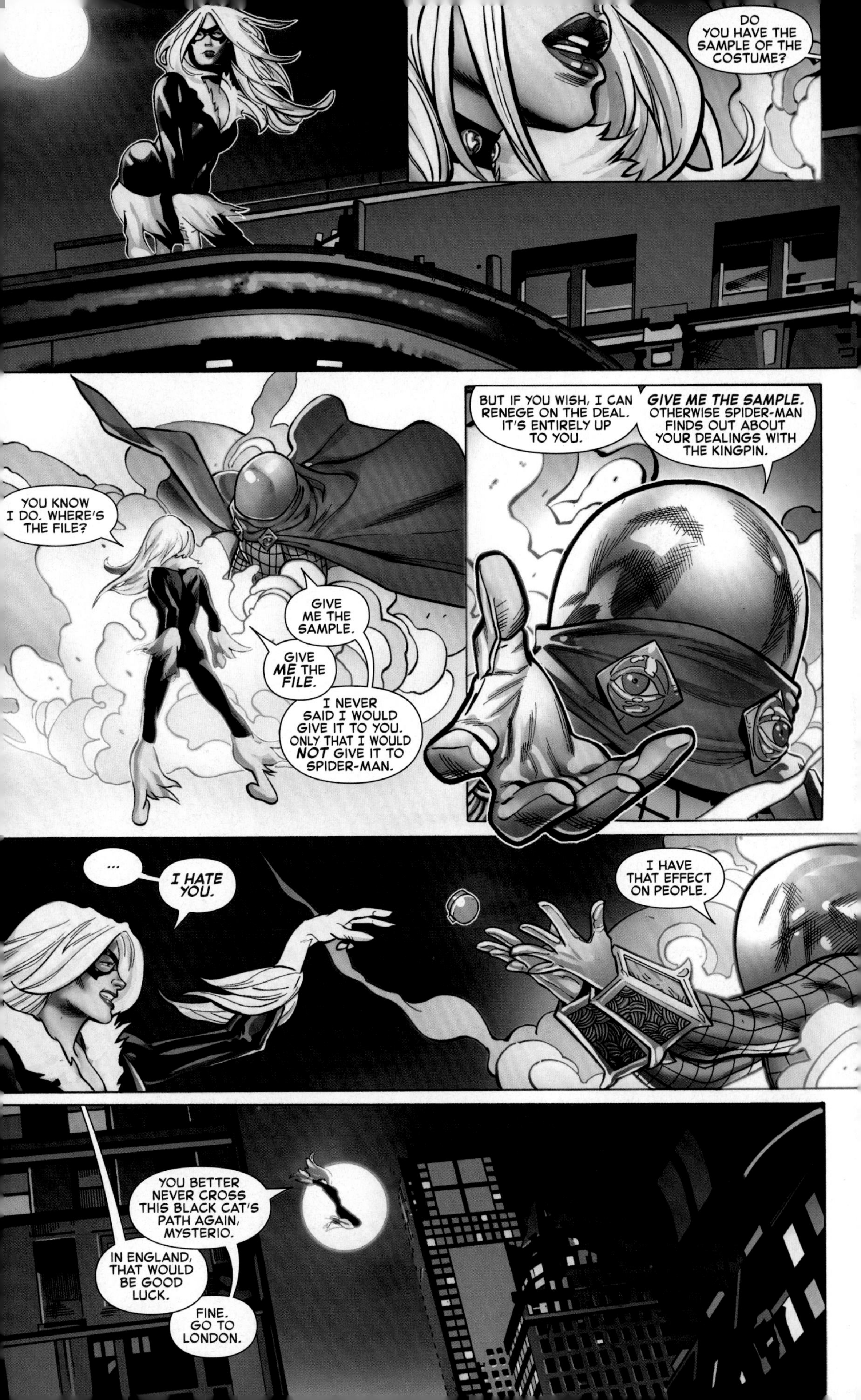
DO YOU HAVE THE SAMPLE OF THE COSTUME?
YOU KNOW I DO. WHERE'S THE FILE?
GIVE ME THE SAMPLE.
GIVE *ME* THE *FILE.*
I NEVER SAID I WOULD GIVE IT TO YOU. ONLY THAT I WOULD *NOT* GIVE IT TO SPIDER-MAN.
BUT IF YOU WISH, I CAN RENEGE ON THE DEAL. IT'S ENTIRELY UP TO YOU.
GIVE ME THE SAMPLE. OTHERWISE SPIDER-MAN FINDS OUT ABOUT YOUR DEALINGS WITH THE KINGPIN.
...
I HATE YOU.
I HAVE THAT EFFECT ON PEOPLE.
YOU BETTER NEVER CROSS THIS BLACK CAT'S PATH AGAIN, MYSTERIO.
IN ENGLAND, THAT WOULD BE GOOD LUCK.
FINE. GO TO LONDON.

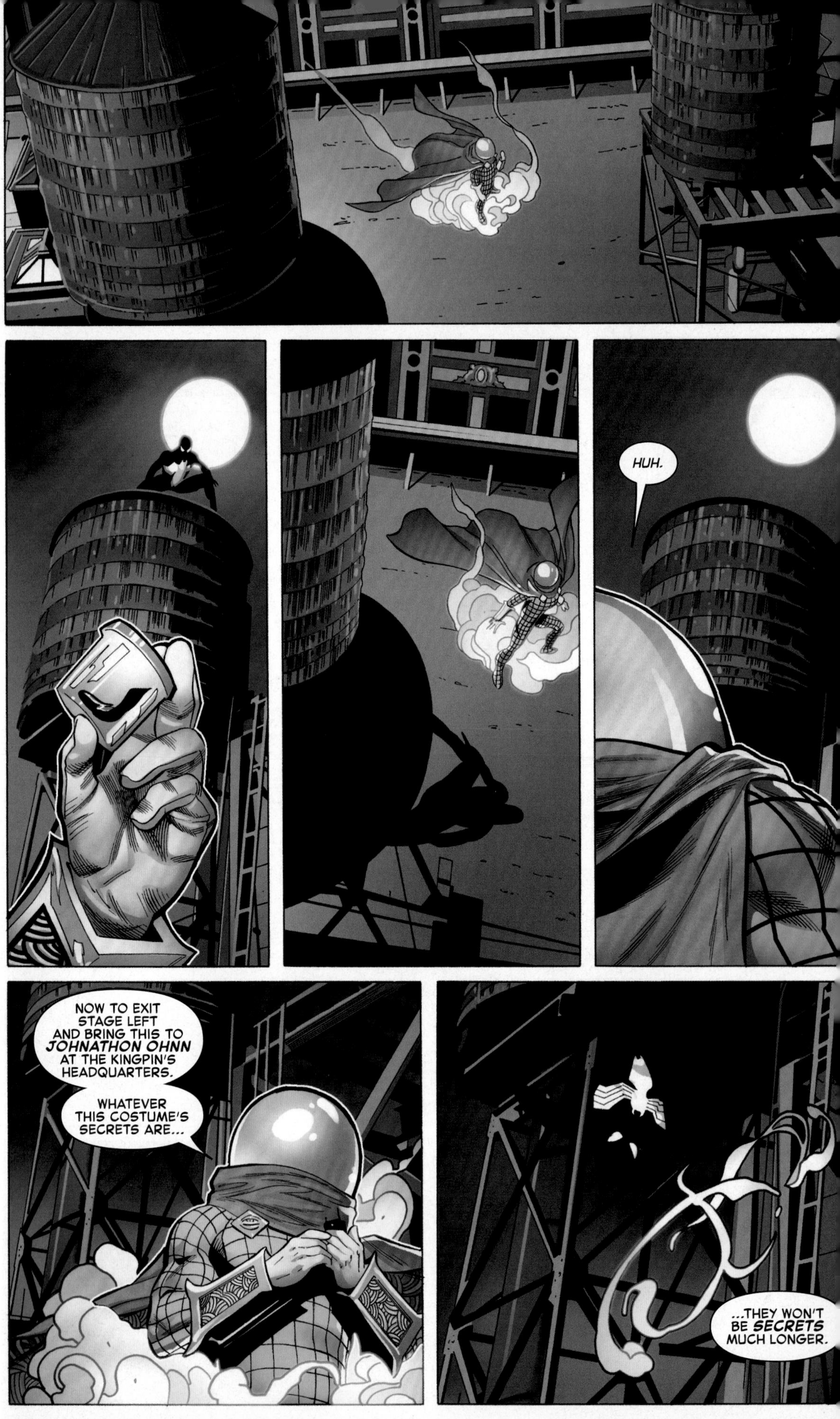
HUH.
NOW TO EXIT STAGE LEFT AND BRING THIS TO JOHNATHON OHNN AT THE KINGPIN'S HEADQUARTERS.
WHATEVER THIS COSTUME'S SECRETS ARE...
...THEY WON'T BE SECRETS MUCH LONGER.

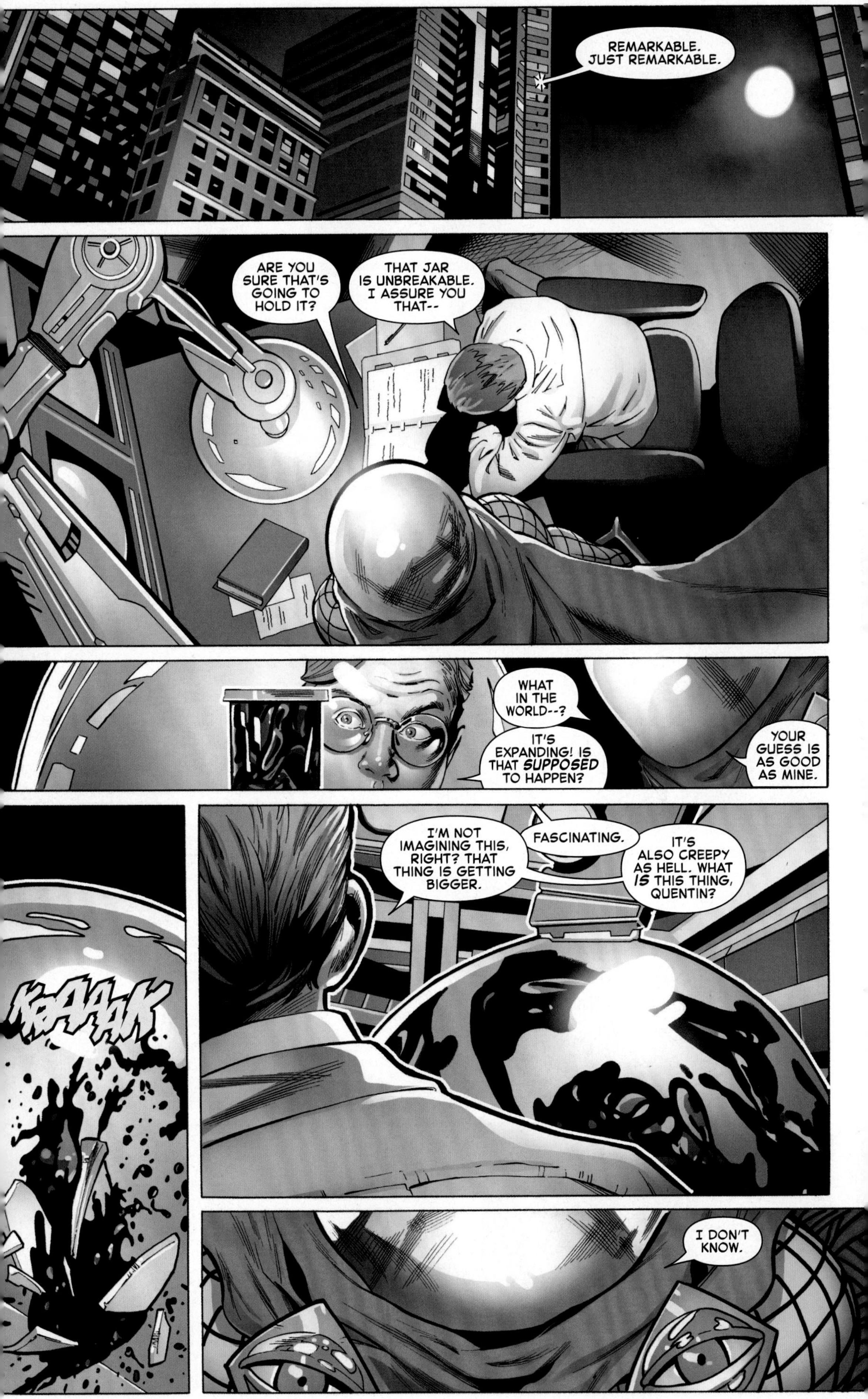
REMARKABLE. JUST REMARKABLE.
ARE YOU SURE THAT'S GOING TO HOLD IT?
THAT JAR IS UNBREAKABLE. I ASSURE YOU THAT--
WHAT IN THE WORLD--?
IT'S EXPANDING! IS THAT SUPPOSED TO HAPPEN?
YOUR GUESS IS AS GOOD AS MINE.
KRAAAK
I'M NOT IMAGINING THIS, RIGHT? THAT THING IS GETTING BIGGER.
FASCINATING.
IT'S ALSO CREEPY AS HELL. WHAT IS THIS THING, QUENTIN?
I DON'T KNOW.

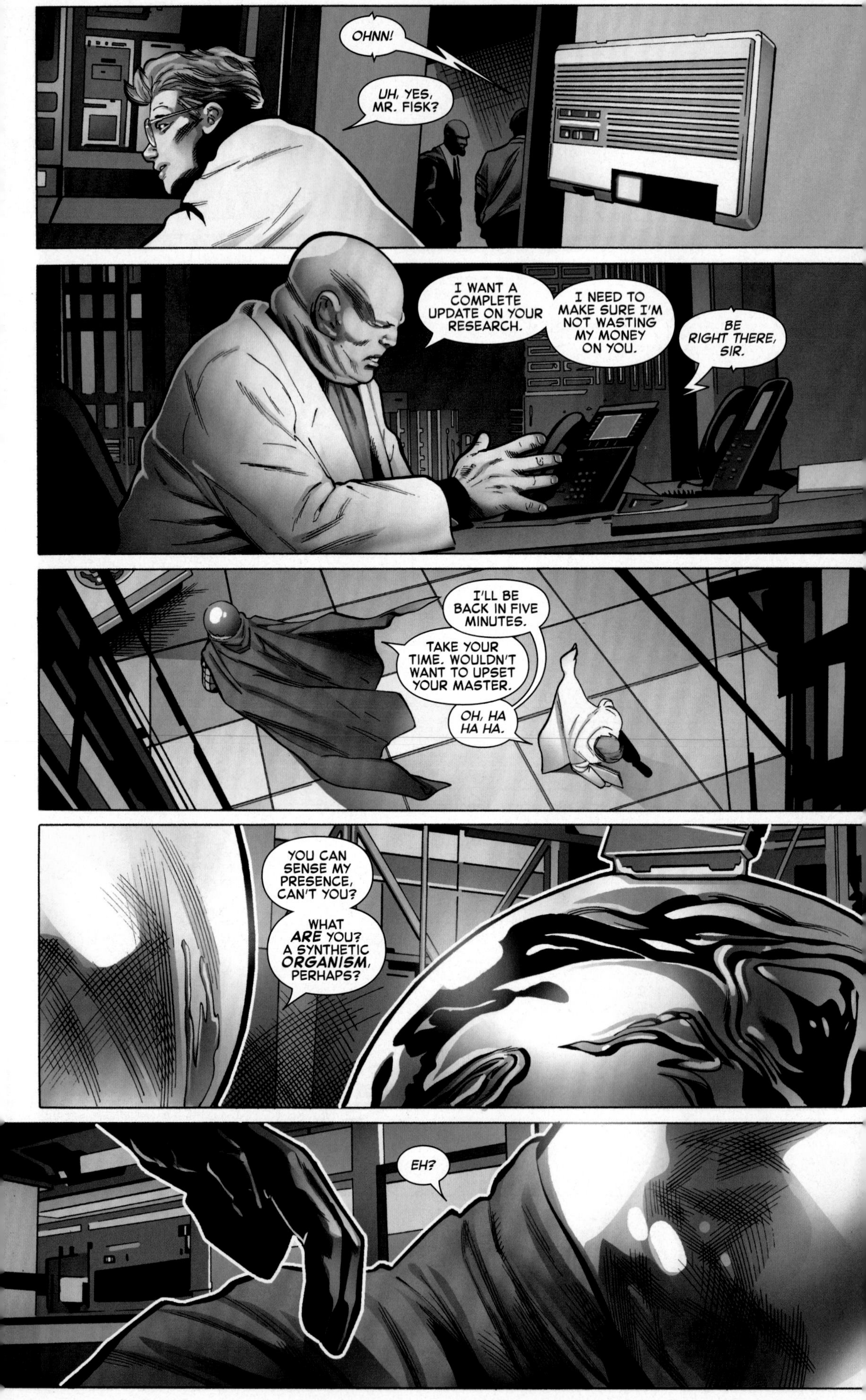
OHNN!
UH, YES, MR. FISK?
I WANT A COMPLETE UPDATE ON YOUR RESEARCH.
I NEED TO MAKE SURE I'M NOT WASTING MY MONEY ON YOU.
BE RIGHT THERE, SIR.
I'LL BE BACK IN FIVE MINUTES.
TAKE YOUR TIME. WOULDN'T WANT TO UPSET YOUR MASTER.
OH, HA HA HA.
YOU CAN SENSE MY PRESENCE, CAN'T YOU?
WHAT ARE YOU? A SYNTHETIC ORGANISM, PERHAPS?
EH?

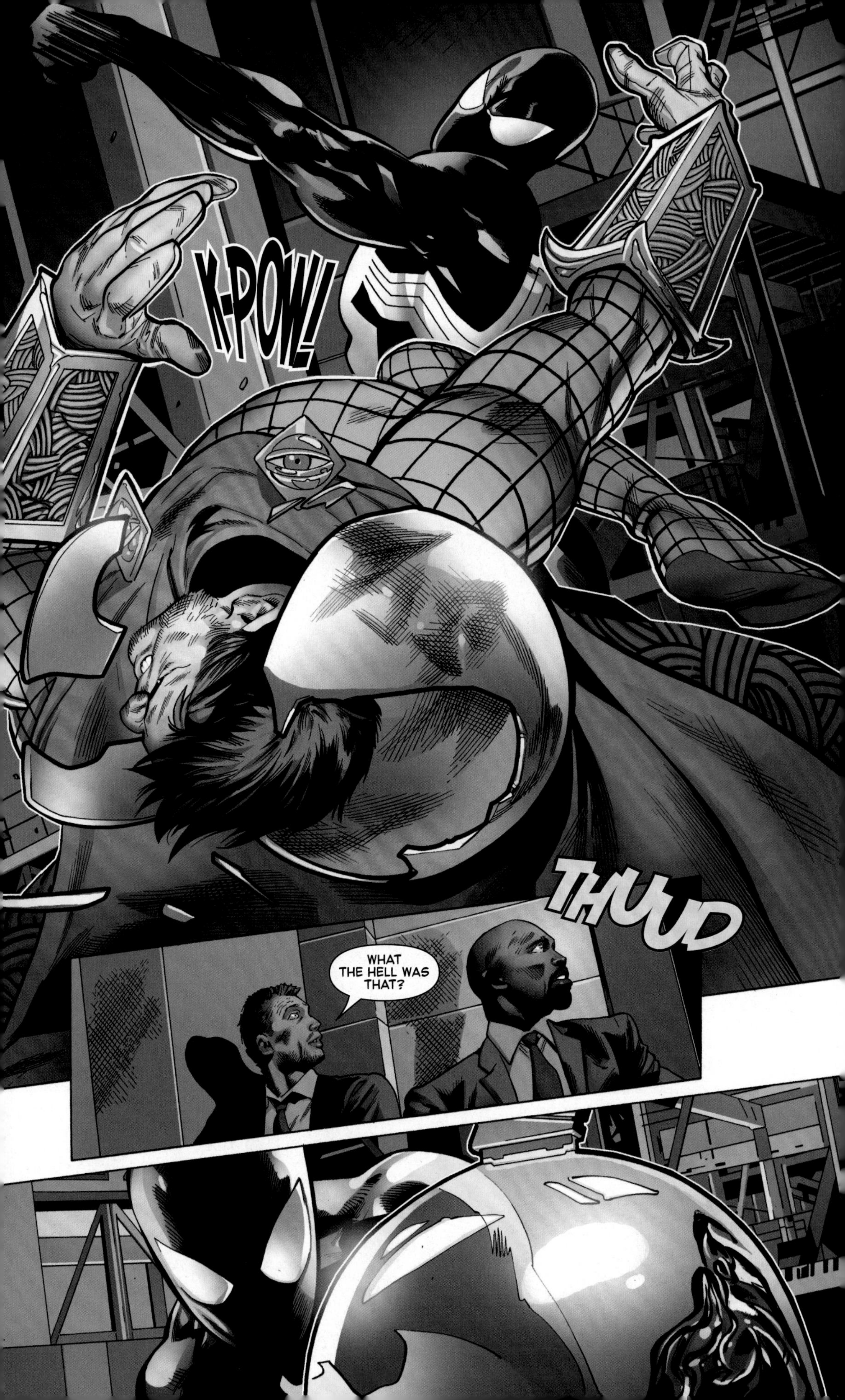
K-POW!
THUUD
WHAT THE HELL WAS THAT?

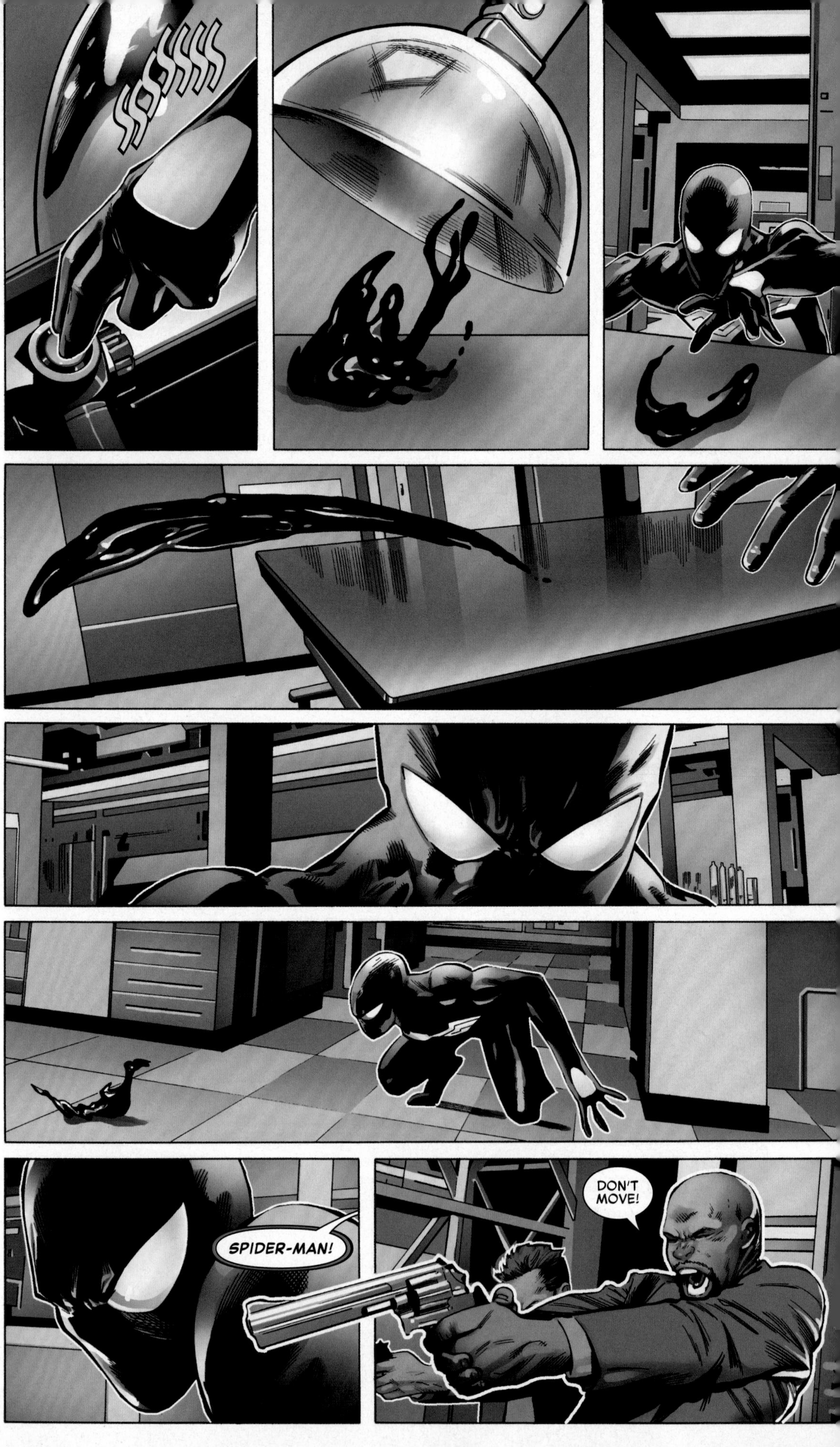
SSSSSSS
SPIDER-MAN!
DON'T MOVE!

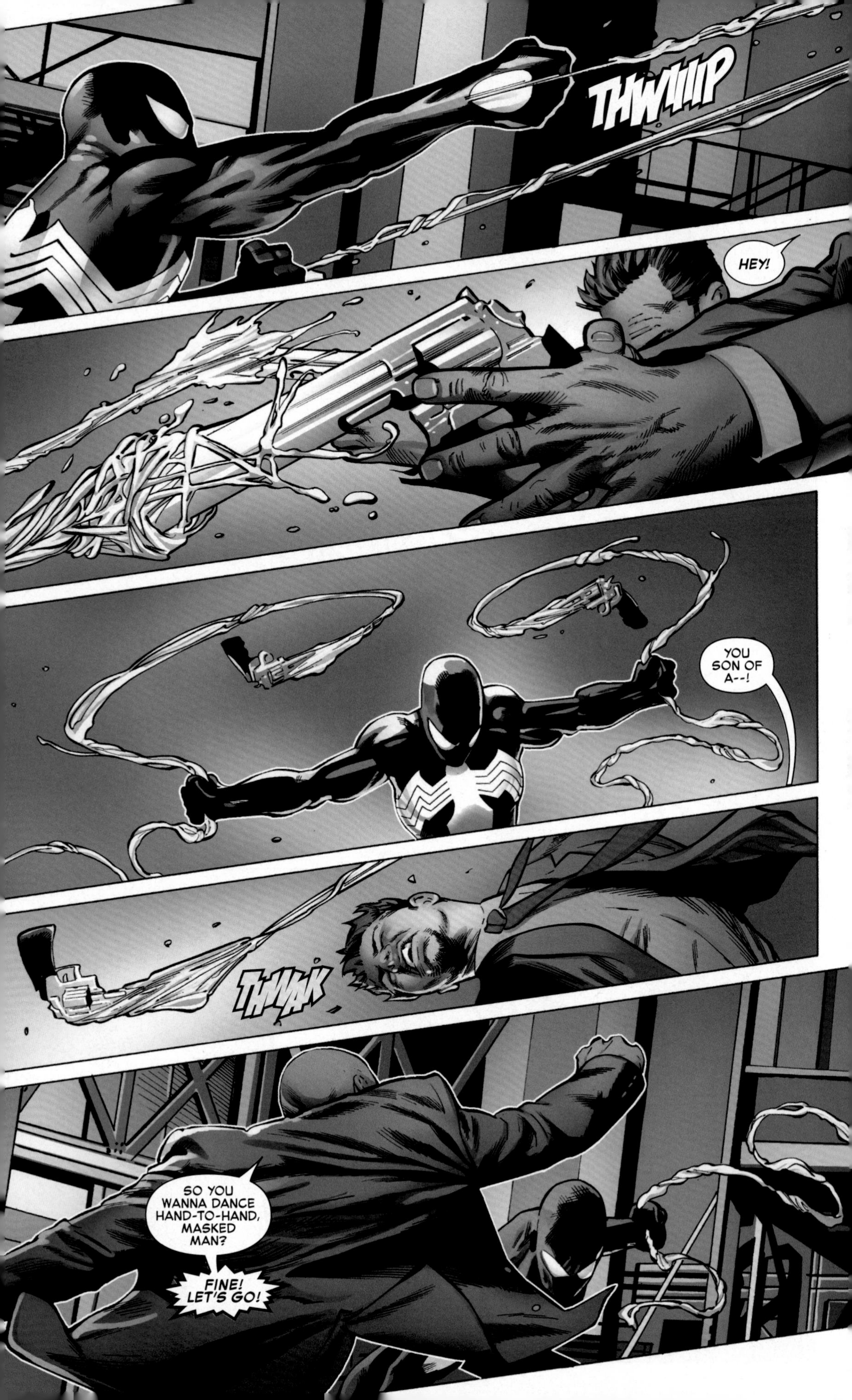
THWIIIP
HEY!
YOU SON OF A--!
THWAK
SO YOU WANNA DANCE HAND-TO-HAND, MASKED MAN?
FINE! LET'S GO!

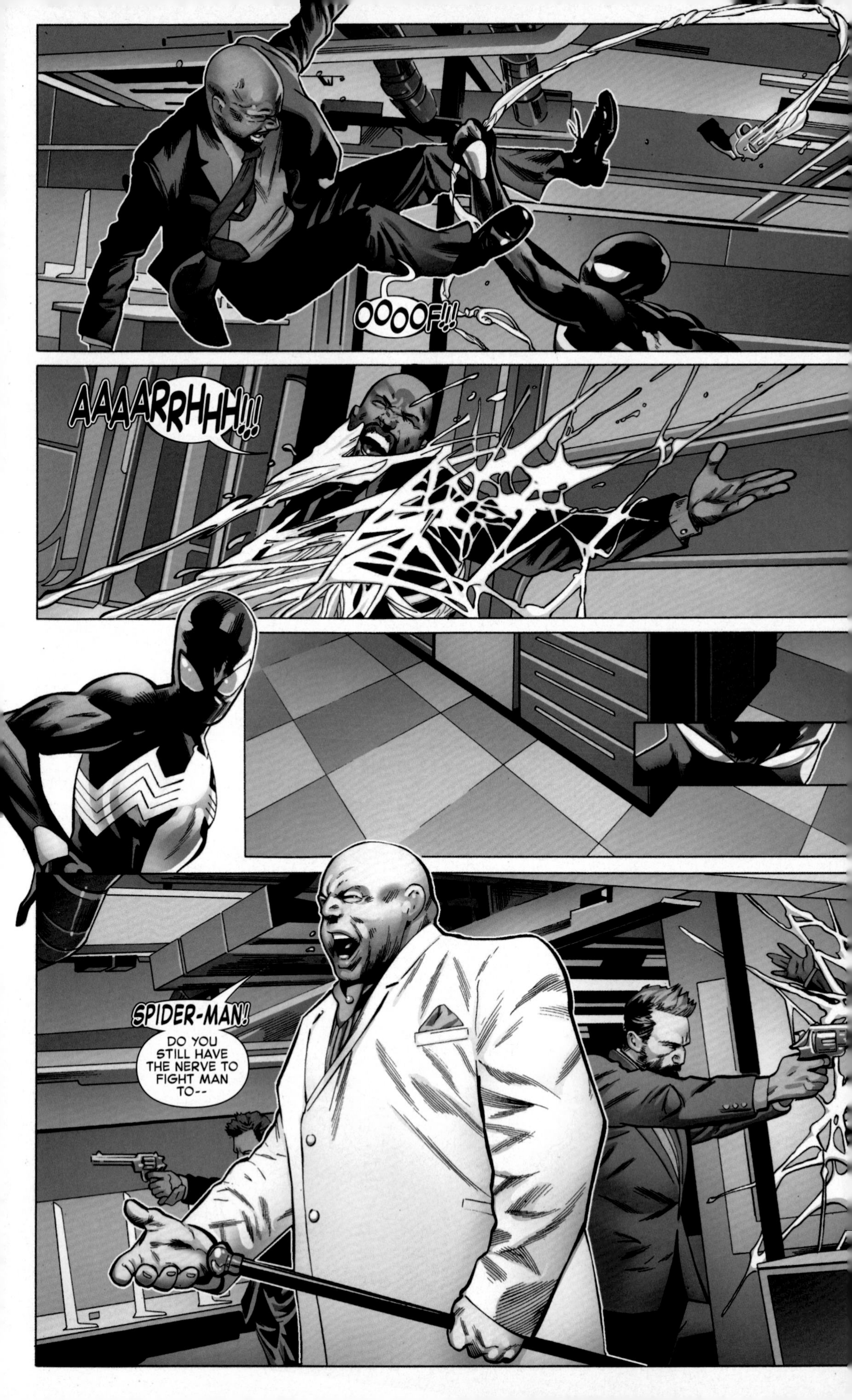
OOOOF!!!
AAAARRHHH!!!
SPIDER-MAN!
DO YOU STILL HAVE THE NERVE TO FIGHT MAN TO--

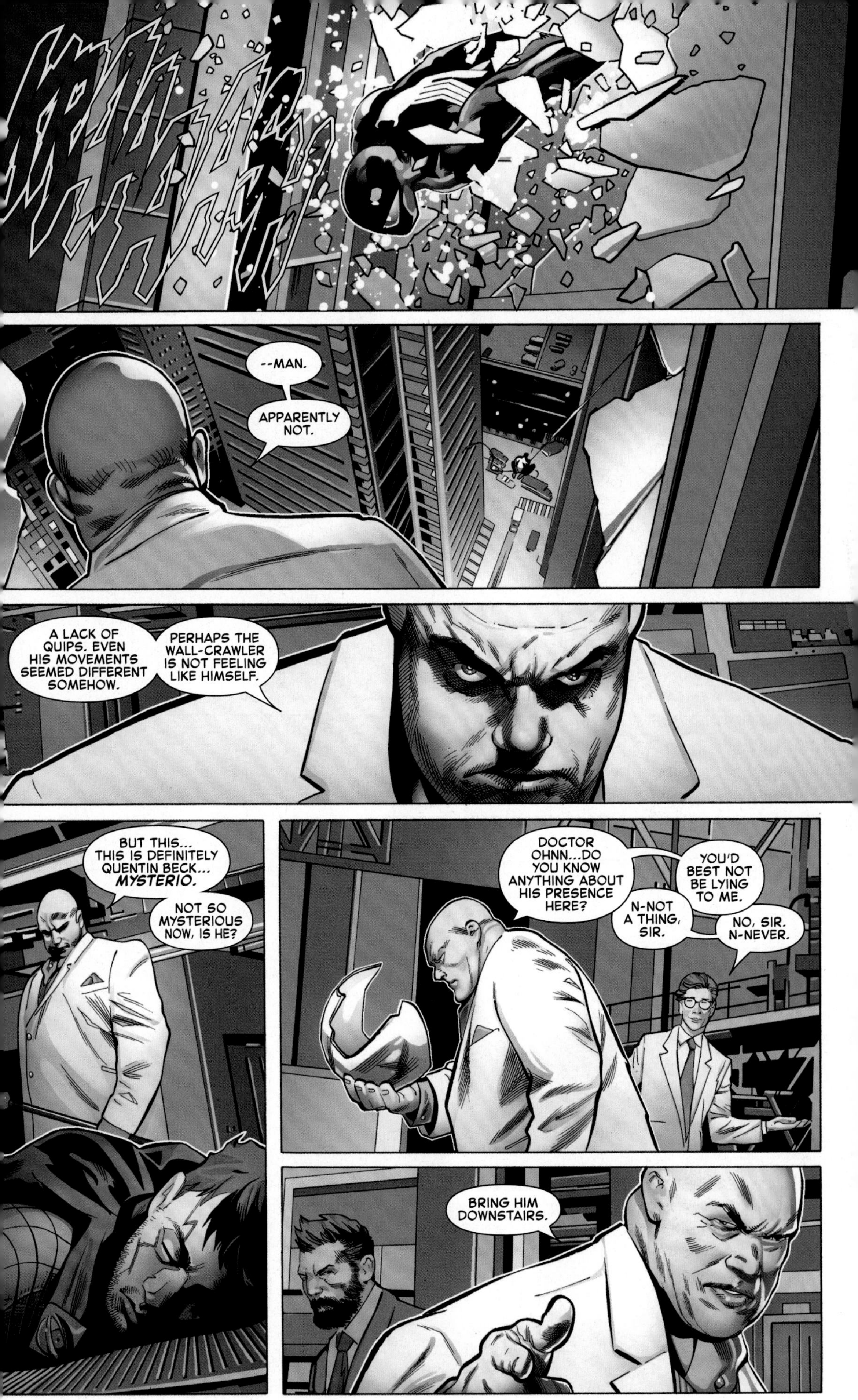
--MAN.
APPARENTLY NOT.
A LACK OF QUIPS. EVEN HIS MOVEMENTS SEEMED DIFFERENT SOMEHOW.
PERHAPS THE WALL-CRAWLER IS NOT FEELING LIKE HIMSELF.
BUT THIS... THIS IS DEFINITELY QUENTIN BECK... MYSTERIO.
NOT SO MYSTERIOUS NOW, IS HE?
DOCTOR OHNN...DO YOU KNOW ANYTHING ABOUT HIS PRESENCE HERE?
N-NOT A THING, SIR.
YOU'D BEST NOT BE LYING TO ME.
NO, SIR. N-NEVER.
BRING HIM DOWNSTAIRS.

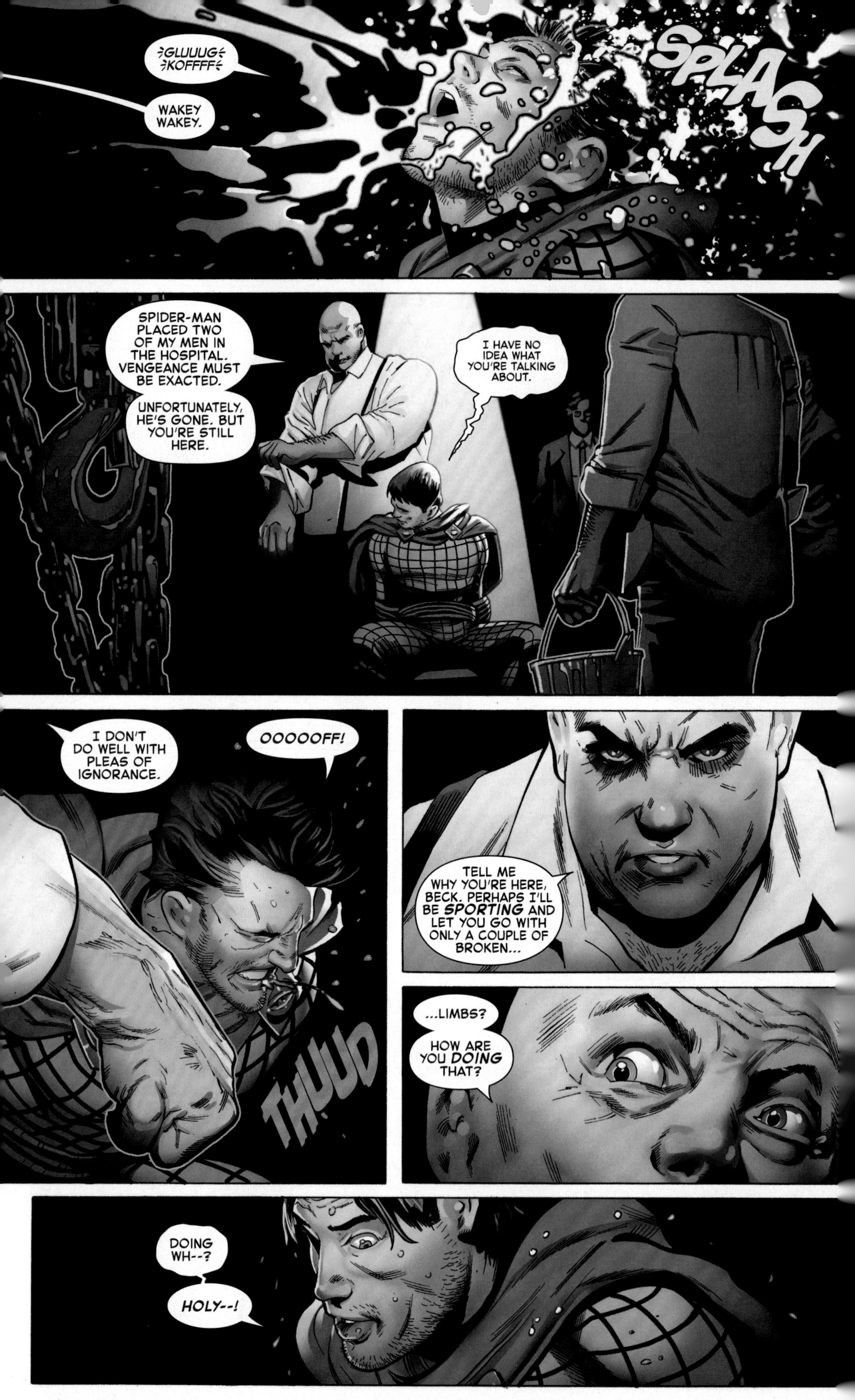

GLUUUG KOFFFF
WAKEY WAKEY.
SPLASH
SPIDER-MAN PLACED TWO OF MY MEN IN THE HOSPITAL. VENGEANCE MUST BE EXACTED.
UNFORTUNATELY, HE'S GONE. BUT YOU'RE STILL HERE.
I HAVE NO IDEA WHAT YOU'RE TALKING ABOUT.
I DON'T DO WELL WITH PLEAS OF IGNORANCE.
OOOOOFF!
THUUD
TELL ME WHY YOU'RE HERE, BECK. PERHAPS I'LL BE SPORTING AND LET YOU GO WITH ONLY A COUPLE OF BROKEN...
...LIMBS?
HOW ARE YOU DOING THAT?
DOING WH--?
HOLY--!

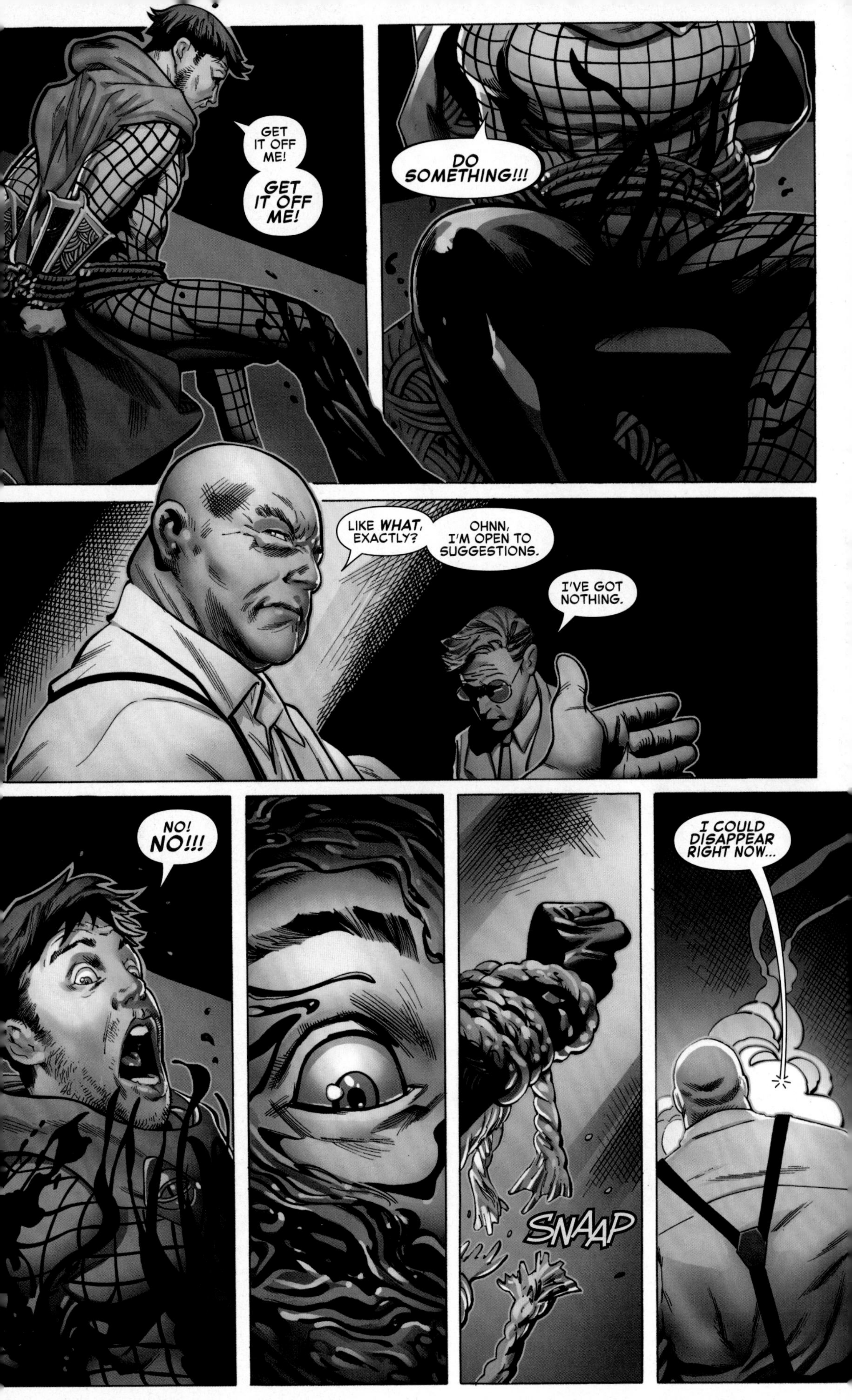
GET IT OFF ME!
GET IT OFF ME!
DO SOMETHING!!!
LIKE WHAT, EXACTLY?
OHNN, I'M OPEN TO SUGGESTIONS.
I'VE GOT NOTHING.
NO! NO!!!
SNAAP
I COULD DISAPPEAR RIGHT NOW...

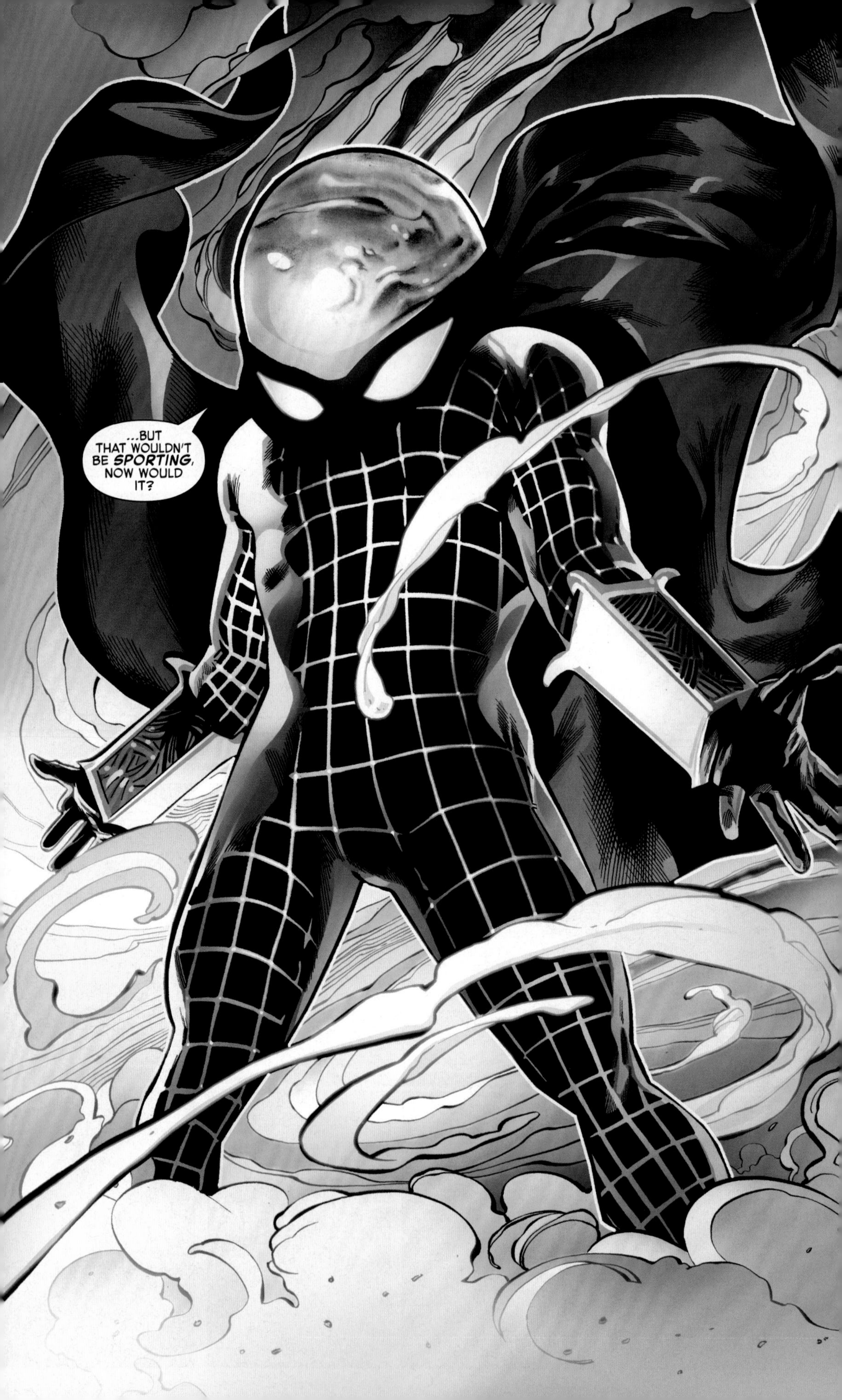
...BUT THAT WOULDN'T BE *SPORTING*, NOW WOULD IT?

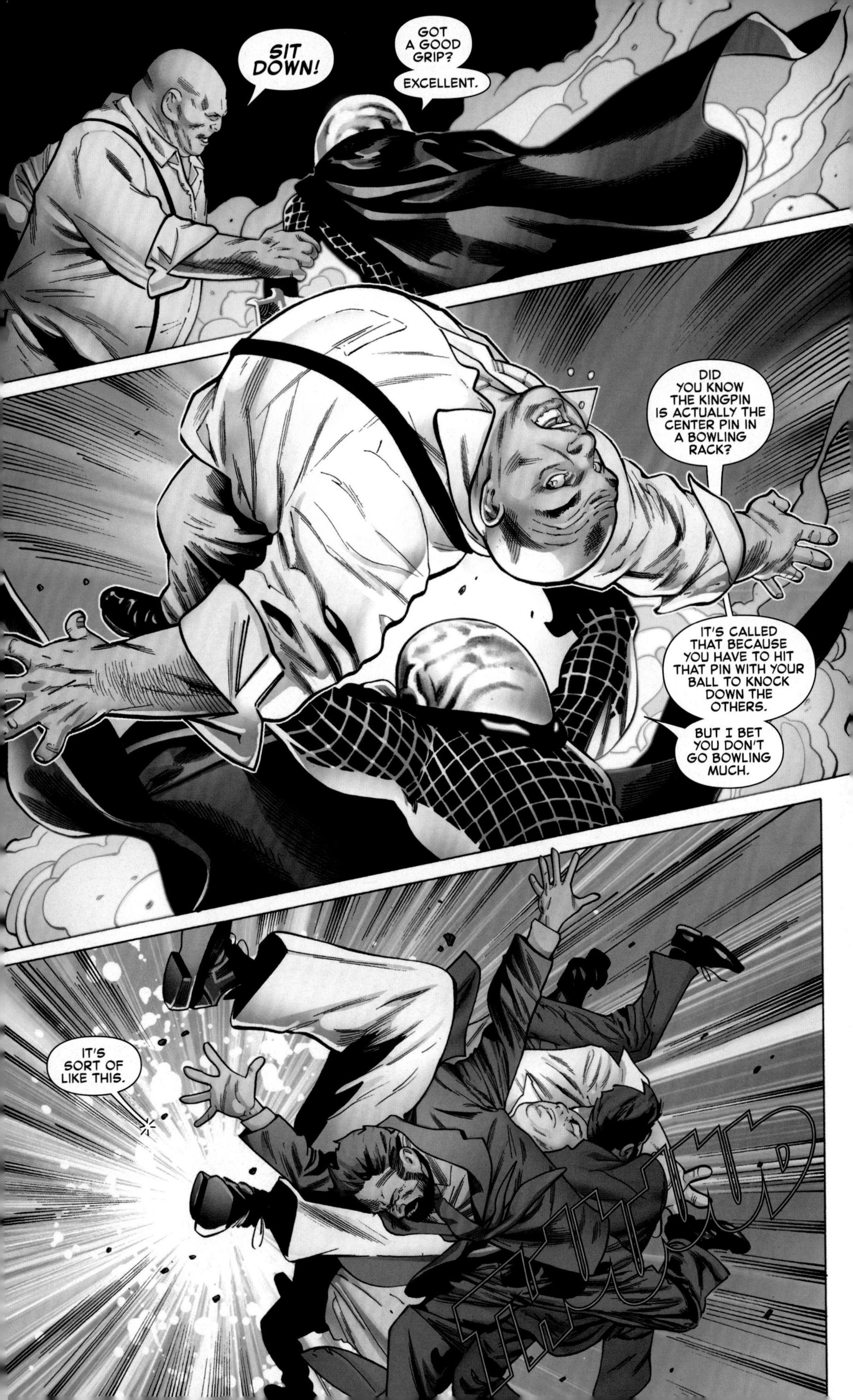
SIT DOWN!
GOT A GOOD GRIP?
EXCELLENT.
DID YOU KNOW THE KINGPIN IS ACTUALLY THE CENTER PIN IN A BOWLING RACK?
IT'S CALLED THAT BECAUSE YOU HAVE TO HIT THAT PIN WITH YOUR BALL TO KNOCK DOWN THE OTHERS.
BUT I BET YOU DON'T GO BOWLING MUCH.
IT'S SORT OF LIKE THIS.

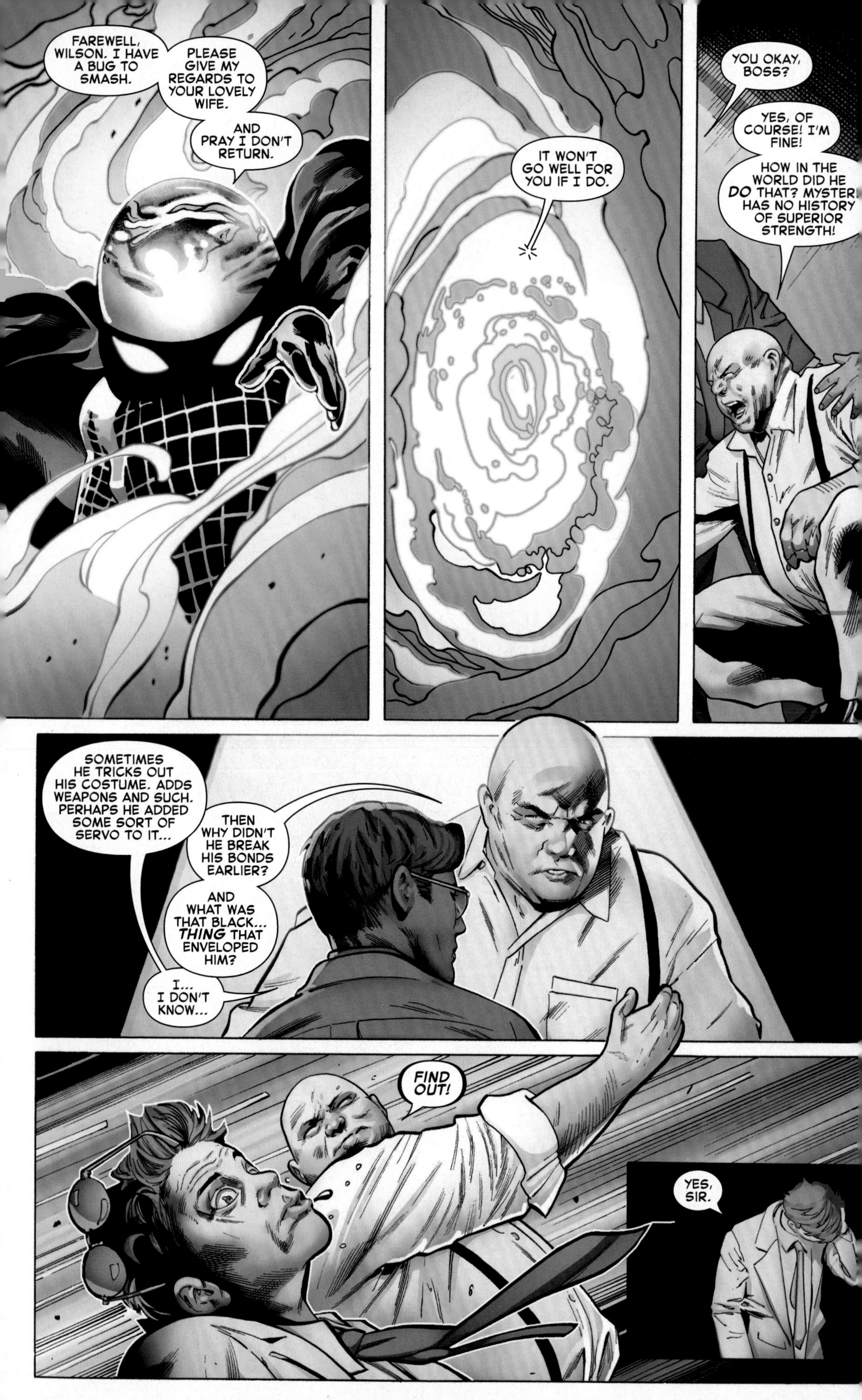
FAREWELL, WILSON. I HAVE A BUG TO SMASH.
PLEASE GIVE MY REGARDS TO YOUR LOVELY WIFE.
AND PRAY I DON'T RETURN.
IT WON'T GO WELL FOR YOU IF I DO.
YOU OKAY, BOSS?
YES, OF COURSE! I'M FINE!
HOW IN THE WORLD DID HE *DO* THAT? MYSTER HAS NO HISTORY OF SUPERIOR STRENGTH!
SOMETIMES HE TRICKS OUT HIS COSTUME. ADDS WEAPONS AND SUCH. PERHAPS HE ADDED SOME SORT OF SERVO TO IT...
THEN WHY DIDN'T HE BREAK HIS BONDS EARLIER?
AND WHAT WAS THAT BLACK... *THING* THAT ENVELOPED HIM?
I... I DON'T KNOW...
FIND OUT!
YES, SIR.

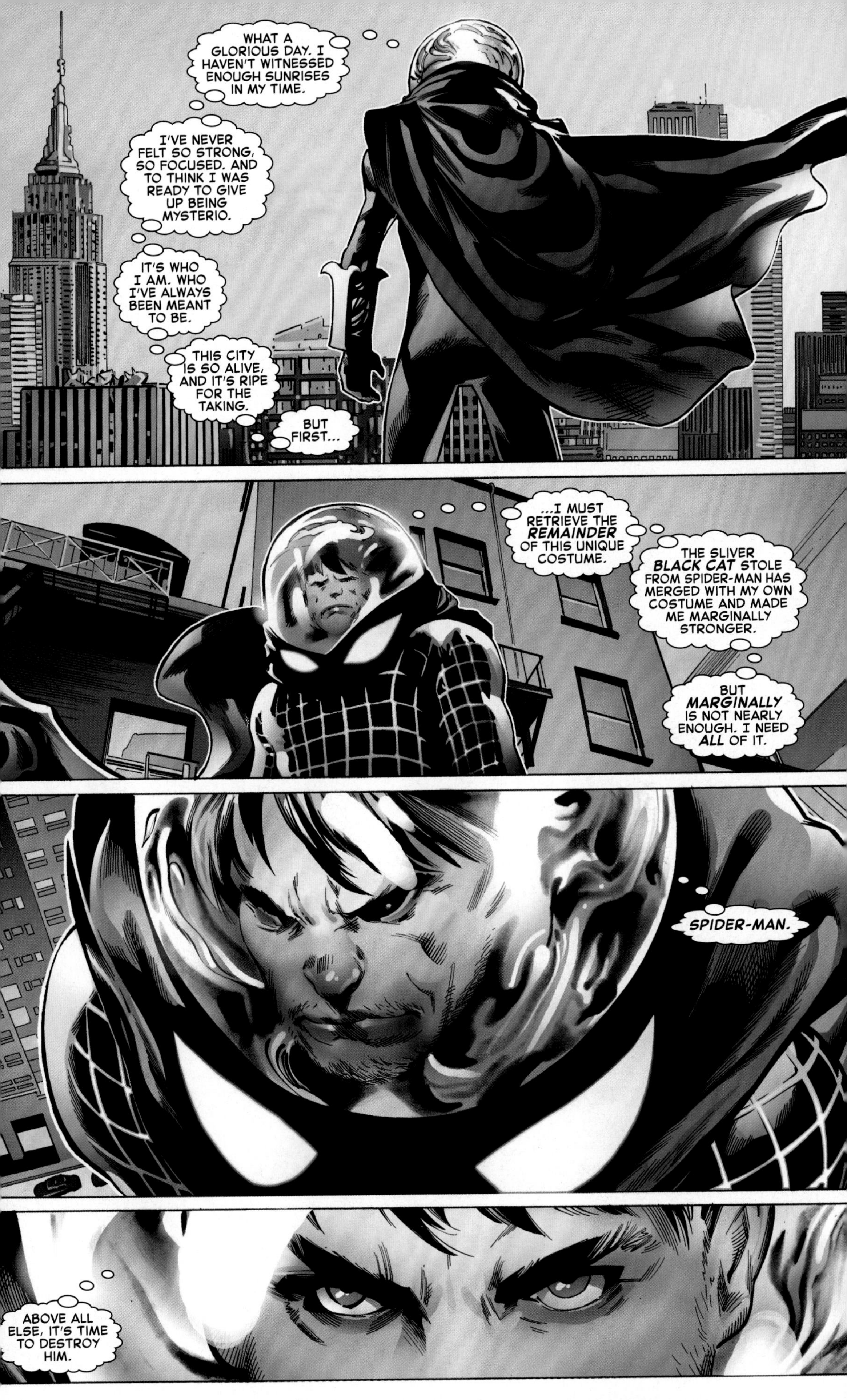
WHAT A GLORIOUS DAY. I HAVEN'T WITNESSED ENOUGH SUNRISES IN MY TIME.
I'VE NEVER FELT SO STRONG, SO FOCUSED. AND TO THINK I WAS READY TO GIVE UP BEING MYSTERIO.
IT'S WHO I AM. WHO I'VE ALWAYS BEEN MEANT TO BE.
THIS CITY IS SO ALIVE, AND IT'S RIPE FOR THE TAKING.
BUT FIRST...
...I MUST RETRIEVE THE REMAINDER OF THIS UNIQUE COSTUME.
THE SLIVER BLACK CAT STOLE FROM SPIDER-MAN HAS MERGED WITH MY OWN COSTUME AND MADE ME MARGINALLY STRONGER.
BUT MARGINALLY IS NOT NEARLY ENOUGH. I NEED ALL OF IT.
SPIDER-MAN.
ABOVE ALL ELSE, IT'S TIME TO DESTROY HIM.

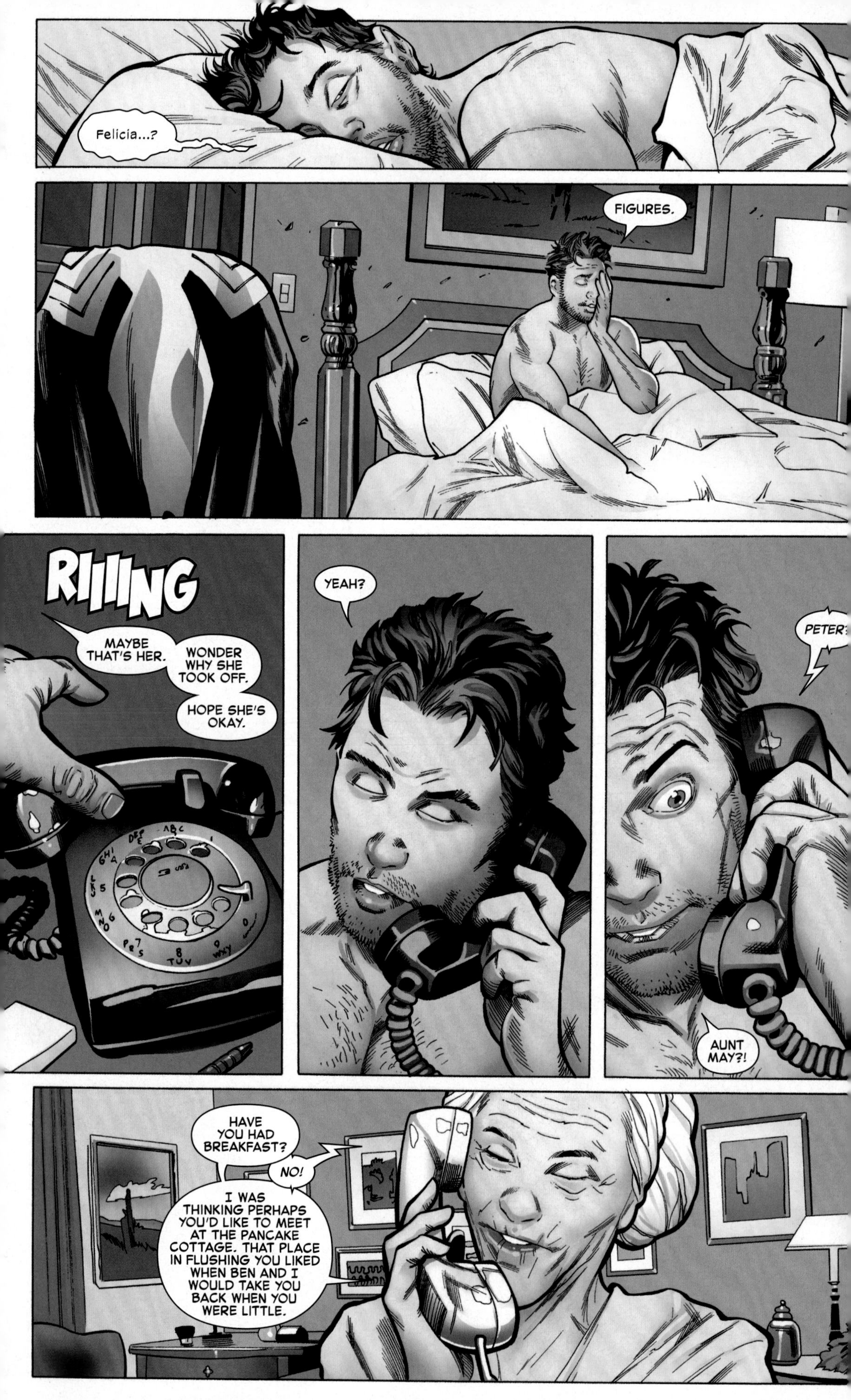

Felicia...?
FIGURES.
RIIIING
MAYBE THAT'S HER.
WONDER WHY SHE TOOK OFF.
HOPE SHE'S OKAY.
YEAH?
PETER?
AUNT MAY?!
HAVE YOU HAD BREAKFAST?
NO!
I WAS THINKING PERHAPS YOU'D LIKE TO MEET AT THE PANCAKE COTTAGE. THAT PLACE IN FLUSHING YOU LIKED WHEN BEN AND I WOULD TAKE YOU BACK WHEN YOU WERE LITTLE.

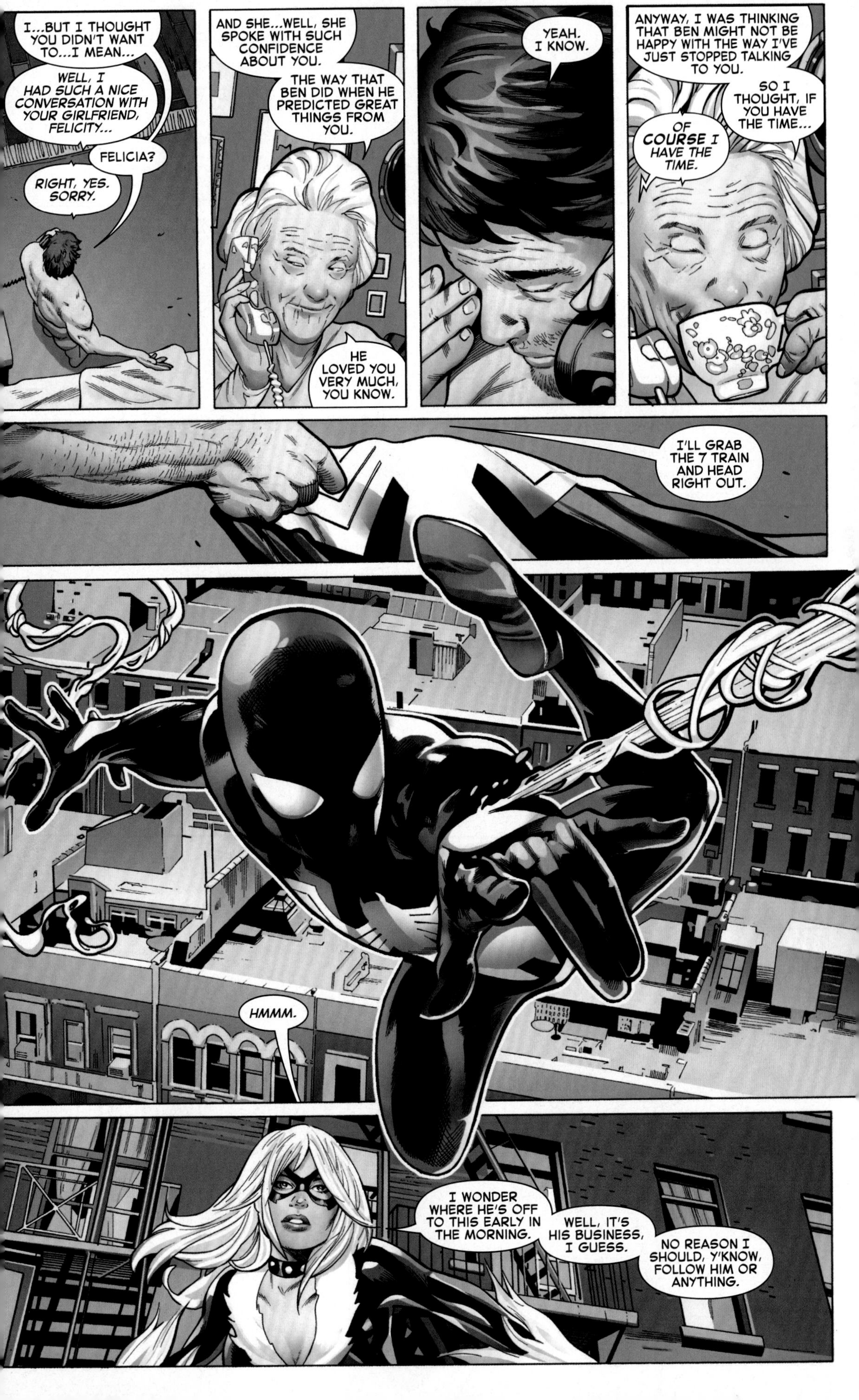
I...BUT I THOUGHT YOU DIDN'T WANT TO...I MEAN...
WELL, I HAD SUCH A NICE CONVERSATION WITH YOUR GIRLFRIEND, FELICITY...
FELICIA?
RIGHT, YES. SORRY.
AND SHE...WELL, SHE SPOKE WITH SUCH CONFIDENCE ABOUT YOU.
THE WAY THAT BEN DID WHEN HE PREDICTED GREAT THINGS FROM YOU.
HE LOVED YOU VERY MUCH, YOU KNOW.
YEAH. I KNOW.
ANYWAY, I WAS THINKING THAT BEN MIGHT NOT BE HAPPY WITH THE WAY I'VE JUST STOPPED TALKING TO YOU.
SO I THOUGHT, IF YOU HAVE THE TIME...
OF COURSE I HAVE THE TIME.
I'LL GRAB THE 7 TRAIN AND HEAD RIGHT OUT.
HMMM.
I WONDER WHERE HE'S OFF TO THIS EARLY IN THE MORNING.
WELL, IT'S HIS BUSINESS, I GUESS.
NO REASON I SHOULD, Y'KNOW, FOLLOW HIM OR ANYTHING.

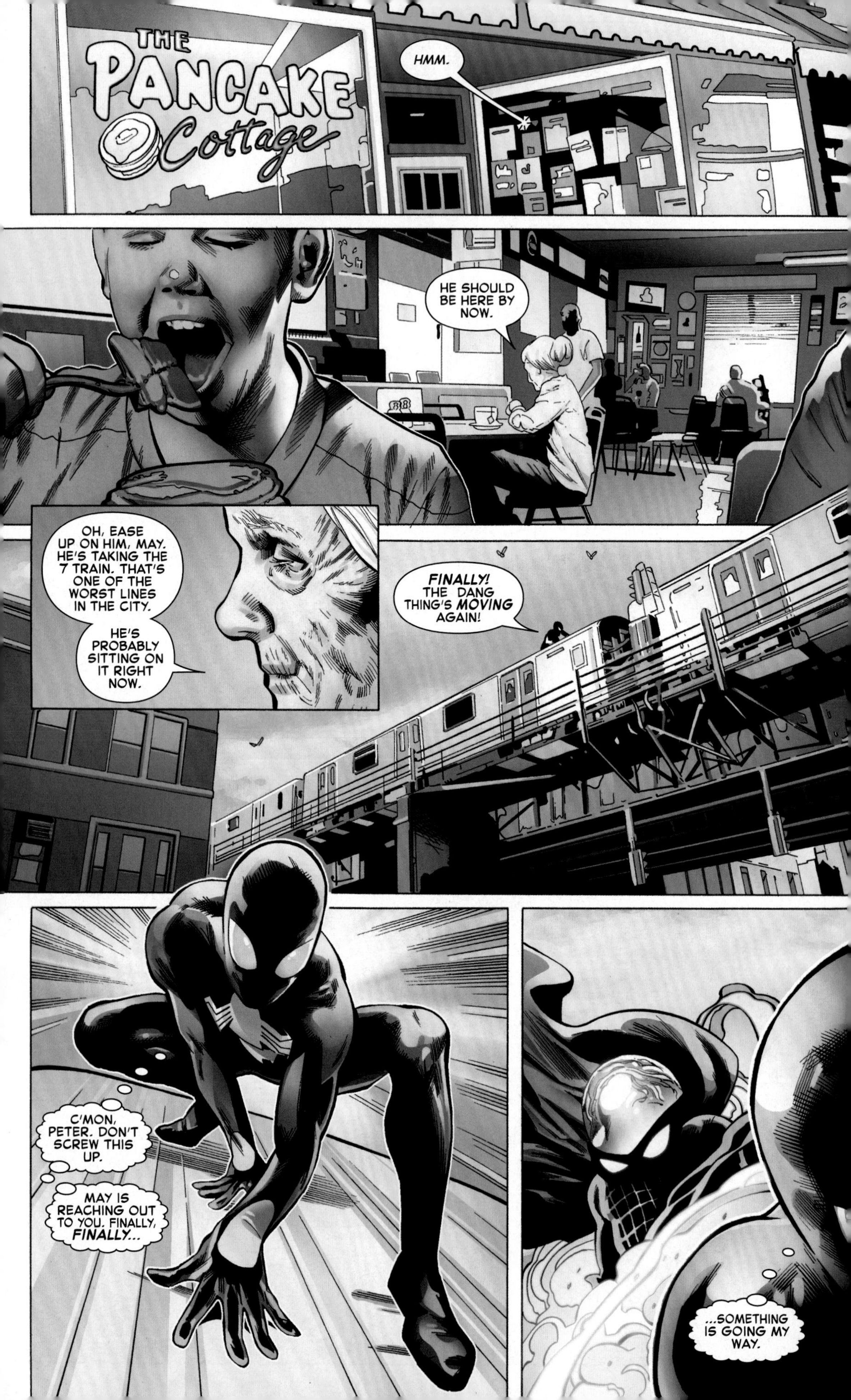
THE PANCAKE Cottage
HMM.
HE SHOULD BE HERE BY NOW.
OH, EASE UP ON HIM, MAY. HE'S TAKING THE 7 TRAIN. THAT'S ONE OF THE WORST LINES IN THE CITY.
HE'S PROBABLY SITTING ON IT RIGHT NOW.
FINALLY! THE DANG THING'S MOVING AGAIN!
C'MON, PETER. DON'T SCREW THIS UP.
MAY IS REACHING OUT TO YOU. FINALLY, FINALLY...
...SOMETHING IS GOING MY WAY.

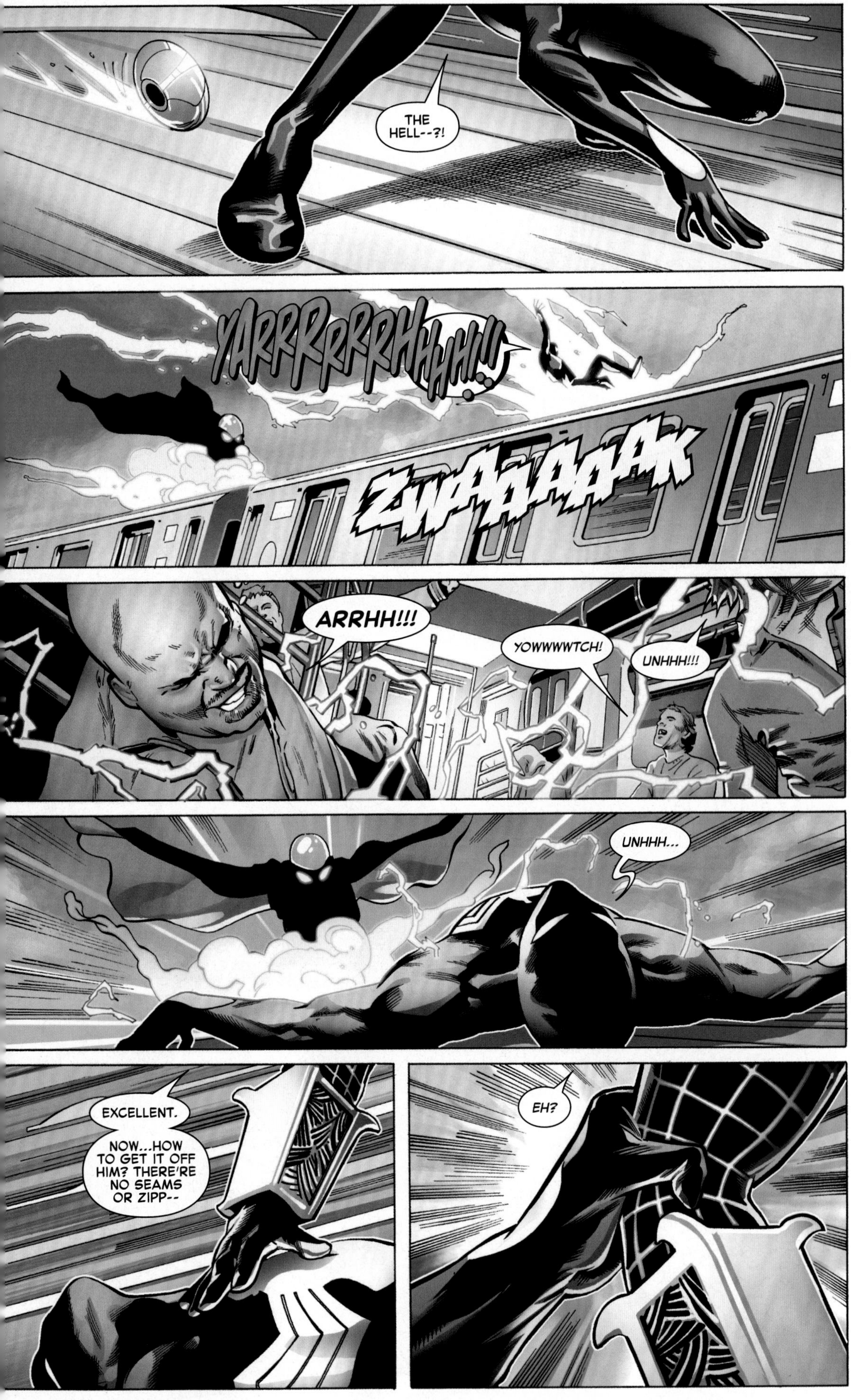
THE HELL--?!
YARRRRRRRHHHHH!!!
ZWAAAAAAK
ARRHH!!!
YOWWWWTCH!
UNHHH!!!
UNHHH...
EXCELLENT.
NOW...HOW TO GET IT OFF HIM? THERE'RE NO SEAMS OR ZIPP--
EH?

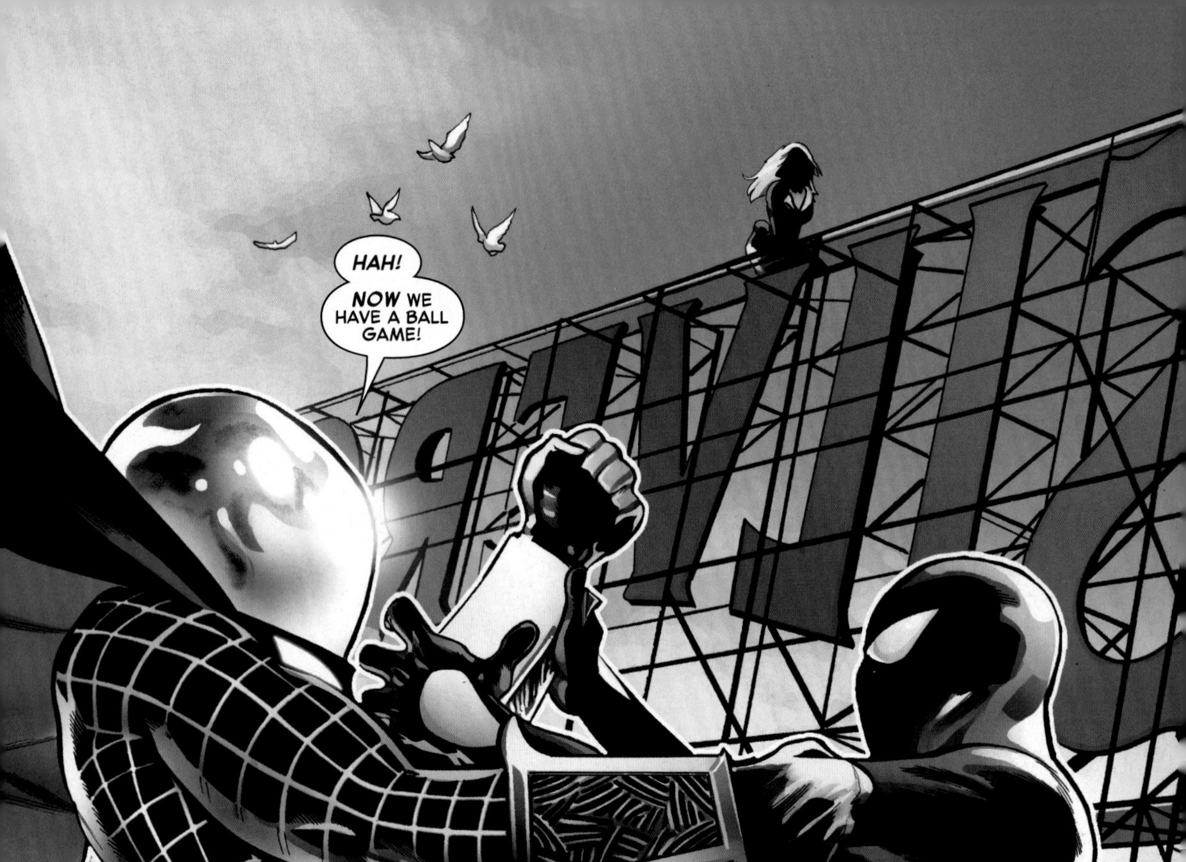
HAH!
NOW WE HAVE A BALL GAME!

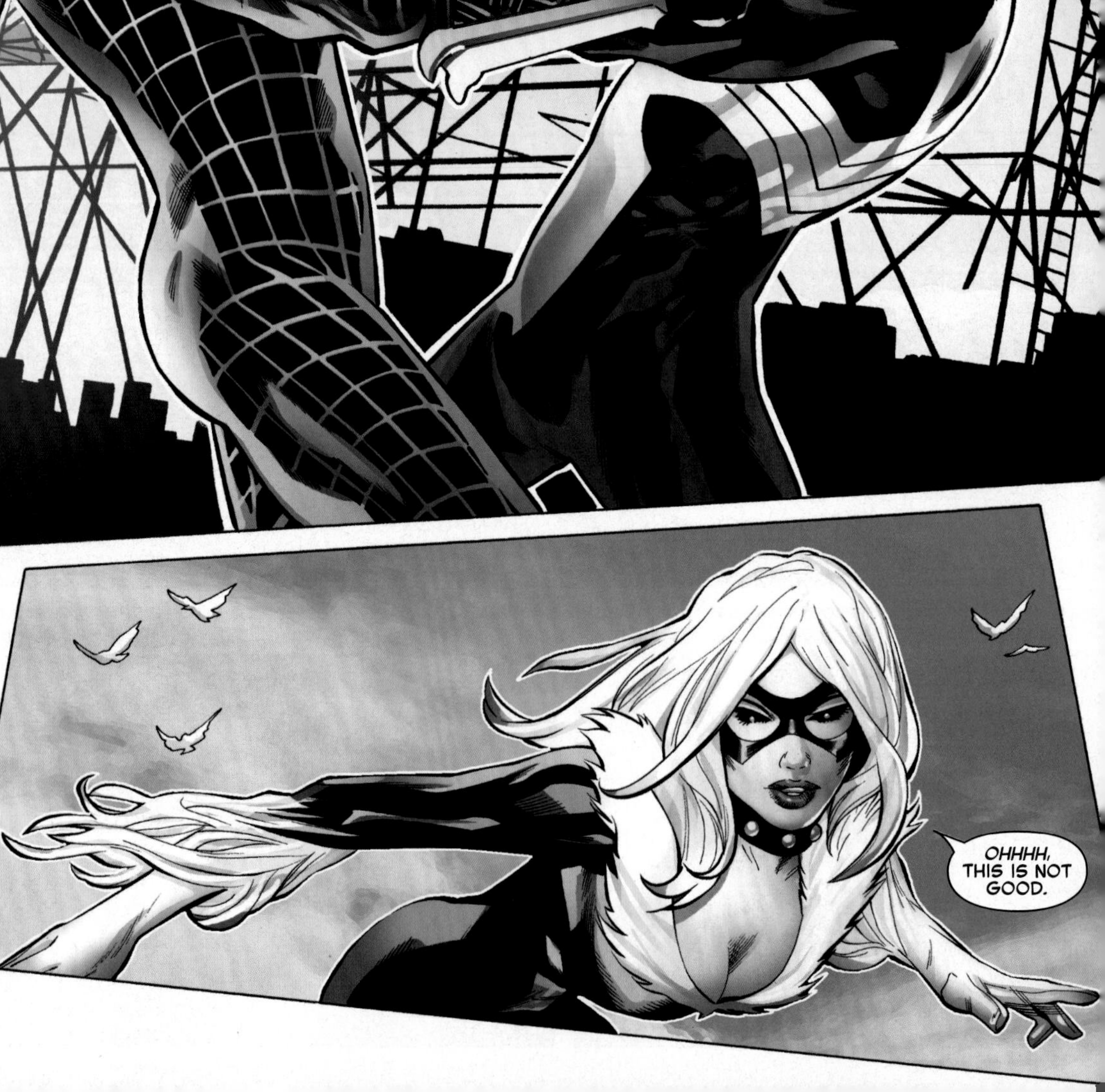
OHHHH, THIS IS NOT GOOD.

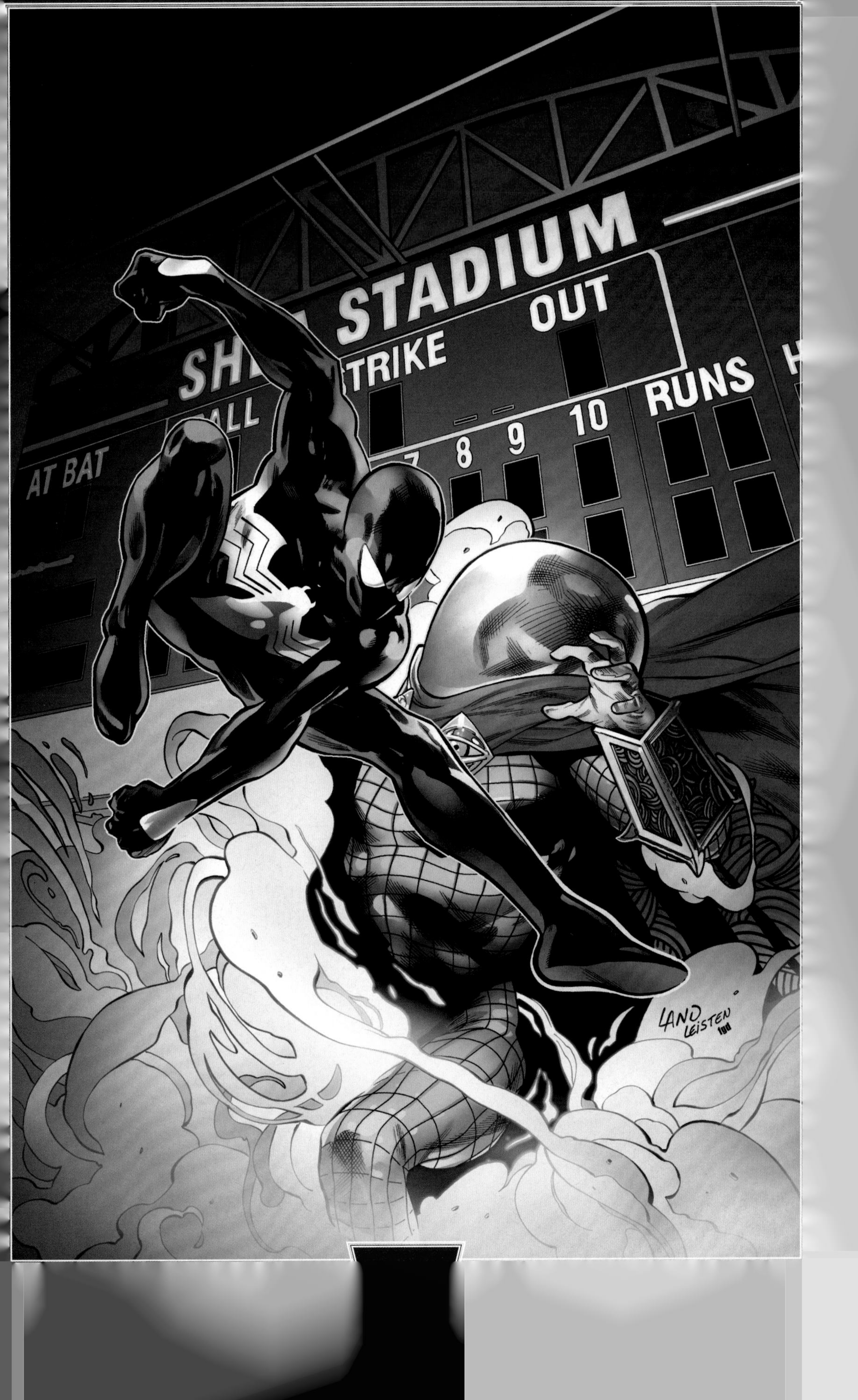
SH
STADIUM
OUT
TRIKE
ALL
AT BAT
7 8 9 10
RUNS
LAND
LEISTEN

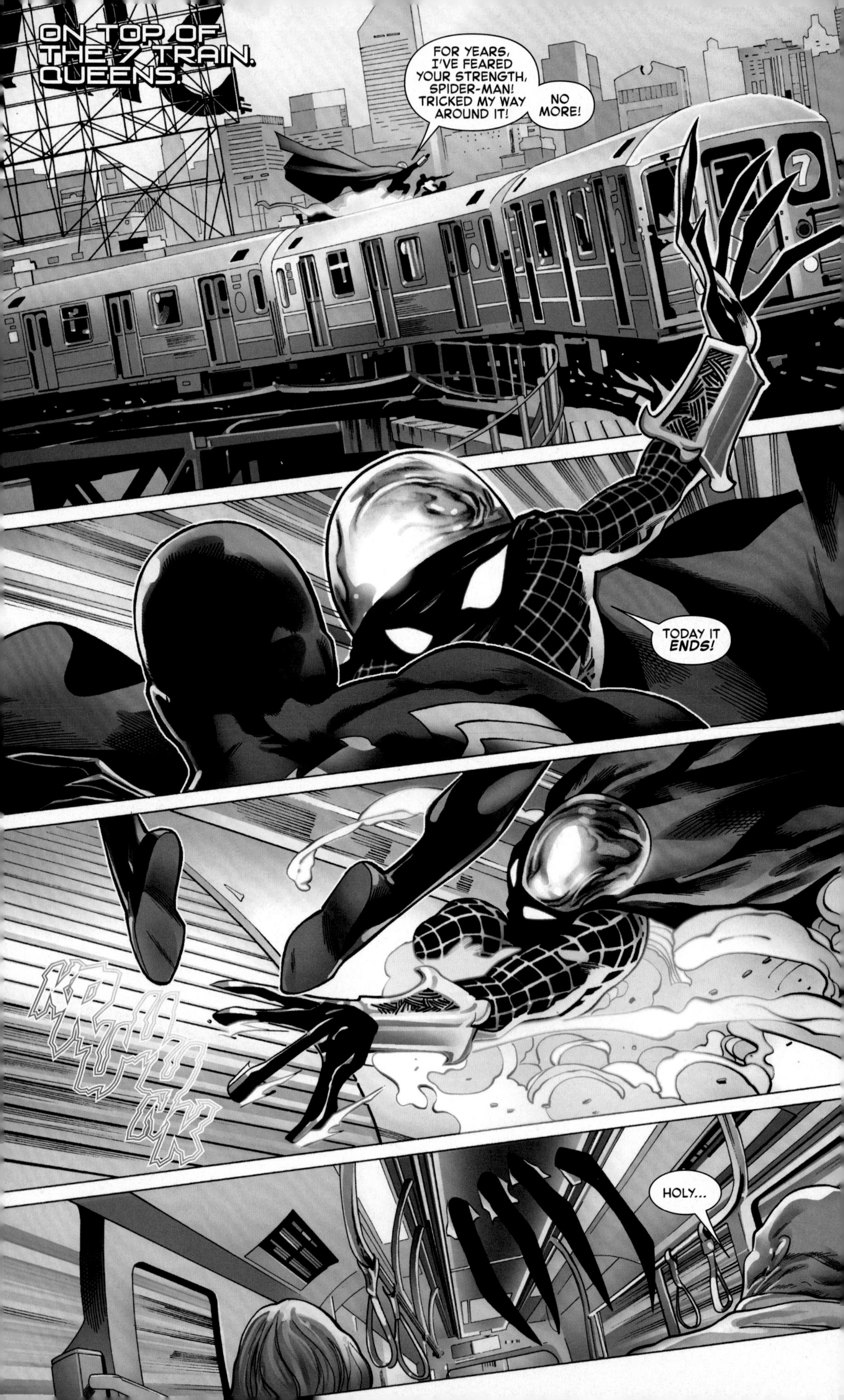
ON TOP OF THE 7 TRAIN. QUEENS.
FOR YEARS, I'VE FEARED YOUR STRENGTH, SPIDER-MAN! TRICKED MY WAY AROUND IT!
NO MORE!
TODAY IT ENDS!
HOLY...

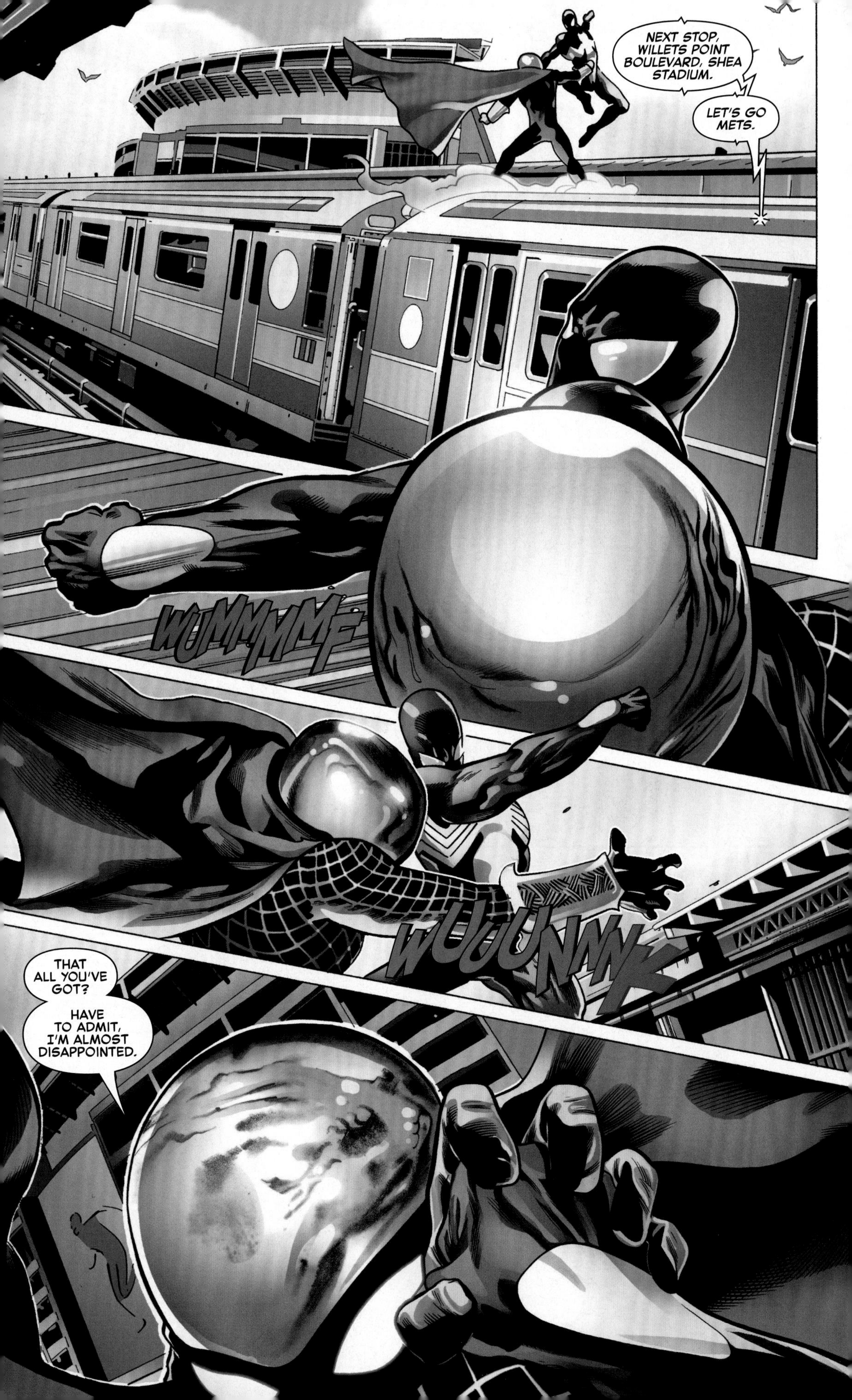
NEXT STOP, WILLETS POINT BOULEVARD, SHEA STADIUM.
LET'S GO METS.
WUMMMMMF
WUUUNNNK
THAT ALL YOU'VE GOT?
HAVE TO ADMIT, I'M ALMOST DISAPPOINTED.

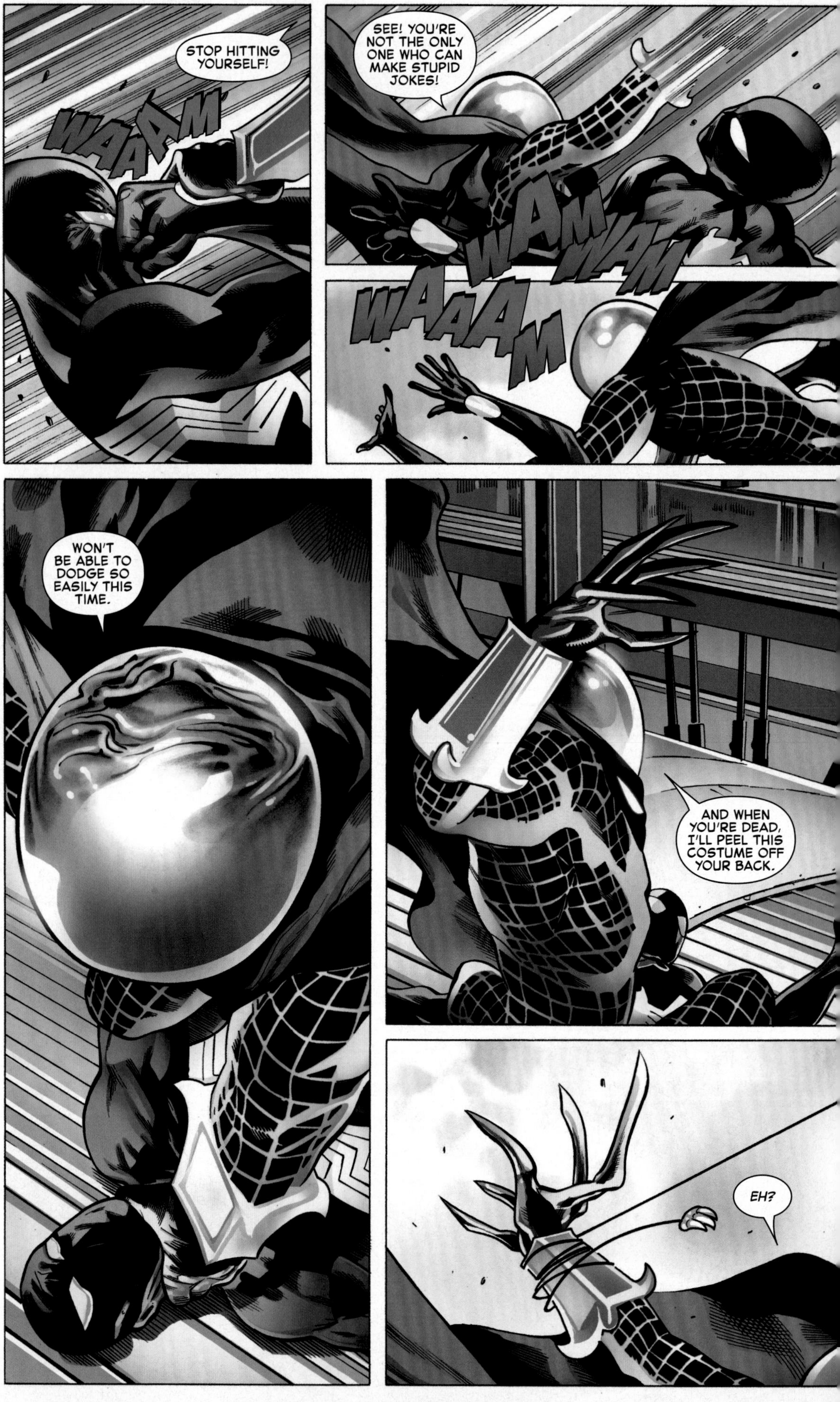
STOP HITTING YOURSELF!
WAAAM
SEE! YOU'RE NOT THE ONLY ONE WHO CAN MAKE STUPID JOKES!
WAM
WAM
WAAAAM
WON'T BE ABLE TO DODGE SO EASILY THIS TIME.
AND WHEN YOU'RE DEAD, I'LL PEEL THIS COSTUME OFF YOUR BACK.
EH?

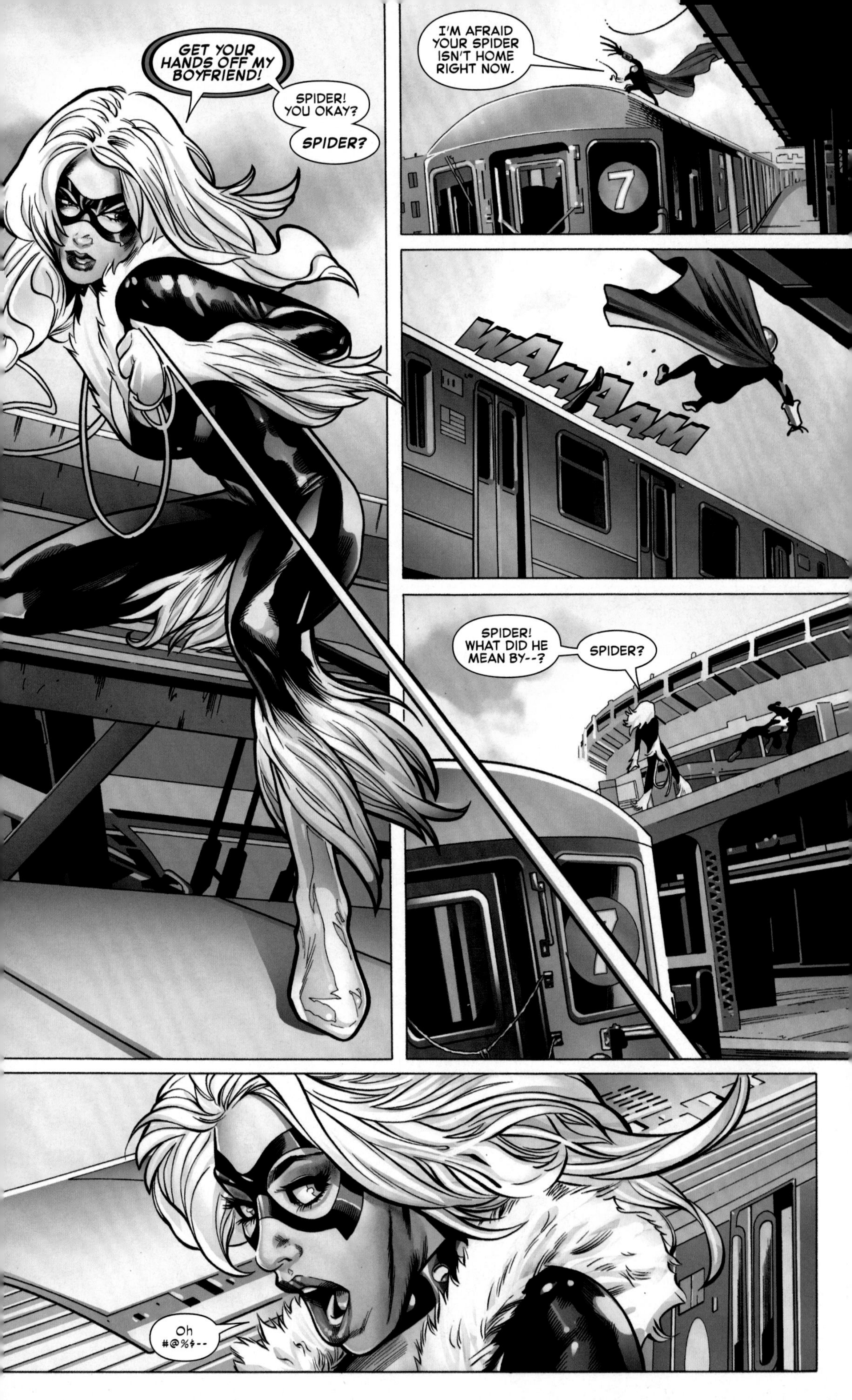
GET YOUR HANDS OFF MY BOYFRIEND!
SPIDER! YOU OKAY?
SPIDER?
I'M AFRAID YOUR SPIDER ISN'T HOME RIGHT NOW.
WAAAAAM
SPIDER! WHAT DID HE MEAN BY--?
SPIDER?
Oh #@%$--

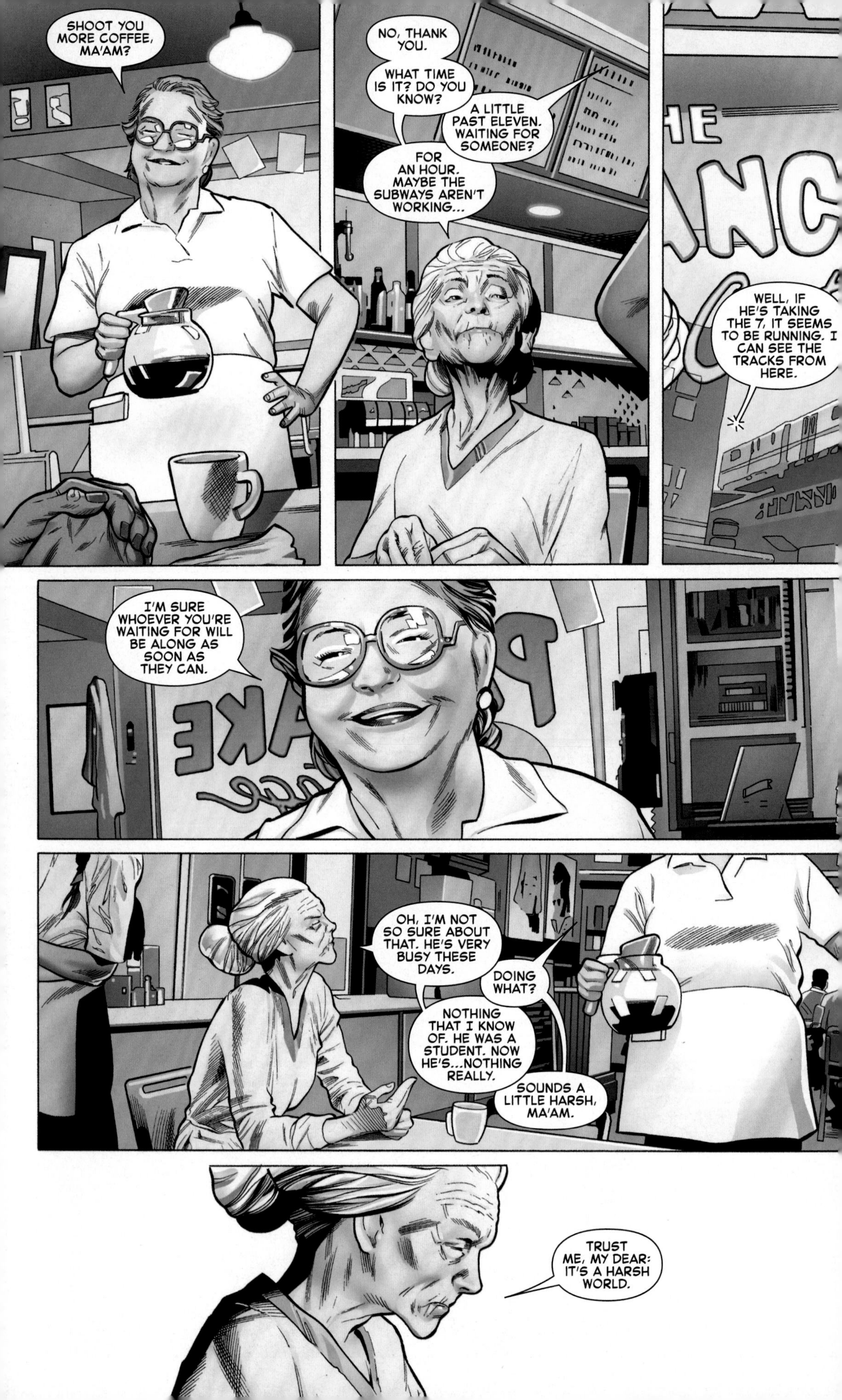

SHOOT YOU MORE COFFEE, MA'AM?
NO, THANK YOU.
WHAT TIME IS IT? DO YOU KNOW?
A LITTLE PAST ELEVEN. WAITING FOR SOMEONE?
FOR AN HOUR. MAYBE THE SUBWAYS AREN'T WORKING...
WELL, IF HE'S TAKING THE 7, IT SEEMS TO BE RUNNING. I CAN SEE THE TRACKS FROM HERE.
I'M SURE WHOEVER YOU'RE WAITING FOR WILL BE ALONG AS SOON AS THEY CAN.
OH, I'M NOT SO SURE ABOUT THAT. HE'S VERY BUSY THESE DAYS.
DOING WHAT?
NOTHING THAT I KNOW OF. HE WAS A STUDENT. NOW HE'S...NOTHING REALLY.
SOUNDS A LITTLE HARSH, MA'AM.
TRUST ME, MY DEAR: IT'S A HARSH WORLD.

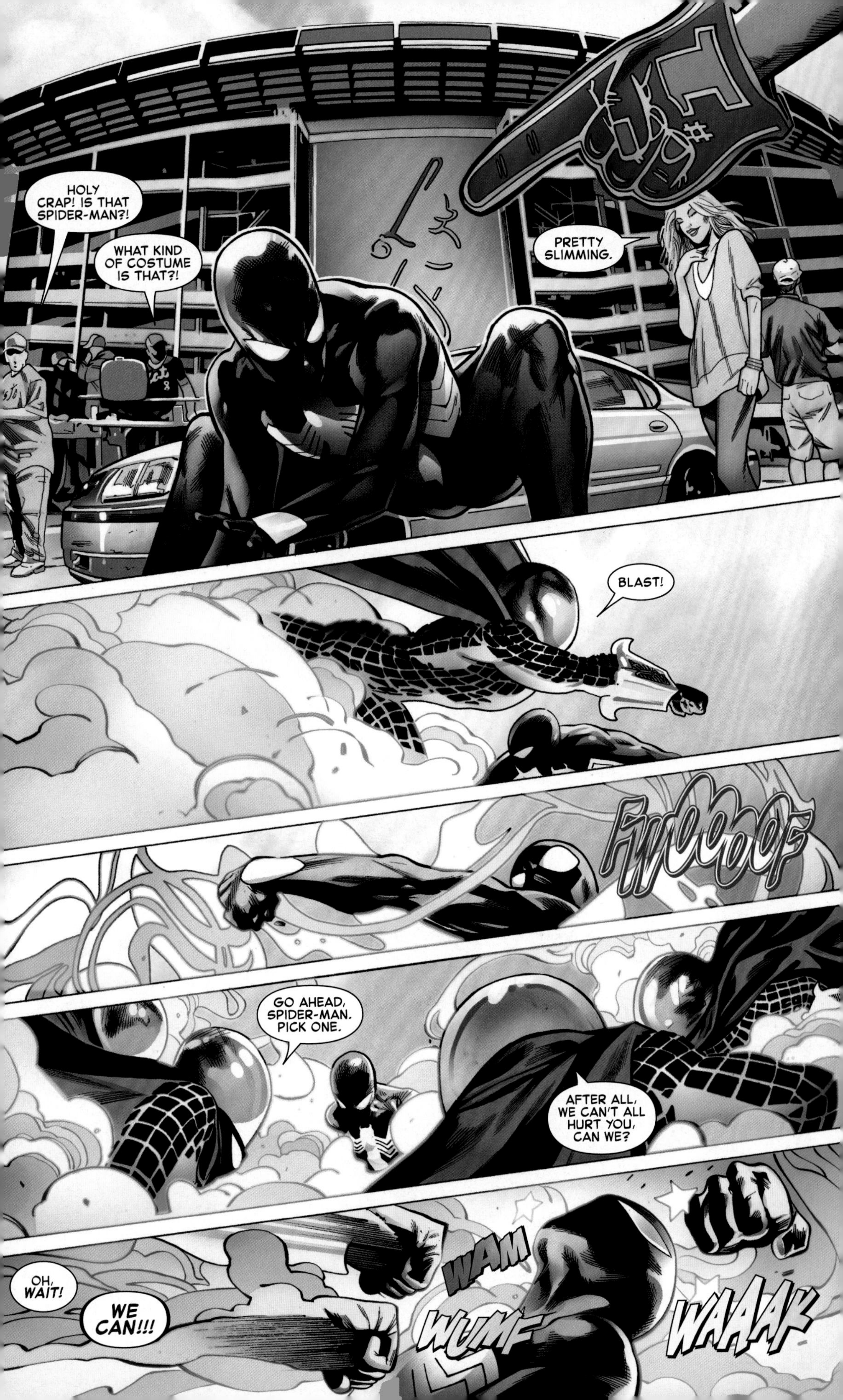

HOLY CRAP! IS THAT SPIDER-MAN?!
WHAT KIND OF COSTUME IS THAT?!
PRETTY SLIMMING.
BLAST!
FWOOOOOF
GO AHEAD, SPIDER-MAN. PICK ONE.
AFTER ALL, WE CAN'T ALL HURT YOU, CAN WE?
OH, WAIT!
WE CAN!!!
WAM
WUMF
WAAAK

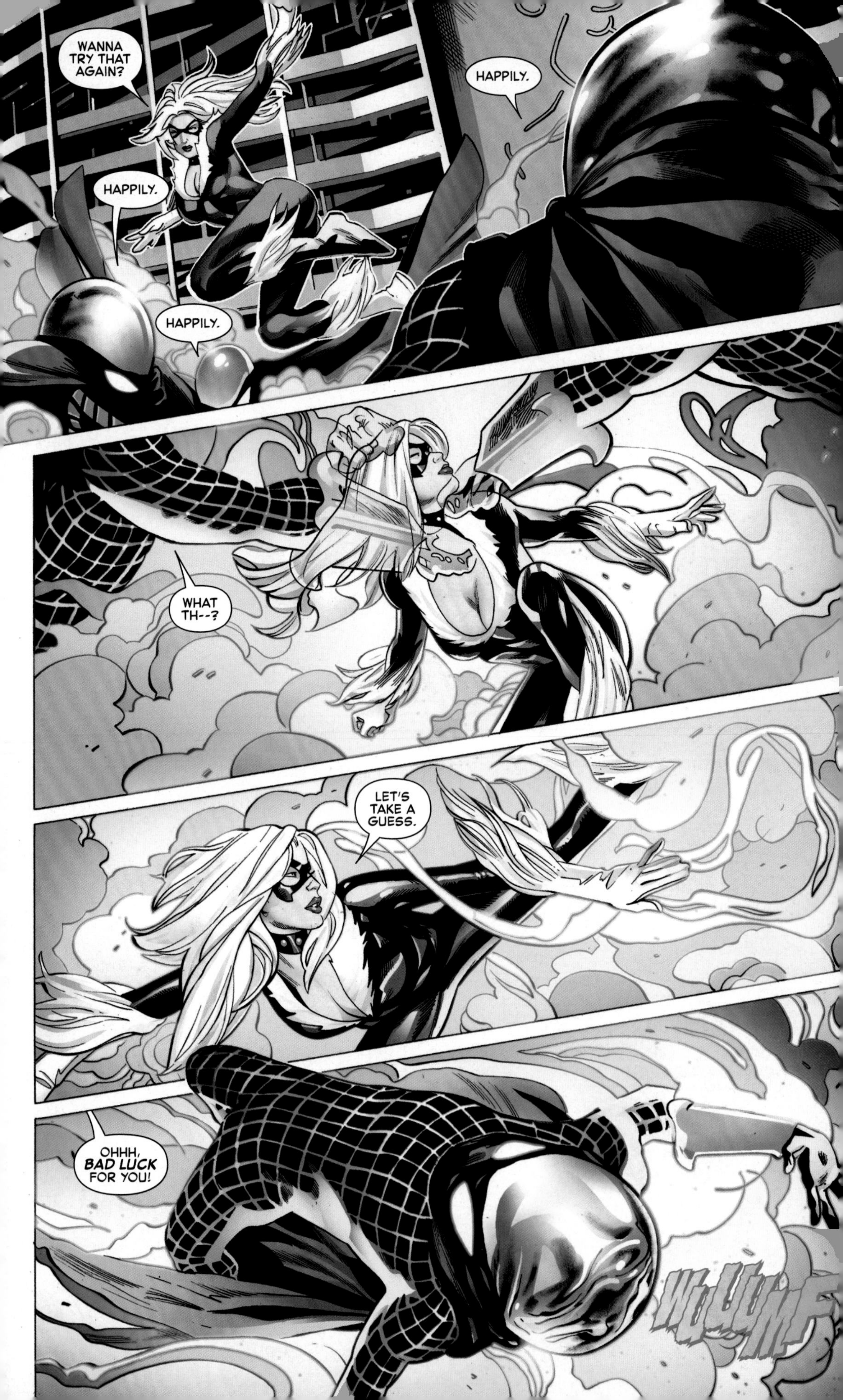
WANNA TRY THAT AGAIN?
HAPPILY.
HAPPILY.
HAPPILY.
WHAT TH--?
LET'S TAKE A GUESS.
OHHH, **BAD LUCK** FOR YOU!
WUUMF

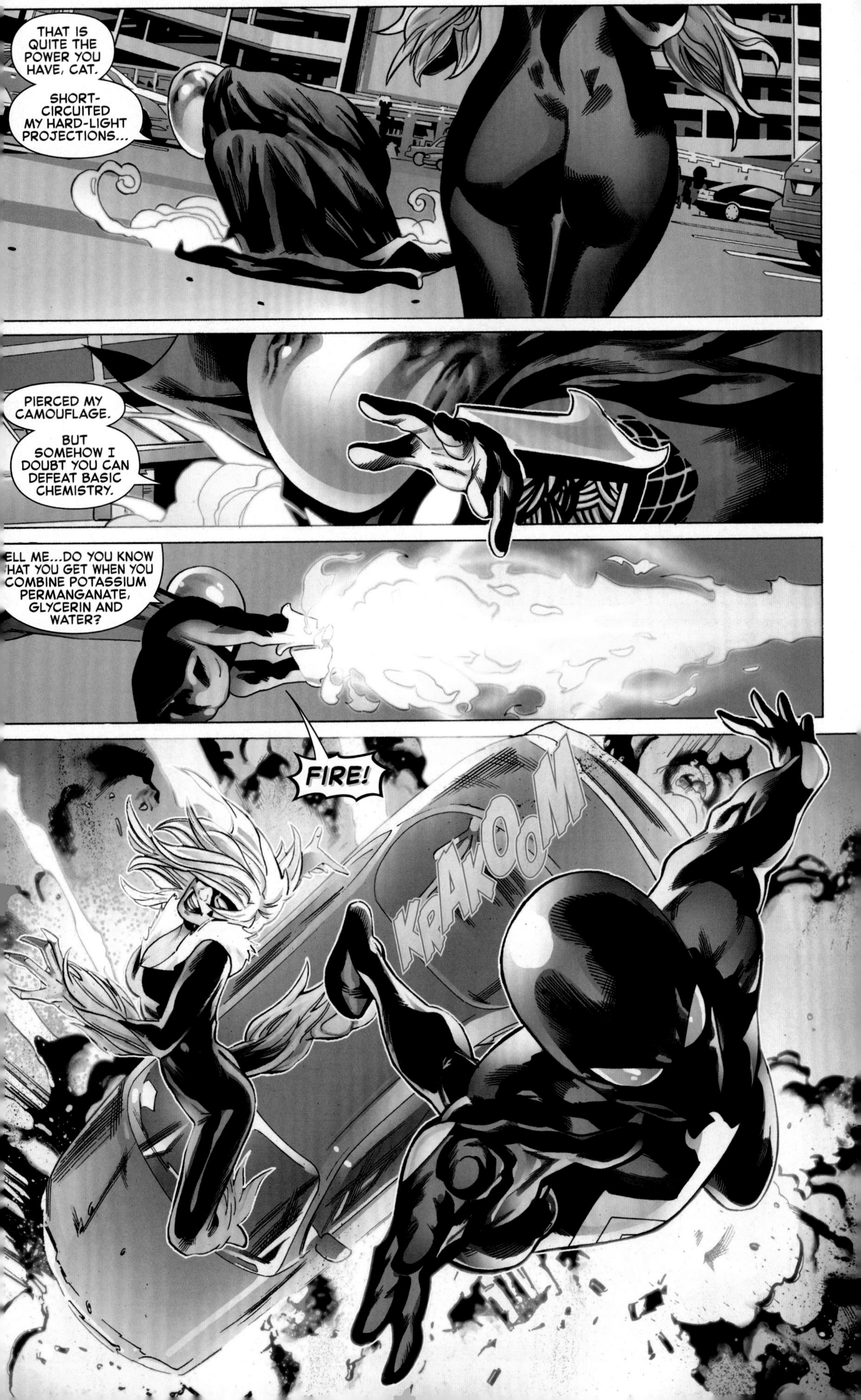
THAT IS QUITE THE POWER YOU HAVE, CAT.
SHORT-CIRCUITED MY HARD-LIGHT PROJECTIONS...
PIERCED MY CAMOUFLAGE.
BUT SOMEHOW I DOUBT YOU CAN DEFEAT BASIC CHEMISTRY.
ELL ME...DO YOU KNOW HAT YOU GET WHEN YOU COMBINE POTASSIUM PERMANGANATE, GLYCERIN AND WATER?
FIRE!
KRAKOOM

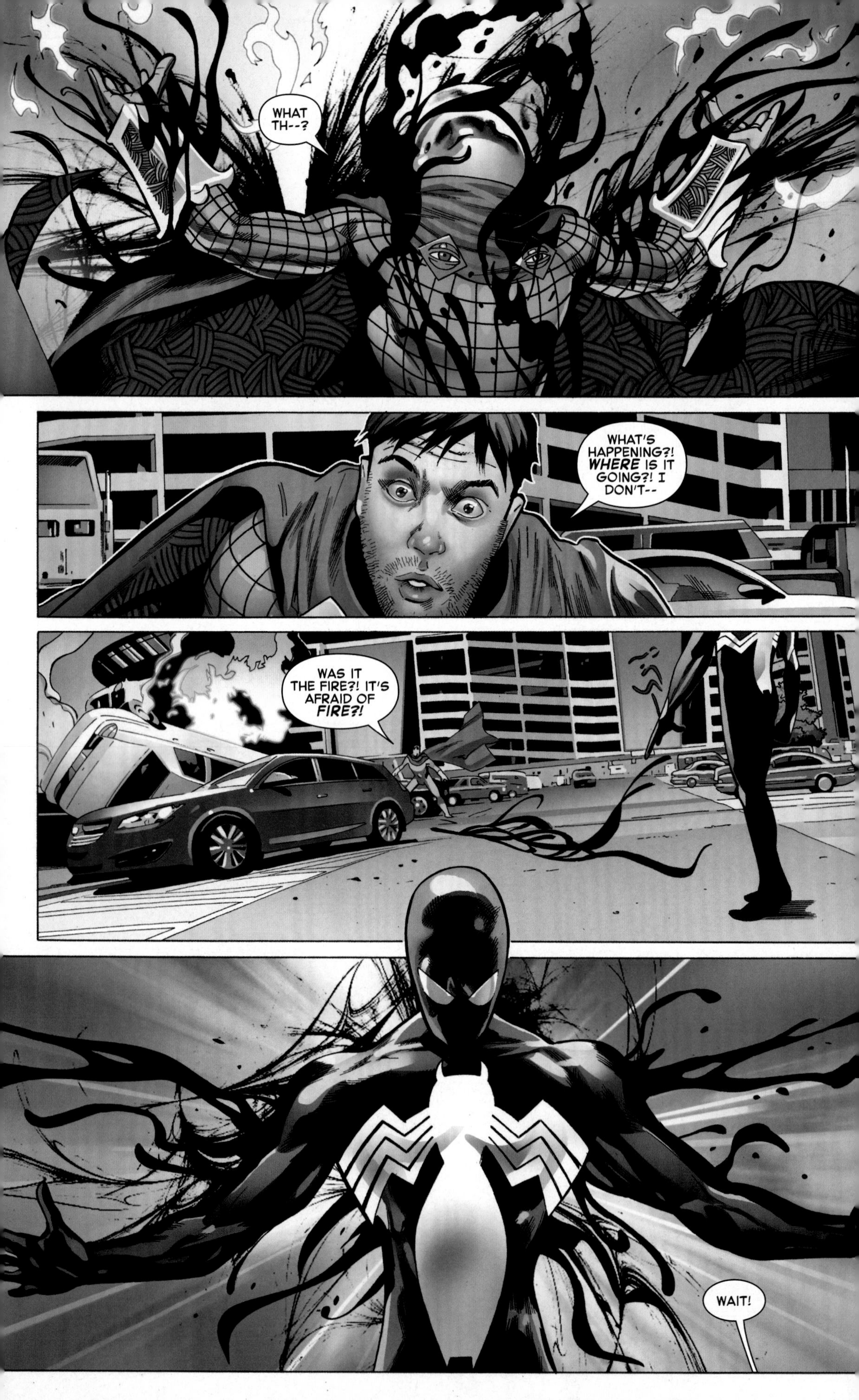
WHAT TH--?
WHAT'S HAPPENING?! WHERE IS IT GOING?! I DON'T--
WAS IT THE FIRE?! IT'S AFRAID OF FIRE?!
WAIT!

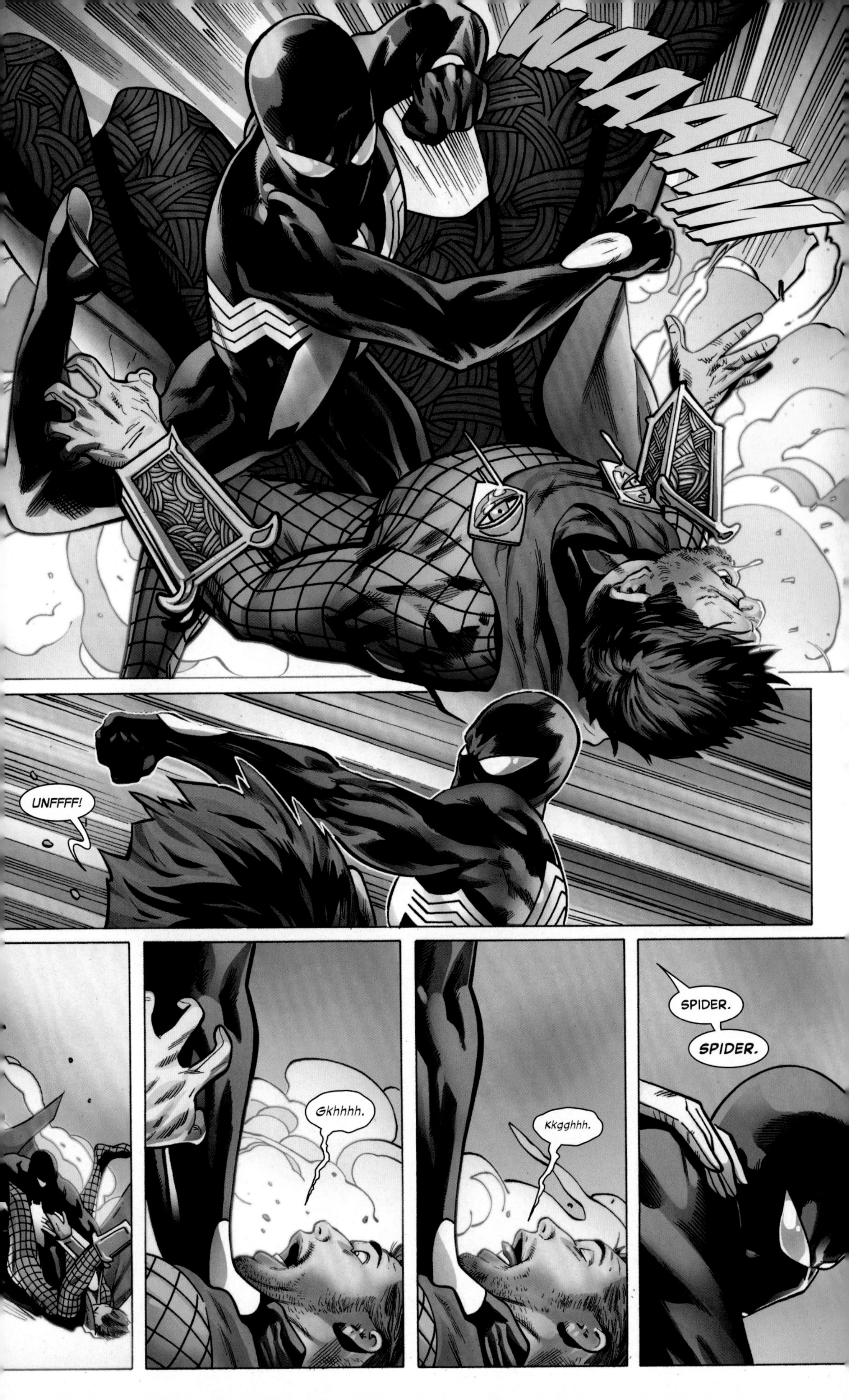
WAAAAM
UNFFFF!
Gkhhhh.
Kkgghhh.
SPIDER.
SPIDER.

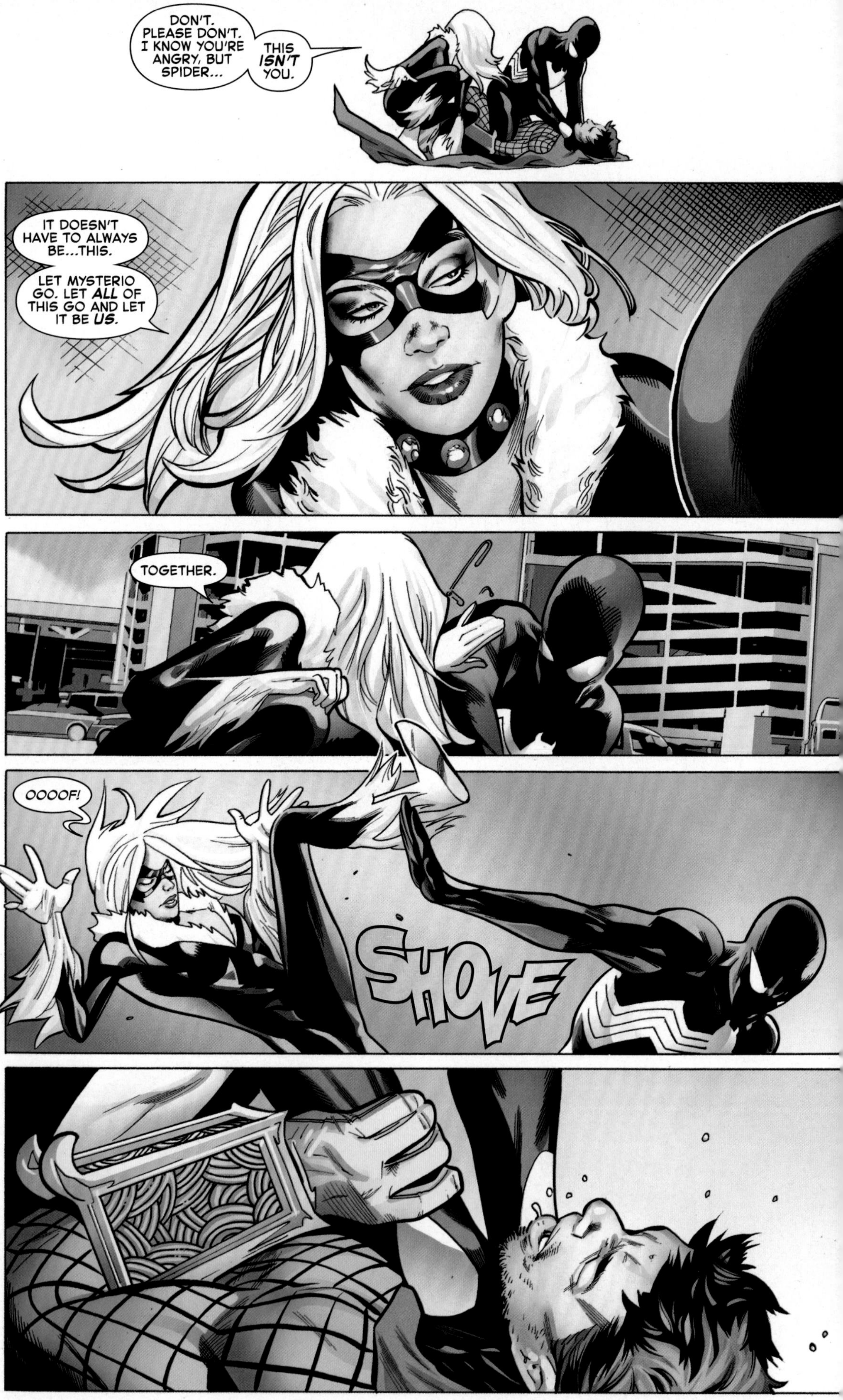
DON'T. PLEASE DON'T. I KNOW YOU'RE ANGRY, BUT SPIDER...
THIS ISN'T YOU.
IT DOESN'T HAVE TO ALWAYS BE...THIS.
LET MYSTERIO GO. LET ALL OF THIS GO AND LET IT BE US.
TOGETHER.
OOOOF!
SHOVE

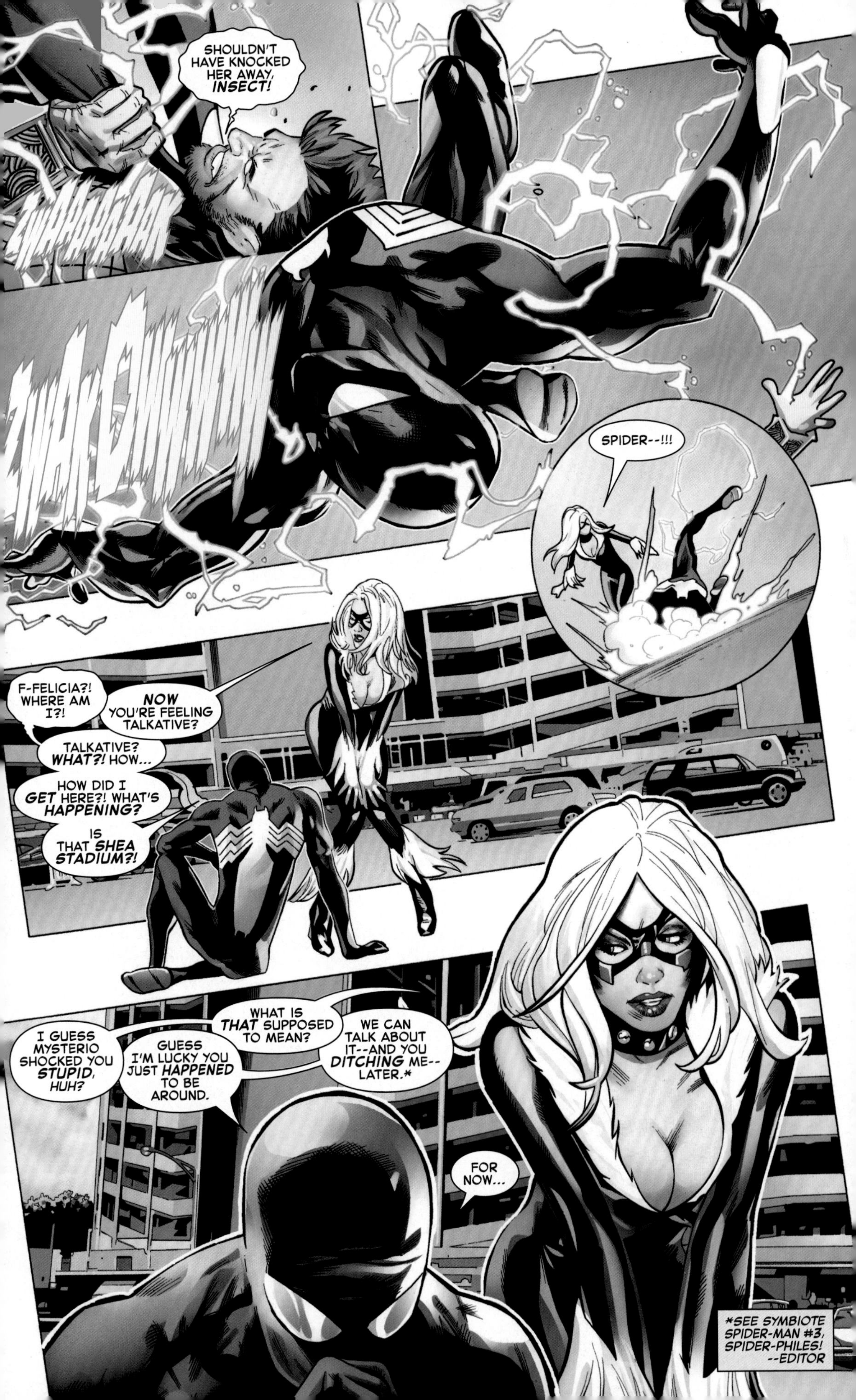
SHOULDN'T HAVE KNOCKED HER AWAY, INSECT!
ZWHHAAAK
ZWAKOWWWWW
SPIDER--!!!
F-FELICIA?! WHERE AM I?!
NOW YOU'RE FEELING TALKATIVE?
TALKATIVE? WHAT?! HOW...
HOW DID I GET HERE?! WHAT'S HAPPENING?
IS THAT SHEA STADIUM?!
I GUESS MYSTERIO SHOCKED YOU STUPID, HUH?
GUESS I'M LUCKY YOU JUST HAPPENED TO BE AROUND.
WHAT IS THAT SUPPOSED TO MEAN?
WE CAN TALK ABOUT IT--AND YOU DITCHING ME--LATER.*
FOR NOW...
*SEE SYMBIOTE SPIDER-MAN #3, SPIDER-PHILES! --EDITOR

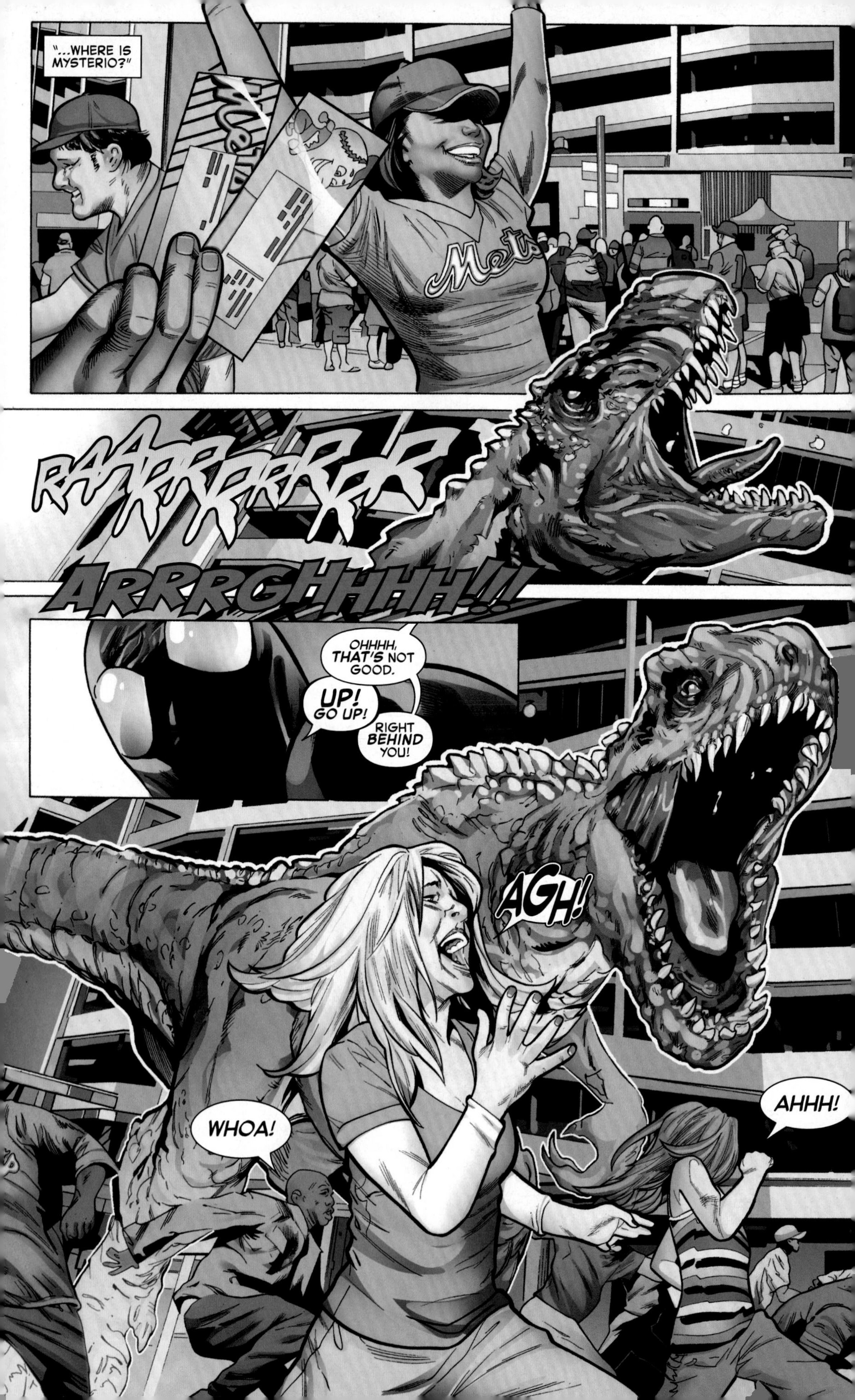

"...WHERE IS MYSTERIO?"
RAAARRRRRRR
ARRRGHHHH!!!
OHHHH, THAT'S NOT GOOD.
UP! GO UP!
RIGHT BEHIND YOU!
AGH!
WHOA!
AHHH!

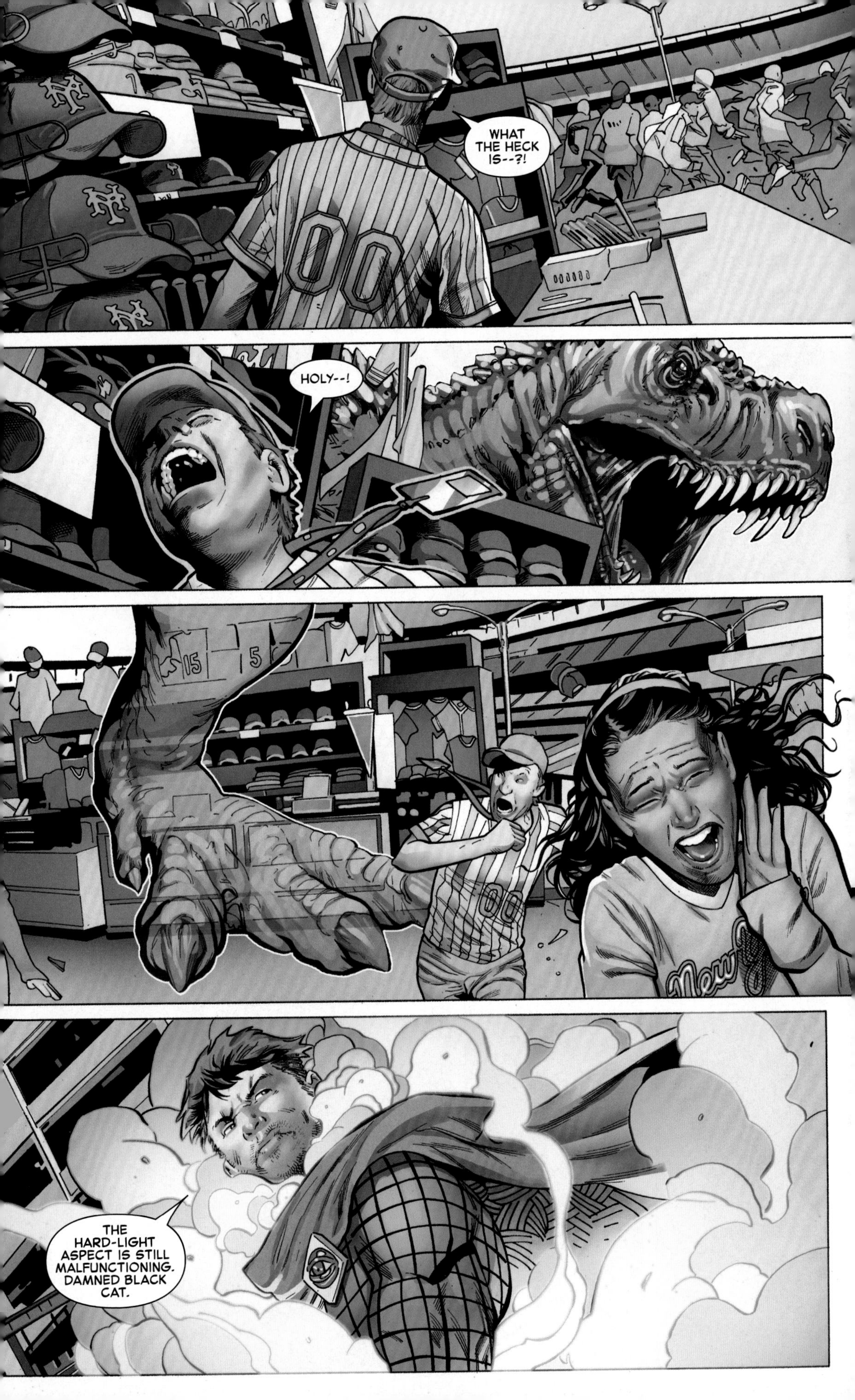
WHAT THE HECK IS--?!
HOLY--!
THE HARD-LIGHT ASPECT IS STILL MALFUNCTIONING. DAMNED BLACK CAT.

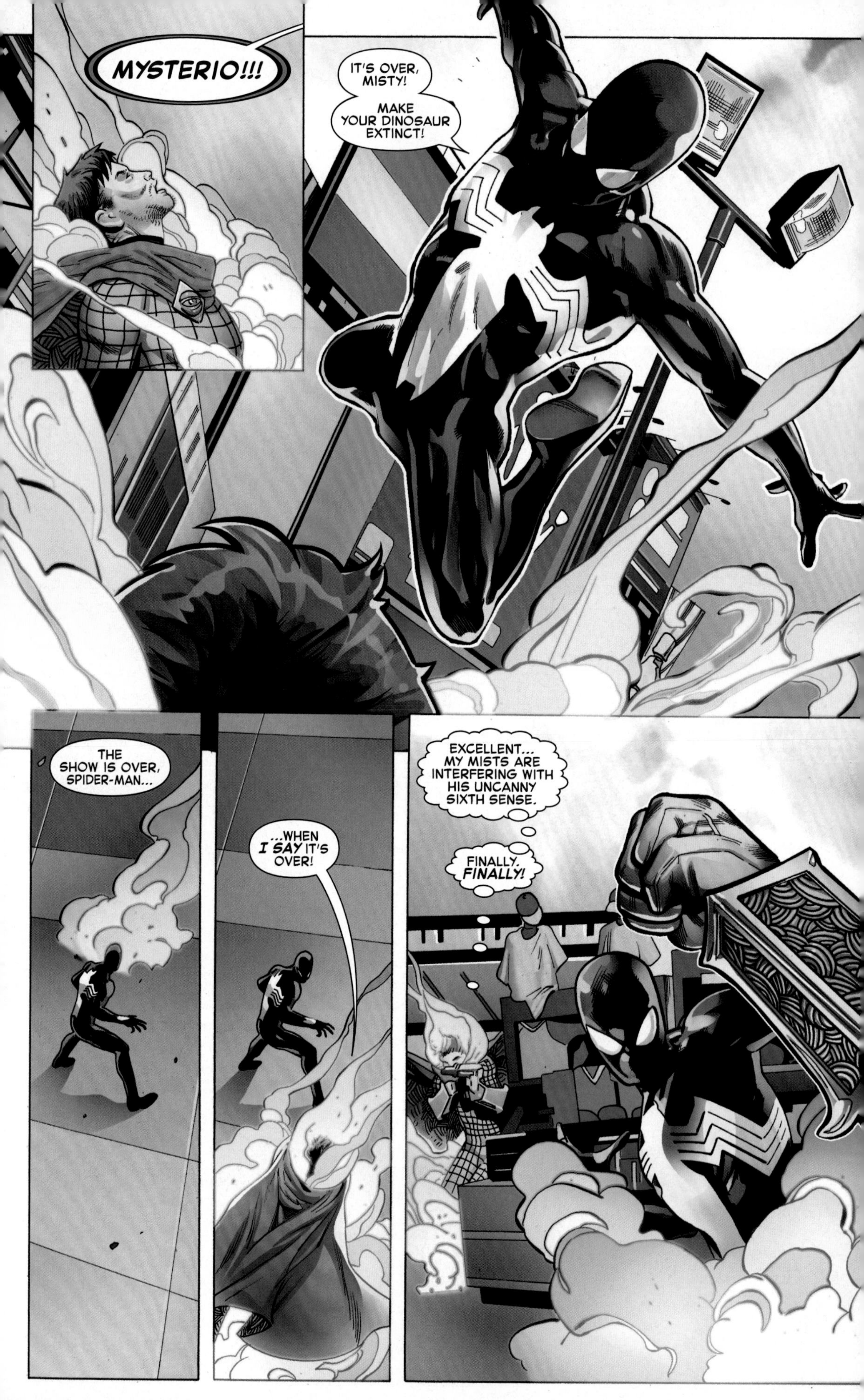
MYSTERIO!!!
IT'S OVER, MISTY!
MAKE YOUR DINOSAUR EXTINCT!
THE SHOW IS OVER, SPIDER-MAN...
...WHEN I SAY IT'S OVER!
EXCELLENT... MY MISTS ARE INTERFERING WITH HIS UNCANNY SIXTH SENSE.
FINALLY. FINALLY!

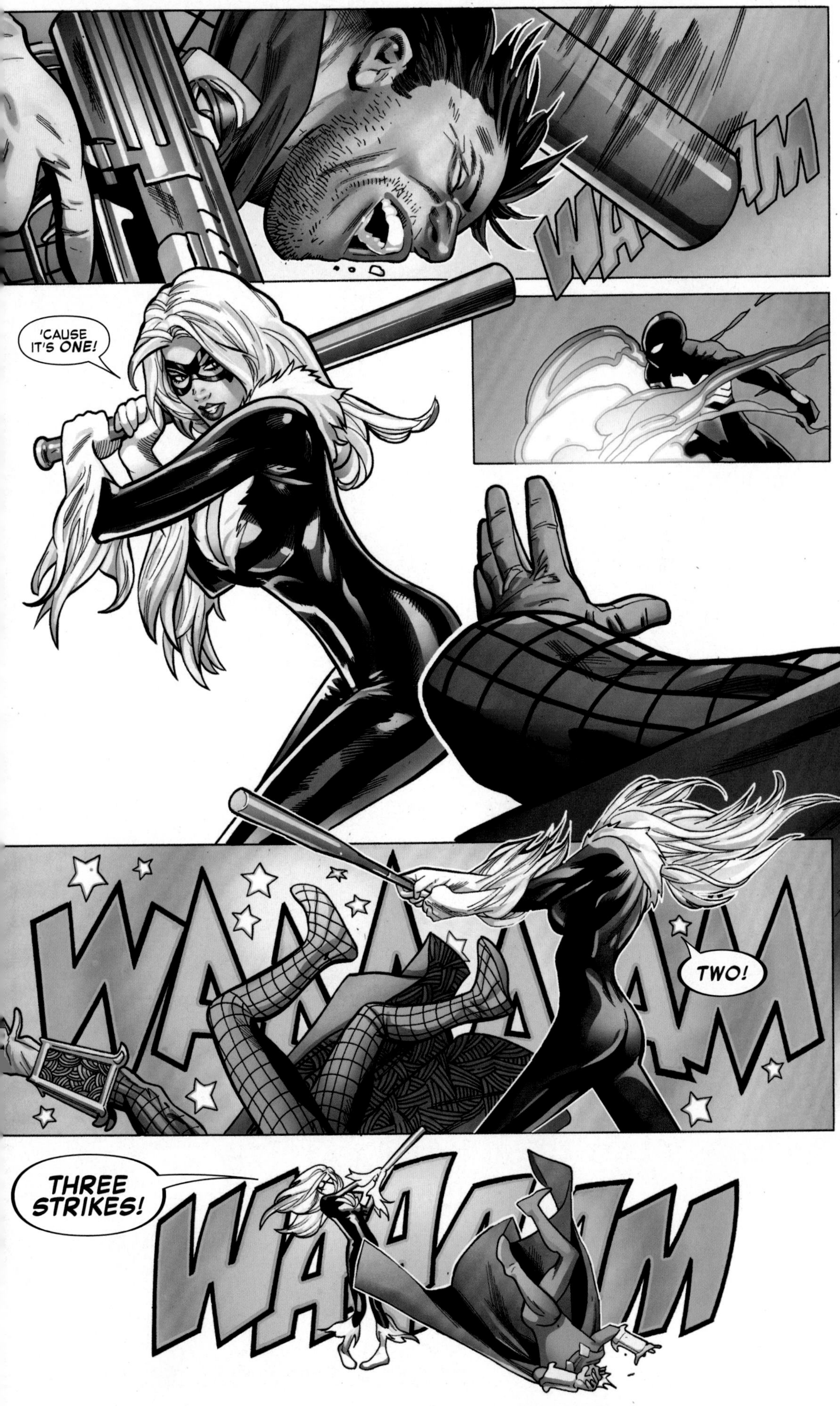
WAAAM
'CAUSE IT'S ONE!
WAAAM
TWO!
THREE STRIKES!
WAAAM

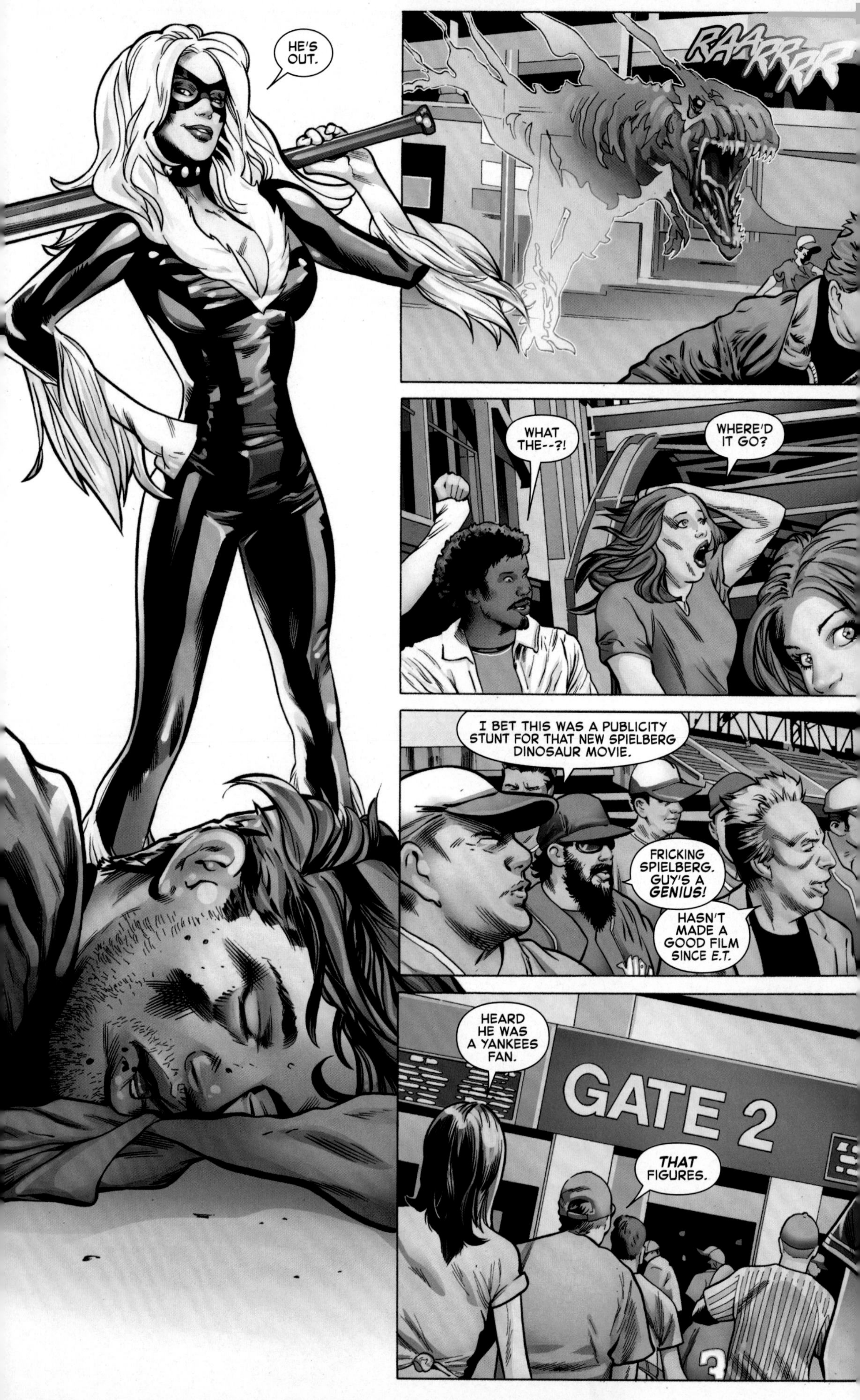
HE'S OUT.
RAAARRRR
WHAT THE--?!
WHERE'D IT GO?
I BET THIS WAS A PUBLICITY STUNT FOR THAT NEW SPIELBERG DINOSAUR MOVIE.
FRICKING SPIELBERG. GUY'S A GENIUS!
HASN'T MADE A GOOD FILM SINCE E.T.
HEARD HE WAS A YANKEES FAN.
GATE 2
THAT FIGURES.

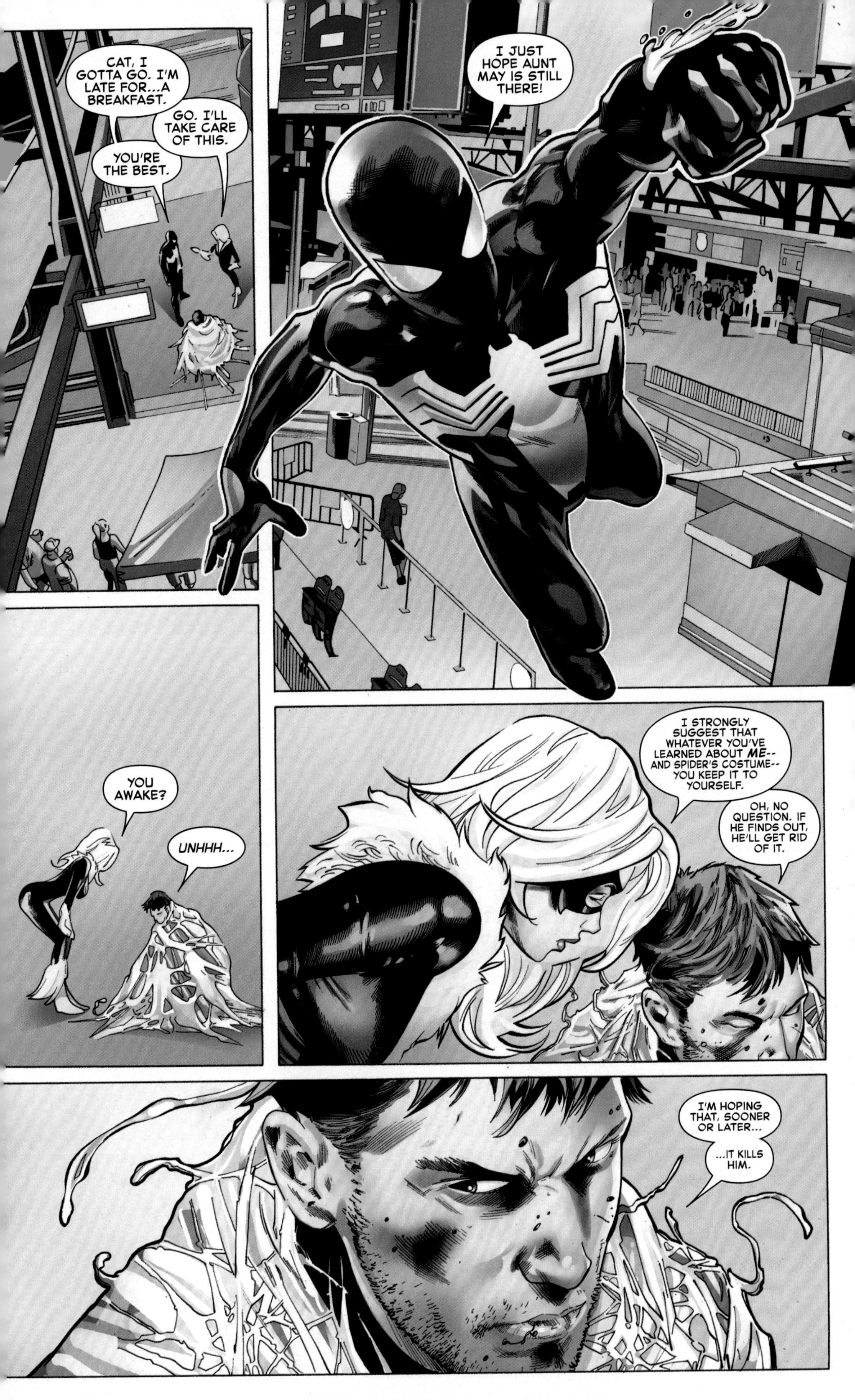
CAT, I GOTTA GO. I'M LATE FOR...A BREAKFAST.
GO. I'LL TAKE CARE OF THIS.
YOU'RE THE BEST.
I JUST HOPE AUNT MAY IS STILL THERE!
YOU AWAKE?
UNHHH...
I STRONGLY SUGGEST THAT WHATEVER YOU'VE LEARNED ABOUT ME-- AND SPIDER'S COSTUME-- YOU KEEP IT TO YOURSELF.
OH, NO QUESTION. IF HE FINDS OUT, HE'LL GET RID OF IT.
I'M HOPING THAT, SOONER OR LATER...
...IT KILLS HIM.

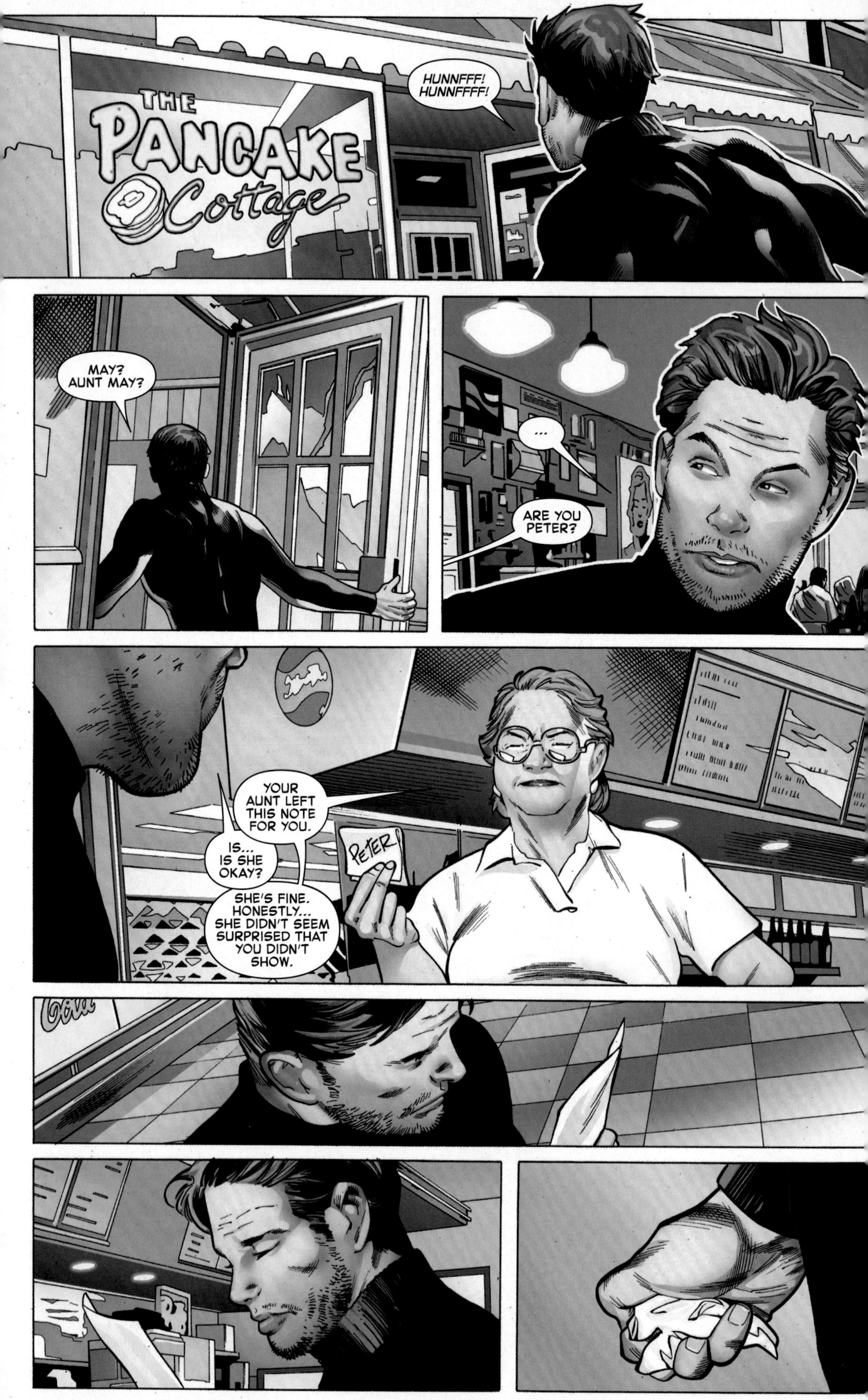
THE PANCAKE Cottage
HUNNFFF! HUNNFFFF!
MAY? AUNT MAY?
...
ARE YOU PETER?
YOUR AUNT LEFT THIS NOTE FOR YOU.
IS... IS SHE OKAY?
SHE'S FINE. HONESTLY... SHE DIDN'T SEEM SURPRISED THAT YOU DIDN'T SHOW.
PETER

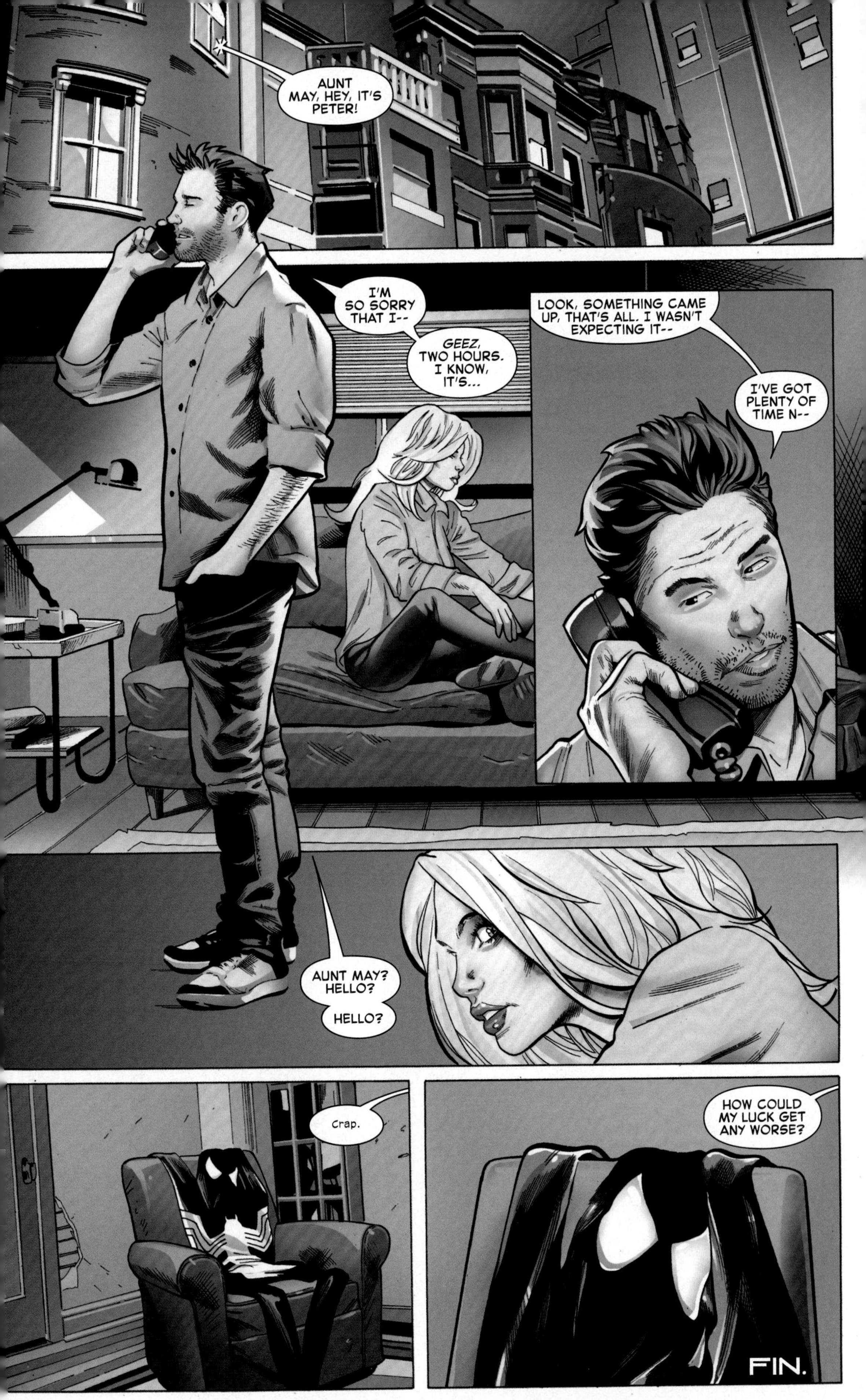
AUNT MAY, HEY, IT'S PETER!
I'M SO SORRY THAT I--
GEEZ, TWO HOURS. I KNOW, IT'S...
LOOK, SOMETHING CAME UP, THAT'S ALL. I WASN'T EXPECTING IT--
I'VE GOT PLENTY OF TIME N--
AUNT MAY? HELLO?
HELLO?
Crap.
HOW COULD MY LUCK GET ANY WORSE?
FIN.

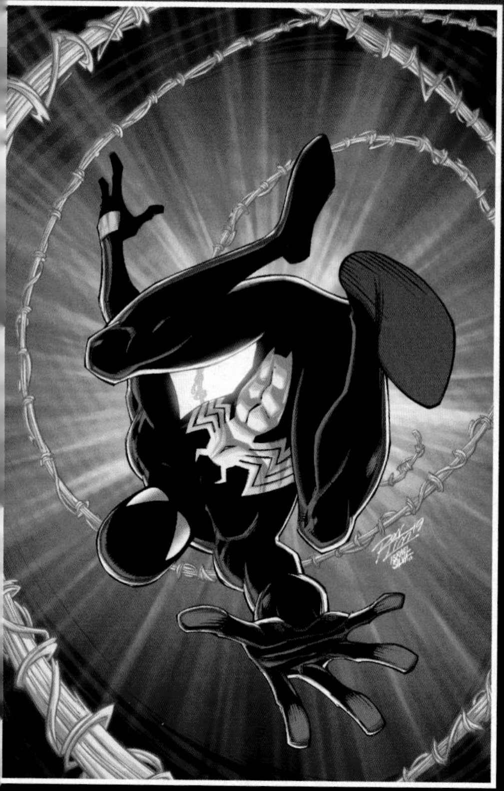

#1 VARIANT BY
RON LIM & ISRAEL SILVA

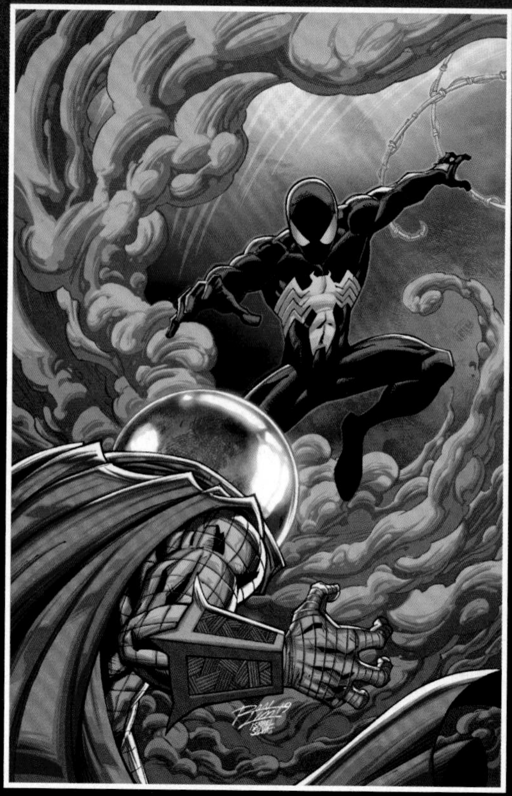

#2 VARIANT BY
RON LIM & ISRAEL SILVA

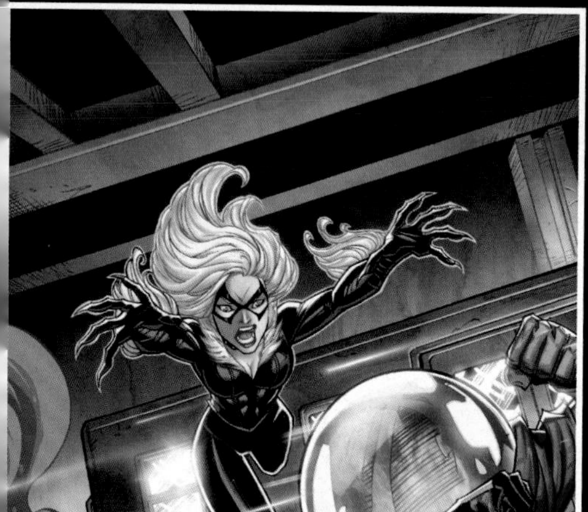

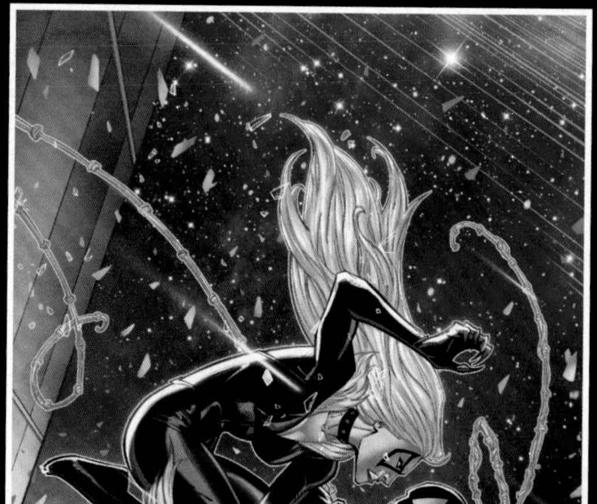

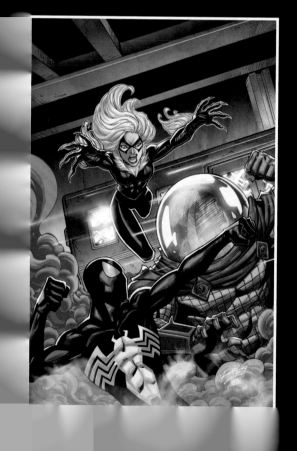

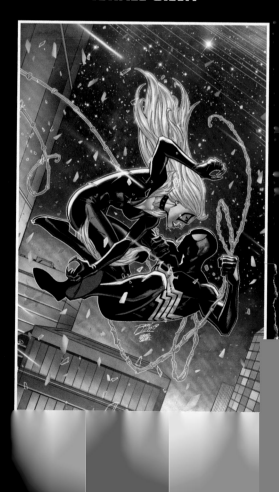

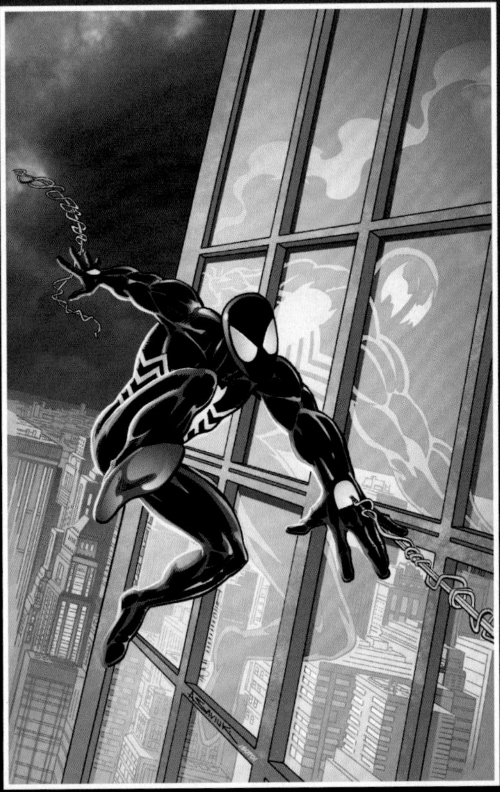

#1 VARIANT BY
ALEX SAVIUK &
CHRIS SOTOMAYOR

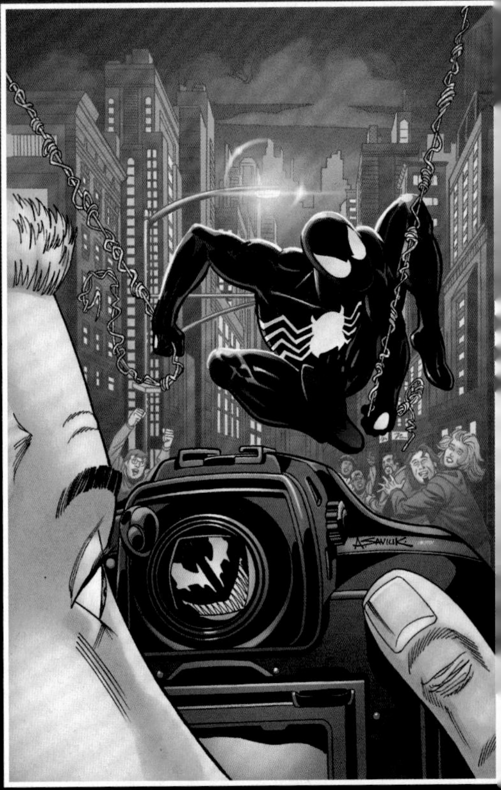

#2 VARIANT BY
ALEX SAVIUK &
CHRIS SOTOMAYOR

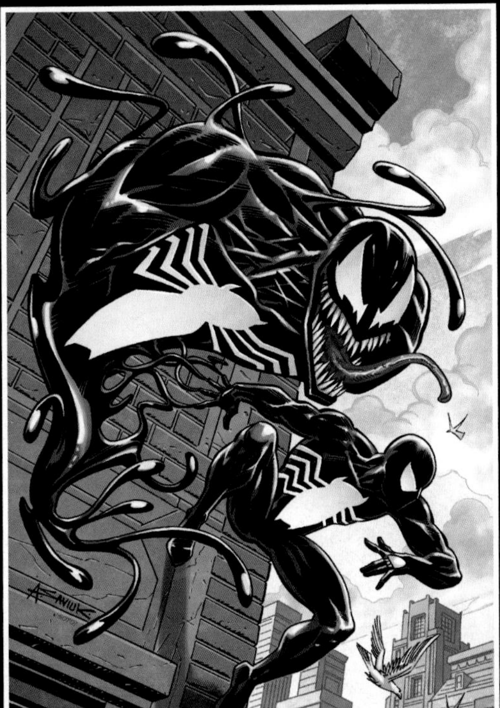

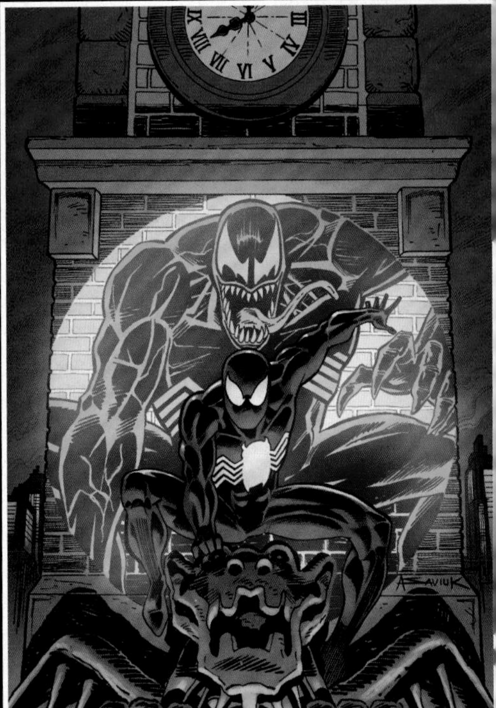

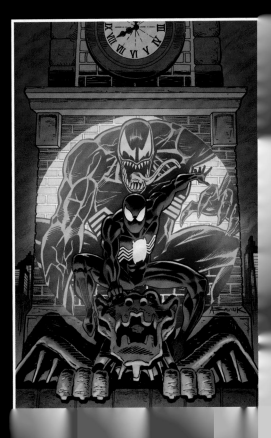

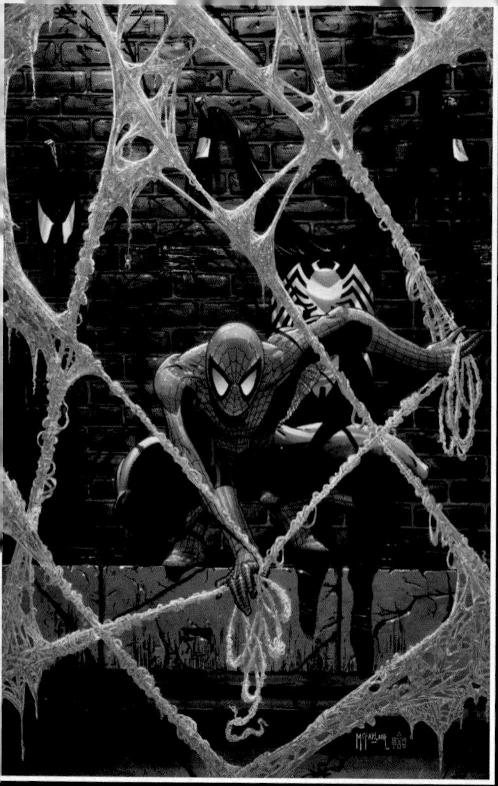

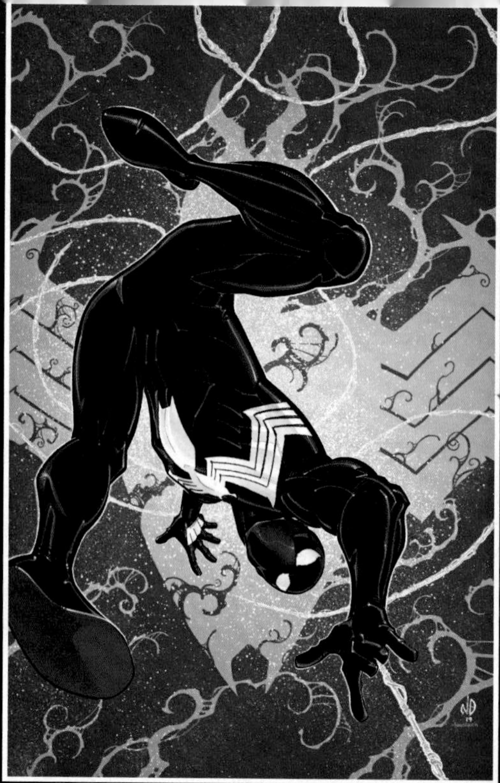

#1 HIDDEN GEM VARIANT BY
TODD McFARLANE *&*
JESUS ABURTOV

#1 VARIANT BY
NICK BRADSHAW *&*
JOHN RAUCH

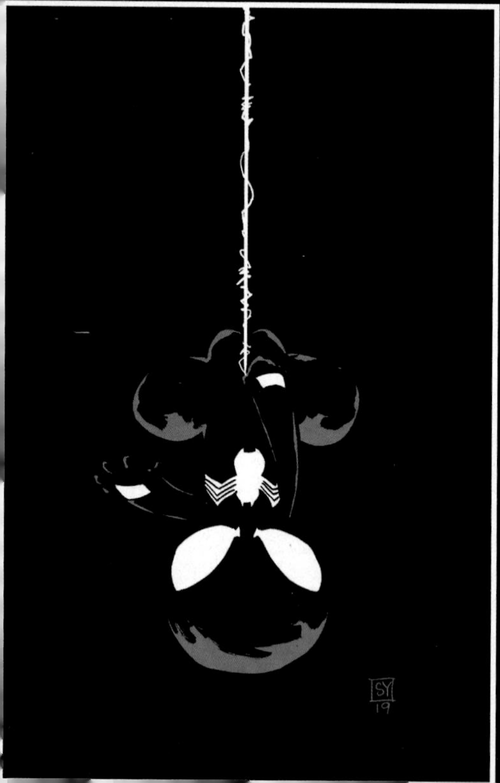

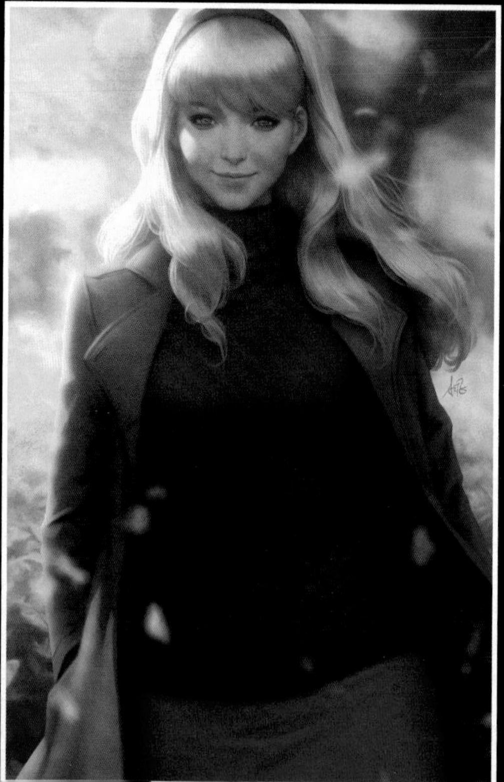

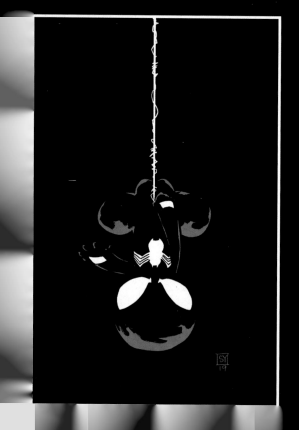